The Day-by-Day COLORING BOOK OF Saints

VOLUME 2
July–December

SOPHIA INSTITUTE PRESS

Manchester, NH

Sophia Institute Press

Box 5284, Manchester, NH 03108

1-800-888-9344

www.SophiaInstitute.com

Sophia Institute Press® is a registered trademark of Sophia Institute.

Day-by-Day Coloring Book of Saints—July–December

ISBN: 978-1-64413-119-0

First printing

Saints Inside

July 1	St. Junípero Serra	August 3	St. Lydia of Philippi
July 2	Sts. Acestes, Longinus, and Megistus	August 4	St. Jean-Marie Vianney
July 3	St. Thomas the Apostle	August 5	Dedication of the Basilica of St. Mary Major
July 4	St. Elizabeth of Portugal	August 6	The Transfiguration
July 5	St. Anthony Zaccaria	August 7	Pope St. Sixtus II
July 6	St. Maria Goretti	August 8	St. Dominic
July 7	Bl. Peter To Rot	August 9	St. Teresa Benedicta of the Cross (Edith Stein)
July 8	Sts. Priscilla and Aquila		
July 9	St. Augustine Zhao Rong	August 10	St. Lawrence
July 10	Bl. Pacificus	August 11	St. Clare
July 11	St. Benedict of Nursia	August 12	St. Jane Frances de Chantal
July 12	St. Veronica	August 13	Sts. Pontian and Hippolytus
July 13	St. Henry II	August 14	St. Maximilian Kolbe
July 14	St. Kateri Tekakwitha	August 15	The Assumption
July 15	St. Bonaventure	August 16	St. Stephen of Hungary
July 16	Our Lady of Mt. Carmel	August 17	St. Hyacinth
July 17	St. Hedwig	August 18	St. Helena
July 18	St. Camillus de Lellis	August 19	St. John Eudes
July 19	St. Macrina the Younger	August 20	St. Bernard of Clairvaux
July 20	St. Apollinaris	August 21	Pope St. Pius X
July 21	St. Lawrence of Brindisi	August 22	The Queenship of the Blessed Virgin Mary
July 22	St. Mary Magdalene		
July 23	St. Birgitta of Sweden	August 23	St. Rose of Lima
July 24	St. Sharbel Makhluf	August 24	St. Bartholomew
July 25	St. James the Greater	August 25	St. Louis IX
July 26	Sts. Joachim and Anne	August 26	St. Melchizedek
July 27	St. Simeon Stylites	August 27	St. Monica
July 28	St. Alphonsa	August 28	St. Augustine of Hippo
July 29	St. Martha	August 29	The Martyrdom of St. John the Baptist
July 30	St. Peter Chrysologus		
July 31	St. Ignatius of Loyola	August 30	St. Margaret Ward
August 1	St. Alphonsus Liguori	August 31	St. Aidan of Lindisfarne
August 2	St. Peter Julian Eymard	September 1	St. Beatrice da Silva

St. Junípero Serra

July 1

St. Junípero Serra

1713–1784 • Spain

Junípero Serra joined the Franciscan friars at the young age of seventeen and later became a priest. He was so intelligent that everyone thought he was going to be an important teacher in Spain. But in his heart, there was something else that he wanted to do: he wanted to be a missionary. There were stories about missionaries teaching the Good News of Jesus to those who had never heard of Him. He thought of all those peoples in the New World—those of North and South America—who had never heard of Jesus and had never been baptized. He wanted to bring the love of Jesus to them.

Fr. Junípero sailed with a group of Franciscans to Mexico. He landed at Veracruz and needed to travel nearly 250 miles to get to Mexico City. The city officials in Veracruz gave the Franciscans horses to make the journey. But Junípero Serra would not take a horse. He chose to go on foot, carrying only a prayer book, to offer his long trip as a sacrifice to God.

On the road, a mosquito bit Junípero Serra's foot, which then became infected. This infection made his journey very hard, and his foot would bother him for the rest of his life. Finally, he reached Mexico City and there preached to the Native Americans for sixteen years.

Fr. Junípero Serra knew that God wanted him to preach the Good News about Jesus even farther west. He traveled to California (this time Fr. Junípero rode on a horse) and founded the Spanish missions. The missions were congregations where the Franciscans told the Native Americans about the Good News that God loved them and that Jesus died for them to save them from their sins.

Not all the Native Americans liked having the Franciscans telling them what to do. And sometimes the Spanish soldiers at the missions did not treat the Native Americans well. Fr. Junípero Serra always defended the Native Americans from the soldiers. Everything he did was out of love. He preached the Faith to the Native Americans because he wanted them to be in heaven with Jesus forever.

Fr. Junípero founded nine missions all over California and spread the Gospel to many who had never heard of Jesus before. He served his beloved Native Americans until he died a holy death.

St. Junípero Serra, help me to do everything out of love for God!

Sts. Acestes, Longinus, and Megistus
July 2

Sts. Acestes, Longinus, and Megistus

d. c. 68 • Rome

Roman soldiers accompanied the Apostle Paul to his martyrdom. The cruel emperor Nero had ordered the persecution of Christians, and so the great Apostle to the Gentiles was to be executed.

But three of the Roman soldiers noticed that there was something very different about the Apostle Paul. Their names were Acestes, Longinus, and Megistus. They had been to many executions, and never before had they seen someone so peaceful and brave going to his death.

As they marched the Apostle Paul down the road outside of Rome, Paul spoke to them about Jesus and how He had risen from the dead. Soon, Paul told the soldiers, Jesus would raise Paul himself from the dead, and he would be with Jesus forever in heaven.

Some of the soldiers scoffed at Paul and called him foolish. But Acestes, Longinus, and Megistus did not. The Apostle Paul looked straight into their eyes, and they saw the joy radiating from his face.

He *believed*.

The three soldiers were awestruck. The Apostle Paul had faith in Jesus. The words he spoke were the truth. Paul knew beyond all doubt that all the suffering he had been through in this life would bring him glory in heaven.

Acestes, Longinus, and Megistus glanced at each other with wide eyes. They realized that the strength of Paul's faith was a treasure beyond this world. They wished to possess such peace and joy even if that meant they, too, would suffer for Jesus.

The time had come for Paul's execution. The Apostle spoke words of peace and forgiveness, and he became a glorious martyr for his love for Jesus. Acestes fell on his knees, and Longinus and Megistus felt the grace of God flooding their souls. The three soldiers knew in their heart of hearts that as he died, Paul had said a prayer for them.

Acestes, Longinus, and Megistus received baptism and became Christians. They, too, suffered under the Roman emperor's persecution, but they knew their suffering would bring them glory in heaven, where they would once again meet the Apostle Paul. In heaven, they would have the greatest of joys: to be with Jesus forever. And so, the three Roman soldiers became glorious martyrs for the Faith.

Sts. Acestes, Longinus, and Megistus, help me wish for the treasure of faith!

St. Thomas the Apostle
July 3

St. Thomas the Apostle

Biblical figure

St. Thomas was one of the Twelve Apostles. He followed Jesus even though he knew it was dangerous. Many fellow Jews wanted to kill Jesus because of His great works and the words that He spoke. But Thomas was loyal and brave. When Jesus traveled to Bethany to raise Lazarus from the dead, Thomas knew that he was in even greater danger because many of Jesus' enemies were there. He decided to go with Jesus anyway, even though he thought he might die. He told the other Apostles, "Let us also go to die with him."

When Jesus was arrested and crucified, Thomas was heartbroken. He was not with the other Apostles when Jesus appeared to them after His Resurrection. The other Apostles joyfully told Thomas that Jesus had risen from the dead!

But Thomas did not believe them.

It was too much to hope that the Master he loved was alive. The Apostles must have been mistaken. He said, "Unless I see the mark of the nails in His hands and put my finger into the nail marks and put my hand into His side, I will not believe."

The next time Jesus appeared to the Apostles, Thomas was there. Jesus knew what Thomas had said, and told him to place his fingers in His nail marks, and his hand at His side.

Thomas uttered a heartfelt, "My Lord, and My God."

Thomas's faith in Jesus was restored at the sight of his Master. Jesus told him that those who believe but do not see are blessed all the more.

At His Ascension, Jesus commanded the Apostles to spread the Good News to the ends of the earth. Thomas traveled all the way to India. There, he founded a Church and baptized many people in Jesus' name. St. Thomas the Apostle died a glorious martyr in India preaching about Jesus, the Master that he loved.

St. Thomas the Apostle, help me to believe in Jesus even if I do not see Him!

St. Elizabeth of Portugal

1271–1336 • Spain

Elizabeth was the daughter of the king and queen of Aragon in Spain. She married King Denis of Portugal and became Portugal's queen. Even though she was queen, Elizabeth prayed, fasted, and took especial care of the poor and the sick.

Elizabeth made many enemies because the nobles thought she did not live a life befitting a queen. But she knew that pleasing Jesus was more important than pleasing the royal court and that a good queen cared for all her people, not just the rich and titled. Her good example brought her husband back to the Faith, as he had been living a sinful life.

As queen, Elizabeth was responsible for maintaining her people's well being in politics. War broke out between her son, Afonso, and her husband, King Denis. They were fighting because Afonso did not believe that his father would name him heir to the throne.

Elizabeth knew she must stop the bloodshed between father and son.

She rode a mule onto the battlefield and placed herself between the dangerous armies of her husband and son. Father and son's anger cooled when they saw the brave queen on her mule facing down their soldiers in the name of love and family. And so, the two agreed to make peace.

After King Denis died, Afonso became king and Elizabeth retired to a monastery of Poor Clare nuns. After many years, she was called to be a peacemaker once more.

This time, her son had marched his troops to fight his son-in-law, Alfonso XI of Castile, who had been treating Afonso's daughter poorly. But Elizabeth knew that even though what Alfonso had done was wrong, war must be stopped. She journeyed toward the battle and once again arranged peace. But now Elizabeth was very old. The exhausting journey brought about her final illness. She died with the title of "peacemaker" and beloved by her country.

St. Elizabeth of Portugal, help me to be a peacemaker for Jesus!

St. Anthony Zaccaria
July 5

St. Anthony Zaccaria

1502–1539 • Italy

Anthony was born to a noble family in Cremona, but when he was only two years old, his father died. Because the family was rich, Anthony's mother wanted her young son to care for those who did not have as much as they did. When the poor would come to them for help, she always had Anthony with her as she gave them alms.

When Anthony grew up, he studied philosophy at university. But those early lessons of caring for the poor stayed with him. He studied medicine and became a doctor.

But healing physical illness was not enough. Anthony felt called to do more to serve others.

So Anthony became a priest. He visited the poor in prison and the sick in the hospitals. He founded an order of men now called the Barnabites and an order of nuns called the Angelic Sisters of St. Paul.

Because he loved Jesus deeply, he wanted everyone to grow in love for Jesus. So he renewed an old tradition of ringing the church bells at 3:00 p.m., the hour of Jesus' death, so that everyone could remember to say a special prayer at that time. He spread the practice of the Forty Hours' Devotion, when people take turns worshiping in front of Jesus in the Blessed Sacrament for forty hours in a row.

When he was thirty-six, Anthony fell ill and knew he was going to die. He returned to Cremona to die in the arms of his beloved mother. Throughout his life, he had found ways of reminding others to pray to Jesus.

St. Anthony Zaccaria, help me to grow in my love for Jesus!

St. Maria Goretti
July 6

St. Maria Goretti

1890–1902 • Italy

Maria Goretti was born into a farming family. The Gorettis were poor and had to share a house with another family, the Serenellis. Maria's father died of malaria when she was only nine, so her mother and older siblings all worked in the fields.

Maria did everything she could to help her family. She did all the chores—the laundry and the cooking—and looked after her baby sister. The Gorettis' life was hard, but the family was happy because they loved each other and they loved Christ.

One day, when Maria was only eleven years old, Alessandro Serenelli came home from the fields because he knew that Maria was home all by herself. He tried to force her to sin impurely with him. She said no and told him that she would rather die, since what he wanted to do was a mortal sin. Because Maria refused to sin, Alessandro did an evil and terrible thing. He stabbed Maria fourteen times. Maria's cries woke her baby sister. When her family came home, they found Maria alive on the floor and rushed her to the hospital.

The doctor saw that Maria's wounds were too deep for him to heal. He asked her to think of him in Paradise. He said this because he knew she would die soon. The next day, Maria forgave Alessandro for what he had done. She hoped that he would be in heaven like her someday. She died gazing on an image of the Blessed Virgin Mary and holding a cross to her chest.

Alessandro went to prison, but he refused to be sorry for what he had done. Then one night, he had a dream. Maria appeared to him and gave him a white lily. But he could not hold the flower. The pure white lily burned his hands. When he awoke, he repented of his sins. Released twenty-seven years later, he visited Maria's mother and begged forgiveness. She forgave him, saying, "If my daughter can forgive him, who am I to withhold forgiveness?"

Maria Goretti was canonized a saint by Pope Pius XII. Her mother and her four remaining brothers and sisters attended the canonization. So did Alessandro. He lived a reformed life and became a lay brother in the Order of Friars Minor. He prayed to Maria every day and called her "my little saint."

St. Maria Goretti, help me to have a forgiving heart!

Bl. Peter To Rot
July 7

Bl. Peter To Rot

1912–1945 • Papua New Guinea

Missionary priests came to the island country of Papua New Guinea and preached the love of Jesus. Many islanders left behind their pagan practices and converted to the Christian Faith. Among these converts was the village chief Angelo To Puia, his wife, and his son, Peter To Rot.

Peter To Rot deeply loved Jesus. He married a Catholic woman named Paula, and their love grew with each passing year as they prayed together and grew in holiness. God blessed them with three children.

Because of his love for Jesus, Peter To Rot became a catechist (someone who teaches the Catholic Faith) to help the missionary priests. The island country did not yet have many priests, so Peter To Rot's work was very important.

But the outbreak of World War II threatened the young Catholic Faith in Papua New Guinea. The Japanese took control of the island country and quickly saw that the Catholic Faith gave strength to the island people. One of the first things they did was to imprison all the missionary priests. Before he was taken away, one priest begged Peter to promise to look after the Catholic faithful on the island. Peter To Rot gave the priest his word.

Peter gathered the people secretly. Together, they would pray and worship God. Peter would teach the people about the Faith and baptize their children. He would remind them of Jesus' love for them and give them courage.

The enemy soldiers knew that if they weakened the islanders' faith, then the people would be easier to control. And so, the Japanese tried to make the people of Papua New Guinea return to their old pagan practices by forcing the men to have more than one wife. Peter To Rot knew that this was wrong. God had commanded marriage to be between one man and one woman. If a man had many wives, then he was sinning against the Sacrament of Marriage.

Peter To Rot knew that he had to keep his promise to the priest to look after his people and defend the Faith.

With great bravery, Peter To Rot stood up and proclaimed that Jesus had said that marriage is between one man and one woman, and that a man could not have many wives. He knew that saying this truth in public meant that he would be put to death. With great peace in his soul, he told everyone, "It is beautiful to die for the Faith." The Japanese arrested Peter To Rot and imprisoned him in a dark cave. Soon, they put him to death, and Peter To Rot became a glorious martyr for the Faith.

Bl. Peter To Rot, help me to remind others of Jesus' love!

Sts. Priscilla and Aquila

July 8

Sts. Priscilla and Aquila

Biblical figures

St. Paul, the Apostle to the Gentiles whose mission was to spread the Gospel of Jesus to Jews and non-Jews alike, had come to Corinth. There, he met a Jewish man named Aquila, who was a tentmaker. Now, Paul was also a tentmaker, and so Aquila invited Paul to his home, where Paul met Aquila's wife, Priscilla. The husband and wife explained that they used to live in Rome, but had come to Corinth because Emperor Claudius had expelled all the Jews from the capital.

Aquila sat Paul down at the table and made sure that he was comfortable, while Priscilla served a wonderful meal. Paul explained to the couple that he had just arrived in Corinth and needed a place to stay. Husband and wife exchanged glances, both thinking the same thing. Together, they invited Paul to stay at their home for as long as he needed.

Aquila, Priscilla, and Paul worked on their tentmaking business, and it might have been during this time that Aquila and Priscilla became Christians, too. When it was time for Paul to leave for Ephesus to continue preaching the Gospel, Priscilla and Aquila traveled with him.

For three years in Ephesus, the couple kept Paul in their home, and Priscilla served all the Christians who gathered to hear him. The couple's home became a little church. There, Christians would pray and read the Scriptures, and Paul would say the Holy Sacrifice of the Mass.

In Ephesus, pagan rioters tried to drive Paul and the Christians out for his preaching, and Aquila and Priscilla returned to their old home in Rome after the death of Emperor Claudius. Unfortunately, Claudius's great-nephew and heir was Nero, a terrible persecutor of Christians whose cruelty caused Priscilla and Aquila to return to Ephesus. But no matter where they went, their home was always a church for Christians.

As Paul continued in his travels, he would write letters (which you can read in your Bible) to the different churches, and in them, he would send his greetings to Aquila and Priscilla and the Christians in their home. Priscilla and Aquila served their fellow Christians until they died holy deaths.

Sts. Priscilla and Aquila, help my home always welcome others with the love of Jesus!

St. Augustine Zhao Rong

July 9

St. Augustine Zhao Rong

d. 1815 • China

St. Augustine Zhao Rong was a Chinese soldier who converted to the Faith. China had outlawed the Catholic Faith in the 1700s because the emperor saw the Faith as threatening traditional Chinese culture. But that did not stop missionaries from coming to China to spread the news of Jesus' love to the Chinese people!

One such missionary was the bishop and saint Gabriel Dufresse. Chinese soldiers arrested him for preaching the Faith, but he still preached to the prisoners and whoever would listen in prison.

One day, a Chinese soldier heard Gabriel Dufresse's words. His name was Zhao Rong. He was impressed by Dufresse's patience under such suffering. The bishop's words touched his heart. He escorted Bishop Dufresse from Chengdu to Beijing, where Bishop Dufresse was martyred.

The Chinese authorities martyred Christians to scare other people from converting to Christianity. But seeing Bishop Dufresse's martyrdom did the opposite for Zhao Rong. The bishop's bravery, patience, and love for Jesus made Zhao Rong want to become a Christian too.

Zhao Rong was baptized and took on the name Augustine Zhao Rong. He went to the seminary and was ordained a priest. He bravely spread the news of Jesus' love and administered the sacraments to the Chinese Christians. Soon, he was arrested. The Chinese authorities tortured him, and he died a glorious martyr for the Faith.

There were many Christians who were martyred in China. The eighty-seven Chinese Catholics and thirty-three missionaries who were martyred from the mid-1600s to 1930 are celebrated as the "Martyr Saints of China" or as "St. Augustine Zhao Rong and his 119 companions."

St. Augustine Zhao Rong, help me to be brave and patient and to love Jesus!

Bl. Pacificus
July 10

© Sophia Institute Press

Bl. Pacificus

c. 1162–c. 1234 • Italy

William was a minstrel and a poet. He was so famous that he was made royal poet of the king's court! He had everything he could wish for—a life full of fame, song, and fun. But he felt that something was missing. Even though his fingers plucked the strings of his lute, and his voice soared into song, his heart was silent. It did not join in the singing.

One day, William heard a man preaching. This man was different than anyone he had ever seen. He wore a threadbare robe and rejoiced in living a life of poverty the way that Jesus had lived. This man was St. Francis of Assisi, and Francis's words of joy and love for creation touched William's heart. A vision appeared before him: Francis stood before him with two swords crossed over his heart. William knew he had found what had been missing in his life. Immediately, William went to Francis of Assisi and asked to join his order. William became a Franciscan friar and took the name Br. Pacificus.

Br. Pacificus became one of St. Francis's companions. The joyful Francis composed the words for many canticles and hymns in praise of God and God's creation, which he called "brother" and "sister." Francis wrote about Brother Sun and Sister Moon; Brothers Wind and Fire; and Sisters Water, Earth, and Death. Br. Pacificus put these words into song. He plucked the strings of his lute and sang Francis's beautiful songs of praise.

Now, when his voice soared in song, his heart joined in. Br. Pacificus's joyful heart sang to the Lord.

St. Francis of Assisi sent Br. Pacificus to start an order of friars in France. When St. Francis died, the pope put the order of Poor Clare nuns (the order of nuns founded by St. Francis and led by St. Clare) into Br. Pacificus's care. He looked after them the way that St. Francis had. Near the end of his life, Br. Pacificus returned to France, and his heart sang songs of praise to God until he died a holy death.

Bl. Pacificus, help my heart sing in praise of God!

St. Benedict of Nursia

July 11

St. Benedict of Nursia

480–547 • Italy

Benedict was born into a noble Roman family. He had a sister named Scholastica (who would also become a saint). When he was a young man, Benedict studied in Rome. Benedict enjoyed his lessons, but he was saddened by the sinful lives of the other young men. He wished to separate himself from such worldliness and find the peace and quiet he needed to know God.

Benedict traveled into the mountains of Italy to a place called Subiaco. There, he found a cave high in the rocks overlooking a lake. He met a monk there who showed him how to become a hermit and who would visit him once a week to bring him food.

For three years, Benedict lived alone in his cave. He matured, growing strong in his relationship with God. He performed many miracles, and his fame spread throughout the area. One time, when he was being tempted to sin, he rolled in a thorn bush until the temptation left him. He said that by wounding his body, he was healing his soul.

When the abbot of a local monastery died, the monks asked Benedict to become their next leader. Benedict warned the monks that they would not like him as their leader. He knew that the monks were undisciplined—their community did not observe any rules.

The monks wanted him anyway.

But Benedict was right: the monks found him and his rules too strict. In order to get rid of their new abbot, the monks tried to poison him! When Benedict prayed over the poisoned wine they had given him, the cup shattered into many pieces!

Benedict left the monastery and instead founded twelve other monasteries in the area—including a famous and magnificent monastery called the Abbey of Monte Cassino, built high on a hill. Scholastica also started a convent nearby, and brother and sister would meet to visit and pray together once a year.

Late in his life, Benedict wrote the Rule of St. Benedict, which is a set of rules that a monastery follows in order to be prayerful and to live together in the love of Christ. They followed the motto *ora et labora*—"pray and work." Benedict died a holy death and is known as the "Father of Western Monasticism."

St. Benedict, help me to pray and work for God!

St. Veronica

July 12

St. Veronica

AD 33 • Jerusalem

A woman stood on the path to Calvary. Jesus, her Lord, would soon come by carrying His Cross. The woman's face streamed with silent tears as she thought about Jesus, whom she loved with all her heart, going to His death on a cross.

Now she could see Him. Slowly and patiently, Jesus dragged the heavy wooden beam that pressed heavy against His shoulder. He was as silent as a lamb being taken to the slaughter.

He stumbled on a rock in His path and fell to the ground. The woman rushed to Jesus and sank on her knees before Him. His precious blood streamed down from the wounds inflicted by the crown of thorns, and sweat covered His brow. The woman took the cloth of her veil and, with great love and compassion, she wiped the blood and sweat from Jesus' face.

The gratitude that glowed in Jesus' eyes pierced the woman's heart with sorrow and joy. She was sorrowful because of Jesus' suffering, but joyful that by her one small act, she was able to show Jesus how much she loved Him and to give Him some small comfort in the midst of His suffering.

Jesus struggled back to His feet, aided by a man named Simon of Cyrene, whom the soldiers had pulled from the crowd to help Jesus carry His Cross.

The woman clutched the veil to her breast as she watched Jesus continue His painful walk to Calvary. The veil was precious to her, now stained as it was by Jesus' drops of blood. She raised the veil to her lips and kissed it. Then she opened the veil and gasped.

There, on her veil, was an image of Jesus' face.

Jesus had miraculously imprinted the image of His face on the woman's veil to give her comfort and to thank her for her kindness and compassion.

Later, the woman would rejoice when she heard the news of Jesus' Resurrection. She kept Jesus' image as a treasure, and many great miracles of healing occurred when people touched her veil and prayed to Jesus.

We call the woman with the veil "Veronica," which means "true image" in Latin, because Jesus gave her the gift of the true image of His face when she compassionately wiped His brow with her veil.

St. Veronica, help me to show Jesus how much I love Him with small acts of love and compassion!

St. Henry II

July 13

St. Henry II

973–1024 • Germany

Henry was the son of the Duke of Bavaria in southern Germany. While his father was in exile for rebelling against the emperor, Henry was raised and educated by St. Wolfgang, the bishop of Regensburg. Studying under such a holy man, Henry loved the Faith and desired to become a priest. But when his father died, Henry was crowned Duke of Bavaria and married Cunigunde of Luxembourg. The two never had children and grew together in holiness. Cunigunde would also become a saint.

Henry's cousin was Otto III, the Holy Roman emperor and the king of Germany. Otto was fighting a revolt in Italy, and he ordered Henry to bring his troops to fight for him. But before Henry arrived, the emperor died. Since Otto III did not have children, Henry claimed the throne, though not all the nobles supported him.

The new king fought many battles to ensure his rule and keep peace in his kingdom. Even though he fought many wars, he never stopped living his Faith. He had his soldiers pray and receive Communion before each battle. In peacetime, he worked hard to reform the Church—making sure that the bishops and abbots did not use money for themselves. Henry and Cunigunde gave most of their wealth to the poor and supported missionary work. Henry built the grand Bamberg Cathedral to spread the Faith to non-Christians in his kingdom.

A new pope, Pope Benedict VIII, was elected, but Roman politicians tried to replace him with a false pope. Benedict VIII asked Henry for help. Henry marched to Rome and made sure that Benedict VIII was recognized as pope. In return, the pope crowned him Holy Roman emperor. At his coronation, Henry received a golden globe inlaid with pearls with a cross on top. This globe was meant to represent the earth. Henry gave this great treasure to the monastery of Cluny.

Never forgetting his desire to live a religious life, Henry tried to order an abbot in his kingdom to make him a monk. The abbot refused. He told the king that God willed Henry to perform his duties as a ruler. Humbled, Henry realized that God wished him to serve as king for the good of his people. Henry became a Benedictine oblate, which meant he was able to dedicate his life to God while remaining a king. Henry died a holy death and was buried in his Bamberg Cathedral. When his wife died many years later, she was buried beside him.

St. Henry II, help me to do the duties that God gives to me!

St. Kateri Tekakwitha

July 14

St. Kateri Tekakwitha

1656–1680 • Modern-day United States of America

Four-year-old Tekakwitha sweated with fever. She was sick with smallpox, and upon her recovery, she discovered that her father, the chief of the Mohawks, and her Christian Algonquin mother had died of the same disease.

The smallpox had left Tekakwitha's face scarred and damaged her eyes, and when her uncle and aunt adopted her, they did not understand the quiet, shy girl. She would go deep into the woods to pray the Rosary, which her mother had taught her, even though her father had forbidden her baptism. Young Tekakwitha wished she could be baptized Catholic with her whole heart.

When Tekakwitha turned thirteen, her uncle tried to arrange her marriage, but the young Mohawk girl refused. At first, her uncle let Tekakwitha have her way, but when she turned seventeen and still refused to marry, he began to get angry.

At around the same time, Jesuit missionary priests arrived to preach to the Mohawk tribe. Tekakwitha went to the Jesuit fathers, asking to be baptized. At her baptism, she took the name Kateri, after St. Catherine of Siena.

Kateri Tekakwitha's people scorned and persecuted her because she was Christian. It became so dangerous and unbearable that Kateri escaped, with the help of other Native American Christians, to the Christian Native American village of Sault St. Louis in Canada. There, Kateri lived a life of deep prayer and intense sacrifice.

Kateri Tekakwitha desired to be Jesus' bride, and she consecrated herself to Him. She loved Jesus so much that when she prayed to Him, her face became radiantly beautiful, as if she were speaking to Jesus face-to-face. All the priests and other Native American Christians were inspired by her holiness. She died of illness at the young age of twenty-four. After her death, the smallpox scars on her face disappeared, and she became known as the "Lily of the Mohawks."

St. Kateri Tekakwitha, help me to love Jesus with my whole heart!

St. Bonaventure

July 15

St. Bonaventure

1221–1274 • Italy

When Bonaventure was a child, he almost died. No one knows if Bonaventure fell sick or was in an accident. What we do know is that his mother prayed to St. Francis of Assisi for a miracle. St. Francis answered her prayer, and Bonaventure was healed, becoming a strong little boy. From that time on, Bonaventure had a special love for St. Francis in his heart.

When he was old enough, Bonaventure joined the Franciscans, the order of poor friars started by his special saint. Bonaventure prayed and studied hard, writing many important books about God and how to live a holy life. He taught at the University of Paris, along with a Dominican monk who also would one day become a great saint: Thomas Aquinas.

Pope Urban IV named a new feast day in the Church, the Feast of Corpus Christi, which is a feast honoring the Body of Christ in the Eucharist. The pope wanted the best and most beautiful prayers and songs composed for the Mass that would celebrate this new important feast.

So Urban IV held a contest.

He asked Thomas Aquinas and Bonaventure each to compose the prayers for the Mass. He would listen to both of them, and then he would choose which prayers to use for the Feast of Corpus Christi.

When the time came, Aquinas and Bonaventure came before the pope. Aquinas stood and read aloud his prayers. Bonaventure listened, clutching his own prayers written on parchment in his hand. The prayers his friend Aquinas had read were perfect. They beautifully described the mystery of the Body and Blood of Christ.

Bonaventure no longer wanted to win the contest. He wanted only the best for the Lord. He ripped up his parchment into tiny little pieces, and when it was his turn to read, he explained that only Aquinas's prayers were worthy of the great Feast of Corpus Christi.

Aquinas also admired Bonaventure's writing. Alone in his cell, Bonaventure was writing a book on the life of St. Francis when Aquinas went up to visit him. Aquinas found Bonaventure in a state of ecstasy, which is a state of great prayer and communion with God. Aquinas softly closed the door and said, "Let us leave a saint to work for a saint."

Bonaventure was made a cardinal by the pope and was also in charge of the Franciscan friars—just like St. Francis once had been. Bonaventure was acting as an adviser to the pope during a church council when he died a holy death, just a few months after his friend Thomas Aquinas. St. Bonaventure, help me always give the best to the Lord!

Our Lady of Mt. Carmel

July 16

Our Lady of Mt. Carmel

Marian Apparition • 1251

Mt. Carmel is a mountain in the Holy Land whose name means "the Garden." It is famous because long ago, the prophet Elijah and his follower Elisha stayed there for a time, and God worked a great miracle for Elijah there.

In the Middle Ages, a group of hermits began an order on the mountain to live like Elijah and Elisha and dedicated themselves to Our Lady. They called themselves the Carmelites. The Carmelites spread all throughout Europe, and many of them went to England.

One of the Carmelite priors in England was St. Simon Stock. Simon earned the name "Stock," which means "tree trunk," because he lived in a giant hollow tree trunk when he was a boy. When he was much older and the prior general of the Carmelites, Our Lady appeared to Simon and gave him the Brown Scapular. Our Lady promised that whoever died wearing the Scapular would be saved.

From then on, the Carmelites wore the Brown Scapular, which is a brown piece of cloth that hangs on both sides of the habit from the shoulders.

When Our Lady of Fatima appeared to Lucia, Francisco, and Jacinta, she once also came to them in the appearance of Our Lady of Mt. Carmel. She wanted to remind all of us that the Brown Scapular is important and can give us many graces.

We, too, can wear the Brown Scapular!

To receive the promise Mary gave to St. Simon Stock, we must do three things: 1. Wear the Brown Scapular. 2. Live lives of chastity. 3. Pray the Little Office of the Blessed Virgin Mary or the Rosary.

Our Lady of Mt. Carmel, pray for and preserve us!

St. Hedwig

July 17

St. Hedwig

1374–1399 • Modern-day Hungary

Hedwig was a beautiful Polish princess engaged to marry William, Duke of Austria. Hedwig and William had known each other since they were children, and Hedwig loved William very much. But then Hedwig's father, the king of both Hungary and Poland, suddenly died. Hedwig's older sister Mary was crowned queen of Hungary, and Hedwig was crowned queen of Poland.

Jagiello, the non-Christian Duke of Lithuania, had heard of Hedwig's great beauty and virtue. He marched to Poland with his soldiers to ask for Hedwig's hand in marriage. Jagiello promised that he and all his people would be baptized Christian if Hedwig became his bride.

The Polish courtiers rejoiced. Jagiello was a strong ruler, and an alliance with him was good for the kingdom. But upon hearing that she should break her engagement, Hedwig burst into tears. She did not want to marry the Lithuanian duke: she wanted to marry William!

Hedwig's mother comforted her and told her that through her marriage to Jagiello, she would bring the entire kingdom of Lithuania to Jesus. She must do her duty as a princess, and she must do her duty to God. But the choice was hers.

Hedwig went to the great cathedral of Krakow and knelt before the crucifix. She begged Jesus to tell her what He wanted her to do. Tears in her eyes, Hedwig poured out her broken heart at the foot of His Cross. Jesus' grace and strength entered Hedwig's heart. When she rose, she was ready to do His will without complaint. She knew that the Lord wanted her to marry Jagiello and give her life to the service of God and to her kingdom.

With great ceremony, Hedwig and Jagiello were married. All the people of Lithuania received the grace of baptism, and Christianity came to Lithuania. Jagiello deeply loved and admired his bride. He was astonished not only by her beauty, but also by her wisdom. He would bring Hedwig to all his negotiations with other leaders and rely on her wise counsel. Queen Hedwig even led the army in defense of the kingdom when he was away. The sick and poor were Queen Hedwig's special care, and she passed many laws to protect them. All the people of Poland and Lithuania dearly loved Queen Hedwig.

Hedwig and Jagiello were childless for many years, and when Queen Hedwig became pregnant, she dedicated that special time to prayer. Her daughter died three weeks after she was born, and Queen Hedwig also died days after, but not before receiving the sacraments and readying her soul. Many miracles were reported by those who visited her tomb.

St. Hedwig, ask Jesus to send His grace and strength into my heart, so I will always do His will!

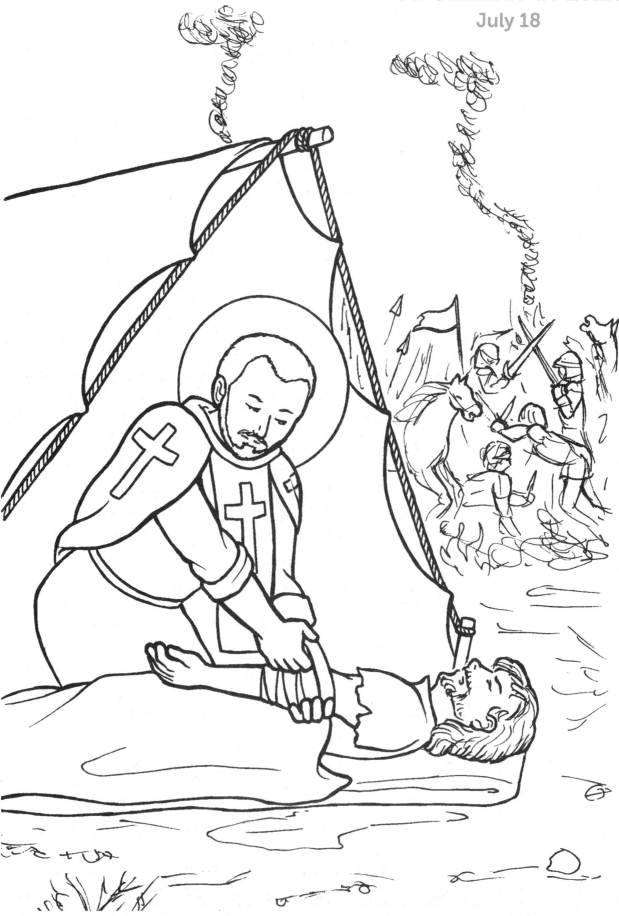

St. Camillus de Lellis

1550–1614 • Italy

Camillus de Lellis was a lonely young boy. His father was a soldier and was never home. His mother died when he was only twelve, and the rest of Camillus's family ignored him.

Because he was all alone, Camillus had a sharp temper and started gambling. At seventeen, he joined the Venetian army as a soldier. He served many years in the military and wounded his leg. When his regiment was disbanded, Camillus had no money because he had gambled it all away.

He had nowhere to go.

So Camillus became a laborer at a Capuchin friary. There, he heard a sermon that touched his heart and inspired him to give his life to Jesus. At first, Camillus tried to become a friar. But his leg wound had never healed. The Capuchins would not accept him because the friary was not a hospital and could not take care of him.

Camillus went to San Giacomo Hospital in Rome. Even though he was a patient at the hospital, he also took care of the sick. He was so dedicated to service that the hospital made him its manager.

While in Rome, Camillus became friends with St. Philip Neri. He told St. Philip that he felt called to start a religious community to care for the sick. St. Philip explained to Camillus that the best way for him to start an order was to become a priest. So that is just what Camillus did, becoming a priest at age thirty-four.

Camillus founded the order of the Camillians to take care of the sick. They made a special vow: "To serve the sick, even with danger to one's own life." On their robes was a large red cross, which became a sign of healing and charity that is used to this day.

Camillus remembered his time as a soldier—how men would lie injured and dying on the battlefield and nobody would help. Camillus and his men decided to risk their lives and tend to the wounded soldiers during battle. When plague struck Rome, Camillus and his men were the first to take care of the sick. Sometimes, Camillus could not walk because his leg wound still bothered him. That did not stop him. He would crawl to visit the sick.

The Camillian order spread all throughout Italy. Camillus went on a tour to inspect all of their hospitals. During the tour, he fell ill and died a holy death.

St. Camillus de Lellis, help me to care for the sick!

St. Macrina the Younger

July 19

St. Macrina the Younger

c. 327–379 • Modern-day Turkey

The maiden Macrina was born to a great family of saints. She was named after her grandmother, Macrina the Elder, who passed on to her son and her grandchildren the teachings of the Faith. Both of Macrina's parents became saints, and her brothers Basil, Gregory, and Peter, also became important saints in the Church.

When Macrina was twelve years old, her father chose a young man for her to marry. But when the young man died before they spoke their vows, Macrina promised never to marry so she could give herself entirely to God. She stayed at home and helped raise her eight younger brothers and sisters. When her father died around the same time that her youngest brother, Peter, was born, Macrina took special care of Peter and showed him how to be holy and virtuous. Peter would become a bishop and eventually a saint.

After Macrina's father had died, the family moved to a new home, where Macrina convinced her mother to live a simpler life and to treat her servants as part of the family. Together, they all lived a Christian life, sharing all of their possessions and caring for the poor.

One day, a mother and father visited the saintly Macrina and her family. The mother held her little girl in her arms, and Macrina saw that the little girl had a festering infection in her eye. Macrina tenderly kissed the little girl's sore and wounded face and told the mother that she had an ointment that would heal their daughter.

When the girl's mother left, she forgot the ointment. She told her husband, who called a servant to return to Macrina's house to fetch it. But before the servant could depart, the mother gave a joyful exclamation and pointed to her daughter's eye. The infection had disappeared! Macrina's prayers to God had miraculously healed their daughter!

When her mother died, Macrina became head of the Christian community that her family led. Near the end of Macrina's life, her younger brother St. Gregory of Nyssa came to visit and found her ill and close to death. Together, they talked of the life to come, and Macrina explained how deeply she longed to be with Jesus, her beloved. She died with a prayer on her lips, tracing the Sign of the Cross over her eyes, mouth, and heart.

St. Macrina the Younger, help me to long to be with Jesus!

St. Apollinaris
July 20

St. Apollinaris

d. c. 79 • Modern-day Turkey

St. Apollinaris was one of the first bishops of the Church. The first pope, St. Peter, made Apollinaris a bishop of Ravenna in Italy. Apollinaris preached the Faith, proclaiming Jesus' love to all people and how He died and rose from the dead on the third day.

But Christianity at this time was illegal. Most people were pagans, which meant that they worshiped many false gods, including worshiping the Roman emperor.

The pagans in Ravenna hunted Apollinaris down. They beat him horribly and threw him out of the city. The Christians of the city looked for their bishop and found him half-dead on the seashore. They hid him so he could recover from his wounds and be safe.

But Apollinaris was the bishop of Ravenna. Jesus had given him the duty of watching over its people and bringing them the Word of God. So he returned to the city.

This time, the pagans tortured him by forcing him to walk on burning coals. Once again, they threw him out of the city.

Apollinaris went back a third time, was caught, and was put on a ship to Greece. There he stayed for many years, preaching and performing miracles. But his heart was with his people in Ravenna. He knew he must watch over his flock, and so he finally returned to the city that had cast him out three times.

At this time, Vespasian was the emperor of Rome. He proclaimed that all Christians must be banished from the city. Apollinaris decided to remain in Ravenna, but stayed in hiding.

One day, he was caught while walking through the city gate. The pagans beat him until he was close to death. For seven days, Apollinaris clung to life. He foretold that the Church would go through even worse persecution, but that in the end, she would triumph! Finally, he died, a glorious martyr for the Faith.

St. Apollinaris, help me to watch over those Jesus puts in my care!

St. Lawrence of Brindisi
July 21

St. Lawrence of Brindisi

1559–1619 • Italy

Ever since Lawrence was young, he knew that he was called to be a priest. He joined the Capuchin friars when he was sixteen and studied at the University of Padua. He had an amazing memory and learned many languages, including Hebrew. He even memorized the entire Bible!

After his studies, he became a priest and preached in Rome and all over Italy. His sermons were for everyone, not just for the learned. He spoke to people kindly, like a father. Because Lawrence spoke Hebrew, the pope asked him to preach to the Jews in Rome. His words won many of them to the Catholic Faith. He also founded monasteries in Germany and Austria and brought many of the Protestants there back to the Faith.

Lawrence was made chaplain of the imperial army. The Ottoman Turks had taken over a city in Hungary, and the emperor was determined to stop the advance of the Muslim army. The Christian army marched to liberate the city, even though they were greatly outnumbered by the Turks.

Lawrence rode at the head of the army, carrying no weapon and holding his crucifix high in the air. Throughout the battle, he stayed on the front lines, crying, "Forward!" and "Victory is ours," remaining completely unharmed. The inspired Christian army defeated the Turks and saved the city. The general of the army said they had won because of great Lawrence.

Soon after the victory, Lawrence was elected vicar general of the Capuchin friars, the highest position in the order. He was elected a second time, but he stepped down from his position. The pope sent him to Germany, where Lawrence preached to the German people.

Even though he was very busy, Lawrence always found time to pray. When he said Mass, he often fell into ecstasies—his heart was so consumed by his love of Jesus that time and everything around him would seem to stand still. He also greatly loved Mary and prayed the Rosary constantly.

Lawrence wished to retire to a monastery, but he was recalled to become a special messenger to the king of Spain. At this point, Lawrence was weak and tired. He knew that he was going to die soon. He served his mission, but was completely worn out and died a holy death a few days later, on his sixtieth birthday.

St. Lawrence of Brindisi, help me to share my faith bravely and kindly with others!

St. Mary Magdalene
July 22

St. Mary Magdalene

Biblical figure

Mary Magdalene lived in Galilee during the time of Jesus' life. She was a great sinner and was even possessed by seven demons! One day, Jesus found her and cast the demons out of her. Mary Magdalene was so very grateful to Jesus and loved Him very much. She followed Him as He preached to sinners, and, with some other women, she took care of Him.

When Jesus was crucified, Mary Magdalene stayed with Him. She remained faithful even though most of Jesus' friends had abandoned Him. She stood at the foot of the Cross, along with Jesus' mother and John, the beloved disciple.

After His death, Jesus was laid in a tomb. Mary Magdalene and some other women went to the tomb to anoint His body with oil according to Jewish custom. But when they looked into the tomb, Jesus was missing. They were shocked and sad because they did not know where Jesus' body was.

Two angels dressed in white told them not to be surprised that Jesus was gone, because He had risen from the dead, as He had told them He would! The women ran to tell the Apostles the news. The Apostles rushed over to see the empty tomb, but afterward they returned home.

Mary stayed behind at the tomb, weeping. Her heart was breaking because she didn't know where Jesus was. She turned around and saw a man standing in front of her. She thought He was the gardener, but it was Jesus, though Mary did not recognize Him.

He asked her, "Why are you weeping? Whom are you looking for?"

"Sir, if you carried Him away, tell me where you laid Him, and I will take Him," she begged Him in reply.

Jesus responded to her request with a single word: "Mary."

At her name, she recognized Jesus and fell at His feet, trying to wrap her arms around Him. But Jesus did not let her touch Him because He had yet to see His Father. Instead, He sent her to His Apostles to tell them the Good News of His Resurrection.

Mary Magdalene ran to the Apostles as fast as her feet could carry her to tell them the Good News that she had seen Jesus and that He had risen from the dead. At first, the Apostles did not know what to think, but when Jesus finally did appear to them, they all believed. Mary Magdalene shared the Good News of Jesus' Resurrection until she died a holy death.

St. Mary Magdalene, help me always to turn to Jesus for forgiveness when I do something wrong!

St. Birgitta of Sweden

July 23

St. Birgitta of Sweden

1303–1373 • Sweden

Birgitta was born to a wealthy noble family in Sweden. Her parents were devout Catholics, but her mother died when Birgitta was young, so she was raised by her aunt. At the young age of ten, Birgitta received a vision of Jesus, sorrowful and suffering, hanging from the Cross. Birgitta cried to Jesus, "Who has done this to you?" Jesus answered, "Those who do not have enough love." From then on, Birgitta knew she must love Jesus with all her heart.

When she was about fourteen, Birgitta married a young man named Ulf. Together they had eight children, among them a girl, Catherine, who would also become a saint.

The king of Sweden summoned Birgitta to be a lady-in-waiting for his new queen, so Birgitta and her husband lived at court. Later, she and Ulf went on a pilgrimage to Compostela in Spain, where the Apostle St. James the Greater is buried. During the pilgrimage, Ulf became sick, and he died soon after they returned.

Birgitta was terribly sad—she loved her husband very much. She had dedicated her life to God by being a good wife and mother. Now she knew that God was asking her to dedicate her life to Him in a different way. She founded the religious community of Brigittines, dedicated to the Most Holy Savior.

All throughout her life, Jesus had appeared to Birgitta in visions. In one vision, an angel, burning with love for God, carried a rod to punish the proud, but instead granted mercy with Jesus' permission. In another vision, Jesus showed Birgitta that a person full of sin is like a ship with devils that let water in to sink it before it can reach its port. Only by carefully watching or by plugging up the holes could the ship safely arrive. These visions and their lessons Birgitta wrote down in a book.

Near the end of her life, Birgitta went on pilgrimage to the Holy Land. She visited all the holy sites where Jesus had walked on this earth. On her return home, she died a holy death in Rome.

St. Birgitta of Sweden, help me to love Jesus with all my heart!

St. Sharbel Makhluf

July 24

St. Sharbel Makhluf

1828–1898 • Lebanon

Sharbel was born in a village in the Lebanese mountains. His father died when Sharbel was only three years old, so he was raised by his pious uncle. His chore was to take care of the family's animals. While out with their sheep, he would find time to pray quietly to God in a nearby cave. He felt closest to God in the silence.

When Sharbel was twenty-three years old, he left his village to enter the Monastery of St. Maroun. He studied hard to become a priest, and for sixteen years he lived in the monastery.

But Sharbel remembered his time praying by himself in the cave. He knew he felt closest to God alone and in silence. So he asked permission to live in a hermitage dedicated to Sts. Peter and Paul. A hermitage is a place where someone can live all alone to pray.

In the hermitage, Sharbel lived a life of prayer and sacrifice. The hermitage was so high up in the mountains that it was very cold in the winter. He slept on a straw mattress and ate only the leftovers from the monastery.

Sharbel greatly loved the Eucharist and would give the nearby villagers Communion. He continued his life of prayer and sacrifice into his old age and died on Christmas Eve after he became suddenly ill while saying Mass.

After his death, a great miracle happened.

Bright light surrounded his grave. The light shone dazzling white for forty-five days. Today many pilgrims come to visit his shrine and pray in silence on the mountain like St. Sharbel.

St. Sharbel, help me to find God in the silence!

St. James the Greater
July 25

St. James the Greater

Biblical figure

Sts. James and John were fishermen, just like their father, Zebedee. One day, James and John were fishing in the Sea of Galilee when Jesus called the brothers to leave their nets to become fishers of men. They left their boat to follow Him.

James and his brother had fiery tempers. One time, they asked Jesus to rain fire on a Samaritan town that had rejected Him! The brothers were called the "Sons of Thunder" because of their temper and zeal.

After they had followed Jesus for a while, the mother of James and John asked Jesus for a special favor—to have one brother sit at Jesus' right hand and the other at His left when He came into His Kingdom. Jesus asked the two brothers if they could drink the cup that He was to drink. "Yes!" they both said. What they did not understand was that Jesus meant His cup of suffering. Jesus said they would drink His cup, but His Father in heaven would choose who would sit on His right and left in glory.

James was one of the three Apostles whom Jesus chose to be with Him at special moments (the other two were his brother John and Peter). These three were with Him during His Transfiguration—when His face changed and His clothes became dazzling white. And they were with Jesus during His Agony in the Garden, though they all fell asleep, too tired to keep watch with Jesus in prayer.

When Jesus was arrested, James ran away in fear with all of the other Apostles except John, who followed Jesus. But James also rejoiced with the other Apostles when Jesus appeared to them after His Resurrection. He followed Jesus' command to baptize all the peoples of the world. It is said that James went to Spain to preach the Good News about Jesus, and that Mary appeared to him on a pillar and there commanded him to build a small church.

Later, James returned to Jerusalem and led the Church in Jerusalem in his mighty, thunderous way. Herod Agrippa, the king in Jerusalem, persecuted the Christians and ordered James be put to death with a sword. James was the first Apostle to be martyred for Jesus. There is a tradition that James's body was miraculously carried back to Spain by angels, and that his body is buried in Compostela. Pilgrims to this day make the long walk to Compostela, carrying shells, to visit St. James's tomb. St. James the Greater, help me to follow Jesus, even when it means drinking His cup of suffering!

Sts. Joachim and Anne

July 26

Sts. Joachim and Anne

1st Century BC–1st Century AD • Galilee

Sts. Joachim and Anne were the parents of the Blessed Virgin Mary and the grandparents of Jesus.

Joachim and Anne had been married for many years but were sad because they were not able to have children. They prayed day and night for a baby, because they knew children were a great blessing.

Imagine the joy in their hearts when a little baby girl was born to them! They named their little girl Mary.

Anne held the sweet little baby close to her heart, and Joachim sang prayers of thanksgiving to God. Together, they taught Mary how to pray and be close to God.

They were so thankful to God that they promised to give Mary to His service. There is a tradition that when Mary was a little girl of three, her parents gave her to the Temple to serve as a temple virgin. There she learned to weave veils, bake the temple bread, and make ready the incense used by the priests.

At the age of fourteen, Mary was betrothed to Joseph. Then, the angel Gabriel appeared to Mary and told her that she was to be the Mother of God. Afterward, Mary visited her cousin Elizabeth to help her with the birth of John the Baptist. When Mary returned, she must have told her mother and father all about what the angel had said and how she was carrying Jesus in her womb. Anne and Joachim knew how special and full of grace their daughter was. They must have trusted God and praised the mystery of His ways.

After Jesus was born and the Holy Family settled in Nazareth, Anne held Jesus close to her heart just as she had held Mary, and Joachim sang prayers of thanksgiving to God. How blessed the holy grandparents were to have Jesus as a grandson!

Sts. Joachim and Anne, please bless my grandparents!

St. Simeon Stylites
July 27

© Sophia Institute Press

St. Simeon Stylites

c. 390–c. 459 • Modern-day Turkey

Crowds of people disturbed the desert hermit Simeon in his cave. Fame of Simeon's holiness and life of sacrifice had spread far and wide. "Didn't the monks at his monastery ask him to leave because his sacrifices were too difficult?" asked one. Another said, "I hear that he is going this whole Lent without food or water."

Simeon sighed. He wished that everyone would let him live his life of prayer and sacrifice in peace so he could better spend time with God.

Then, one day, he had an idea. He built a pillar nine feet high with a platform resting on top. From that time on, he lived atop the pillar, praying and fasting all day and night. The Greek word for "pillar" is stylos, and that is why Simeon is known as Simeon Stylites.

People still came to visit Simeon, even when he was up on his pillar. He would speak to them, write them letters, and give them holy advice. But now he was not set upon by crowds, but set apart from them. His pillar was a constant reminder to others that the most important thing was a life of prayer and sacrifice for God.

As the years went by, the pillar was built higher and higher. First it was nine feet, then eighteen, then thirty-three, and finally sixty feet high! Simeon lived at the top of his pillar for thirty-seven years. God gave Simeon the strength to endure this life of sacrifice because that was Simeon's special calling from God.

Fellow monks would come to visit him. They would climb up a long ladder to give Simeon the little food he ate and to pray with him. Twice a day, he would go to the edge of his pillar to preach. Many people came to hear his preaching, including three different emperors. All knew that Simeon was a holy man and close to God. Simeon Stylites died a holy death atop his pillar.

St. Simeon Stylites, help me always to remember the importance of prayer and sacrifice for God!

St. Alphonsa
July 28

St. Alphonsa

1910–1946 • India

Seven-year-old Anna Muttathupadathu received Jesus in her First Holy Communion. At that moment, she knew that she belonged to Jesus completely and that she wanted to become His bride and enter the convent. But her aunt—who was taking care of her, as Anna's parents had died—had other plans for Anna. She began making arrangements for Anna's marriage. Poor Anna did not know what to do. She poured her heart out in prayer to God, asking Him to let her become a nun and be His bride alone.

When Anna reached marriageable age, she fell into a pit of burning chaff. The embers badly burned and disfigured Anna's feet. Despite her suffering, Anna realized that now she could enter the convent, because she thought no man would want to marry her with her burned feet.

Anna entered the Franciscan order and took the name Alphonsa. She taught the children in the convent school their catechism. Often, she suffered terrible illness and weakness because of her injured feet. But she offered all of her suffering to God in prayer. Finally, the wounds in her feet grew so terrible that everyone feared she would die. But God had not yet called His suffering bride to Him in heaven. Alphonsa prayed a novena to God and miraculously recovered.

Yet suffering was to be Alphonsa's path toward holiness. She fell ill with fever and later pneumonia. Her body was so weak that when a thief entered her room and frightened her, Alphonsa fell into shock and lost her memory. After a year, her condition was so bad that a priest gave her the Sacrament of the Anointing of the Sick. But when she received the healing sacrament, her memory returned.

All throughout her suffering, Alphonsa never complained. Despite her terrible pains, her words to her fellow sisters were always kind and full of love. During the last year of her life, she developed a tumor that filled her days with agony. But she endured the pain with a joyful smile. She realized that she could offer her suffering for the good of other souls, and she said, "I consider a day in which I have not suffered as a day lost to me."

Alphonsa lived a life of joyful prayer and sacrificial suffering until she died a holy death. Immediately upon her death, God granted many miracles to those who asked St. Alphonsa to pray for them. Many of these miracles were for the children in her convent's school, especially for those children that suffered from wounded feet.

St. Alphonsa, help me to offer all of my suffering to God in prayer!

St. Martha
July 29

St. Martha

Biblical figure

Jesus was friends with a family in Bethany: two sisters, named Martha and Mary, and their brother, Lazarus. Jesus would come to their home to rest and eat. One of these times, Martha busily prepared dinner for Jesus. She bustled about, checking and rechecking that the house was tidy and the food keeping warm. She wanted to impress all the guests!

Jesus arrived and she still was not ready. But where was her sister Mary? Surely, she should be helping her serve Jesus? Martha peeked into the room where Jesus was—and there was Mary, sitting at Jesus' feet! Martha was indignant. Why should she be doing all the work? Martha complained to Jesus, "Lord, do you not care that my sister has left me by myself to do the serving? Tell her to help me."

Jesus raised His eyes toward Martha and said in a gentle voice, "Martha, Martha, you are anxious and worried about many things. There is need of only one thing. Mary has chosen the better part, and it will not be taken from her." Jesus' kind but firm words reminded Martha that nothing, not even a fine dinner, was more important than listening to Jesus Himself.

Sometime later, her dear brother, Lazarus, fell ill. Martha and Mary sent news to Jesus, asking Him to come. They were confident that Jesus would heal their brother, just as He had healed others.

But Jesus did not come. And Lazarus died.

Martha wept and wept. She did not understand why Jesus had not come to save Lazarus! Four days later, Martha heard that Jesus was on the road to visit them. She rushed out to meet Jesus and begged Him to explain why He had not come. Jesus told Martha, "Your brother will rise." Then He asked her if she believed that whoever had faith in Him would live.

Martha said from her heart, "Yes, Lord."

Martha and her sister took Jesus to Lazarus's tomb. But when Jesus commanded that they take away the stone covering the entrance, Martha protested. Lazarus had been dead for so long that his body would now smell. Still she did not understand what Jesus was about to do.

Jesus spoke again in His kind but firm voice, "Did I not tell you that if you believe, you will see the glory of God?" Trusting Him, they opened the tomb. Then Jesus called out, "Lazarus, come forth!" And Lazarus walked out alive from his tomb. Martha rejoiced to witness so great a miracle and knew that her faith in Jesus would always keep Him first in her heart. St. Martha, help me to know in my heart that nothing is more important than Jesus!

St. Peter Chrysologus
July 30

St. Peter Chrysologus

406–450 • Italy

A young deacon named Peter stood at the edge of a delegation to the pope. This group had come all the way from Ravenna to present the man they wished the pope to appoint as their next bishop. This was an important role because, at that time, Ravenna was the capital of the Western Roman Empire. The emperor and empress would listen to the new bishop's preaching. The day before, most unexpectedly, the pope had turned away the chosen man and told the people of Ravenna to return with all of their clerics, great and small. The young deacon was present because his bishop had asked him to join, but he was not expecting anything important to happen to him. Little did he know that God had different plans.

The pope looked at the man everyone thought should be the next bishop of Ravenna. Then, his gaze sought out every man in the group, until he saw the young deacon Peter. To everyone's surprise, the pope proclaimed that he would ordain Peter the next bishop of Ravenna. No one was more surprised than Peter himself!

At first, everyone in the delegation was upset. They did not want Peter to be the next important bishop. Peter did not blame them. In fact, he did not want to be the next bishop either. He knew that being bishop would be a heavy burden, and he did not know if he was the right man for the job!

But then the pope explained that the night before he had received a vision. The first pope—St. Peter—and the first bishop of Ravenna—St. Apollinaris—had appeared to him. The two saints had told him not to appoint as bishop the man the delegation would present but had shown him Peter instead. Once the pope recognized Peter in the crowd, he knew he had found their next bishop. After they heard this, everyone's grumbles turned into praises for God. Their new bishop was especially chosen by heaven!

Soon, the people in Ravenna discovered that their new bishop had a great gift for speaking. Bishop Peter kept his sermons short and his words clear so that everyone could pay attention. He encouraged the people to receive Holy Communion every day, to pray, and to fast. The emperor and the empress listened to Bishop Peter's sermons and were impressed by his words. The people called Peter "Chrysologus," which in Greek means "golden speaker," because of the wisdom and beauty of his sermons.

Peter Chrysologus served the people of Ravenna as bishop until he died a holy death. St. Peter Chrysologus, help me to use the gifts God gave me in His service!

St. Ignatius of Loyola
July 31

St. Ignatius of Loyola

1491–1556 • Spain

A Spanish knight, Ignatius of Loyola dreamed of winning fame through great deeds. But during a fearful battle, an enemy cannonball ripped through his leg, and he was carried to a nearby castle. There, he was ordered to stay in bed so his leg could heal. To pass the time, he asked for books about knights and their brave adventures to win their ladies fair. But the castle did not have books about knights; instead, it had books about the holy adventures of the saints.

Ignatius read page after page on the saints and realized that the saints were brave and performed great deeds for God. Now he wanted to perform great deeds like those of the saints, winning fame for God instead of himself.

After his leg healed, Ignatius spent three days going to confession. In the chapel, he hung his sword and dagger over an image of Our Lady and kept watch through the night, which was a custom among knights. In this way, Ignatius dedicated his new life to God.

Afterward, Ignatius withdrew to a cave, where he spent a year in prayer. Here, he began to write about the experiences of his soul. His writings would later become a famous book, the *Spiritual Exercises*. Then, Ignatius set off for the Holy Land, braving the sea, pirates, and shipwreck so he could walk the land where Jesus had lived. But right when he arrived, the Franciscans in charge sent him straight back home, since war and persecution had made it too dangerous to visit the Holy Land.

Ignatius returned to Spain and became a humble student so that he could be a priest. Ignatius was older than most students in the university, but he won over many friends—including the future saint Francis Xavier—to join him in his mission to perform great deeds for God. Ignatius and his men decided to go to Rome and offer their service to the pope.

Just before entering the city, Ignatius received a mystical vision of Jesus and God the Father, who told him that they would favor Ignatius in Rome. Soon after, Ignatius said his first Mass in Rome and founded the Society of Jesus, also known as the Jesuits, who took a special vow of obedience to the pope. The Jesuits would become great missionaries, performing many deeds in the service of God and of the Church. Ignatius of Loyola watched over the Society of Jesus until he died a holy death.

St. Ignatius of Loyola, help me perform great deeds for God!

St. Alphonsus
Liguori
August 1

St. Alphonsus Liguori

1696–1787 • Italy

Raised by good Catholic parents, Alphonsus was a bright boy and quick in his studies. His father made him practice the harpsichord (a musical instrument similar to the piano) three hours every day. When he was thirteen, he played harpsichord as skillfully as a professional musician. His love for music stayed with him as he grew up. At the opera, Alphonsus would take off his glasses so that he could not see the singers, but only hear the music.

Alphonsus became a brilliant lawyer, and hardly ever lost a case. Then, one day, he took a very important case and suffered a crushing defeat because of a mistake he made. Alphonsus was humiliated. The judge and the other lawyers tried to make him feel better, but it was no use. Alphonsus no longer wanted to practice law. He realized that being a lawyer had made him much too proud, and that was why he was so upset when he lost. Now he understood that God was asking him to lead a humble life. But he still did not know exactly what God wanted him to do.

One day, he was visiting the sick in the hospital when a miraculous flood of light surrounded him. The building and ground seemed to shake, and a voice spoke inside his heart, saying, "Leave the world and give yourself to me." Immediately, he went to a nearby church and knelt before a statue of Our Lady. He would do as the voice commanded him: he would give up the world and become a priest.

After he was ordained, Alphonsus served the peasant people, especially the goatherds in the mountains, whom no one else preached to. When he was still a young priest, he started an order that would become known as the Redemptorists. He wrote many important books that taught others to live good and holy lives. Later in Alphonsus's life, the pope made him a bishop.

In his early seventies, Alphonsus suffered from a terrible fever that left him paralyzed. His neck was so bent that it pressed against his chest. For the rest of his life, Alphonsus had to drink his meals through a tube. But he offered his suffering to God until he died a holy death.

St. Alphonsus Liguori, help me listen to God's call and give myself to Him!

St. Peter Julian Eymard

August 2

St. Peter Julian Eymard

1811–1868 • France

Jesus loves us all so much that He came down from heaven, ate with us, talked with us, and even died for us. When He returned to heaven, Jesus promised He would never leave us. One of the ways He keeps this promise is by staying with us in the Blessed Sacrament of the Eucharist. The Eucharist is Jesus' Body and Blood that looks and tastes like bread and wine. Jesus is with us in the Eucharist at every Mass and in the tabernacle at your Catholic church. You can go to your church and sit and talk to Jesus in the Blessed Sacrament. One saint that especially loved Jesus in the Blessed Sacrament was St. Peter Julian Eymard.

Once, when Peter was a young boy in France, he went to his church carrying a small stool, which he then climbed up on in order to bring himself level to the tabernacle. His sister found him there and asked him why he was resting his head beside the tabernacle. He explained that he was trying to be close to Jesus and listen to Him.

Peter later became a priest. One day, he was carrying the Blessed Sacrament for a two-hour-long procession in honor of the Body of Christ. The grace of Jesus flooded his soul with such a strong love for the Blessed Sacrament that it brought tears to his eyes. To Peter, the procession seemed to race by in a single moment. His love for Jesus in the Eucharist was so great that he could have stayed with Him there forever.

Soon after, Peter went on a pilgrimage and returned with the conviction that he should start an order of priests dedicated to the Eucharist, and so he founded the Congregation of the Blessed Sacrament. Soon, a group of nuns and laypeople followed, all dedicated to adoring Jesus in the Blessed Sacrament.

If anyone ever went to Peter seeking comfort and strength, he would point to Jesus in the Eucharist! Peter worked very hard to tell others how much Jesus loved them and how Jesus waits patiently for each and every one of us to go to Him and spend time with Him in the Eucharist. Peter wrote many reflections on the Blessed Sacrament, and he explained that if we go to Jesus in the Blessed Sacrament, then we will receive special graces because Jesus wishes to share His love for us very much. Peter spread devotion to the Eucharist until he died a holy death.

St. Peter Julian Eymard, help us to go to Jesus in the Blessed Sacrament for comfort and strength!

St. Lydia of Philippi
August 3

St. Lydia of Philippi

Biblical figure

On the Sabbath, Lydia gathered with the rest of the women to pray by the riverbank on the outskirts of the Macedonian city of Philippi. She was a seller of purple-dyed cloth. Purple was a royal color and hard to come by.

Her entire household—children and servants—had come with her to pray. Two men also came to the riverbank to join the women at their prayers. They were strangers to the city, and Lydia had never seen them before. The older man's name was Paul, and the man who accompanied him was named Silas.

Paul was a great preacher, and Lydia listened in fascination as Paul told them all about Jesus the Christ, the Messiah, who had died and yet had risen on the third day. He told them about how he had once persecuted the followers of Jesus, until Jesus Himself had appeared to him in a dazzling light on the road to Damascus. Paul told them about how he had been blinded and then healed. Now he was traveling to spread the fire of love for Jesus.

God's grace filled Lydia's soul. Her heart was opened to Paul's words, and she believed that Jesus was the Son of God and that He had died out of love for her. Lydia asked to be baptized, and Paul baptized her and her entire household at the banks of the river. Lydia became Paul's first convert in Europe.

Gratitude filled Lydia's heart. God had sent this man, Paul, to tell her the Good News of His love and salvation. "If you consider me a believer in the Lord," she said to Paul, "come and stay at my home."

Paul and Silas stayed with Lydia and her household. While in the city, Paul and Silas were beaten by a crowd and thrown in jail for preaching about Jesus. After they were set free, Lydia took care of them for as long as they remained at Philippi to share God's Word with her people. Lydia was a follower of Jesus until she died a holy death.

St. Lydia, ask God to give me the grace always to open my heart toward Him!

St. Jean-Marie Vianney
August 4

St. Jean-Marie Vianney

1786–1859 • France

Growing up on a farm in France, Jean-Marie Vianney was better at plowing fields than studying. He had not gone to school when he was little, so as he grew up, learning was a painful struggle. But Jean-Marie had a good reason to work hard at his studies. He wanted to become a priest.

To become a priest, Jean-Marie had to pass an exam to enter the seminary (where you study to become a priest). Once inside the seminary, he would have to study philosophy, theology, and Latin to learn about the Faith. Jean-Marie knew he was not very smart, but that did not stop him from working hard. His teachers worked hard to help him too. They knew that Jean-Marie was not their smartest student. But they knew he was something more important. They knew he was holy. They knew he would make a wonderful priest.

Jean-Marie failed his first examination for the seminary. Still, he did not give up. Three months later, he passed the examination on his second try and soon became a priest at age twenty-nine. But even though he was now a priest, Jean-Marie's struggles were far from over.

Jean-Marie became the parish priest of a little town called Ars. The people of Ars did not pray, and the church was empty. But the people were curious about their new priest. First one person, and then another, went to Mass to hear Jean-Marie preach. His preaching was different from that of other priests they knew. His words were holy but also full of common sense. Slowly, the pews in church filled as more and more people went to Sunday Mass.

The townspeople also went to Jean-Marie for confession. His simple, holy words filled them with sorrow for their sins. If someone forgot to confess a sin, Jean-Marie could miraculously see into that person's heart and remind him about the forgotten sin. Jean-Marie's fame as a confessor spread. People from other towns throughout France and even from different countries all flocked to Ars to confess their sins to Jean-Marie Vianney. So many people were lined up that Jean-Marie would hear confessions sixteen and sometimes eighteen hours a day!

Near the end of his life, Jean-Marie's voice grew so faint it could barely be heard. But still people came to confession so that their sins could be forgiven and so that they could hear Jean-Marie's words of holiness and common sense. Jean-Marie Vianney served the people of Ars until he died a holy death.

St. Jean-Marie Vianney, help me to feel sorry for my sins!

Dedication of the Basilica of St. Mary Major

August 5

Dedication of the Basilica of St. Mary Major

352–366 • Italy

There are many beautiful and grand basilicas in Rome, "the Eternal City" whose bishop is the pope. One of the most beautiful and grandest is the great basilica in honor of Mary called St. Mary Major.

The inside of the basilica shines like a precious treasure. Above rows of columns run colorful images telling the story of Mary's life. Pictures made up of thousands of gleaming tiles in blue, red, and gold cover the arch. The boards of Jesus' holy manger were brought to Rome from the stable in Bethlehem. This wood has been gathered into a silver manger and placed in the crypt under the altar of the basilica.

There is a legend that a wealthy couple, without any children of their own, prayed to Mary to ask her what they should do with their riches.

One warm summer night, Our Lady appeared to them in a vision and told them to build a great church on the place that would be covered with snow.

The next morning, the couple rushed to Pope Liberius and told him about their vision. Imagine their surprise when the pope exclaimed that he had received the same vision! Pope Liberius called together a magnificent procession, and they marched through the city in search of Our Lady's snow. Sure enough, despite the summer heat, a blanket of glistening snow covered the summit of the Esquiline Hill, one of Rome's famous seven hills.

The Roman couple rejoiced over the miracle of snow in the Roman summer and generously gave of their riches to build a great church to God in honor of Mary at the top of the hill.

Once a year, on the Feast of the Dedication of St. Mary Major, a shower of white rose petals is scattered from the top of the basilica's dome in memory of the miraculous snowfall from Our Lady of the Snows.

Our Lady of the Snows, help me to give my best to God!

The Transfiguration

August 6

The Transfiguration

The Lord's Feast

Peter, James, and John followed Jesus up the steep climb to the top of Mt. Tabor. The three disciples felt honored. Jesus had especially chosen them out of the Twelve to accompany Him.

But the climb was hard and long. After some time, they reached the top, and, as Jesus went to pray to His Father, the disciples collapsed to the ground—they were so tired—and fell asleep. A presence stirred them in their sleep, and they slowly opened their eyes. What they saw startled them fully awake.

Jesus was speaking to two other men. But He was not the Jesus that they knew. His face had transformed to become great and splendid. His robe was dazzling white, and they could not look at it directly—it shone so brightly.

As Jesus continued speaking to the two men, the disciples understood that these men were Moses and Elijah, two great prophets from long ago. The disciples felt wonder, awe, and a little bit of fear.

When Peter saw these holy prophets with Jesus, he offered to build them three tents in case they wanted to stay. He realized that he was blabbering and that he did not really know what he was saying. He was so overcome by the wonder of it.

A luminous cloud descended from above and cast a shadow over Jesus, Moses, and Elijah. A mighty voice spoke forth from the cloud and resonated in the disciples' bones and hearts. "This is my chosen Son," it said. "Listen to Him."

Then the cloud disappeared, and along with it disappeared Moses and Elijah. Once again Jesus looked the way He usually did. His robe was worn and stained with travel. His face was the face of the Master, of their friend. Jesus told them not to tell the others what had happened; not until He had risen from the dead.

The disciples remained silent and did not tell the other disciples what they had seen when they rejoined them at the base of the mountain. They did not really understand what had happened, and it was not until after Jesus died and rose from the dead that they told the others about Jesus' Transfiguration.

As happened whenever they witnessed a great miracle, Peter, James, and John wondered who Jesus really was, because at that time they did not understand that Jesus was the Son of God and God Himself. But they knew that the Father had spoken. And they knew that they must listen to Jesus always. Dear Jesus, help me to listen to you always!

Pope St. Sixtus II
August 7

Pope St. Sixtus II

d. c. 258 • Rome

Sixtus II was pope when the emperor Valerian began mercilessly persecuting Christians. The punishment for being Christian was banishment, slavery, or even death. Sixtus knew he must lead and protect the Christians in his care, even at the risk of his own life.

In the dark and secret catacombs, the Christians gathered to avoid capture. The catacombs were underground burial places where other Christians, many of whom had died for the Faith, were laid to rest. There, Christians would celebrate Mass and pray at the tombs of the saints.

Pope Sixtus II and his deacons were saying Mass in the Catacombs of Praetextatus in Rome. Without warning, Roman soldiers burst upon them. The Christian faithful huddled together in fear. They had been discovered and knew that they would be put to death. A Roman soldier raised his sword, about to strike one of the Christians.

Pope Sixtus II stepped forward. In a commanding voice, he ordered the Roman soldier to halt.

Sixtus II was the pope and the leader. He declared that it was only right that he be the first to die for Christ, and he offered himself in place of his flock. He knew that his example would give strength and hope to the other Christians, so that they could face death with courage in their hearts and remain faithful to Jesus, the Good Shepherd who died for His flock—all of us.

Pope Sixtus II became a glorious martyr for Christ, and his brave deacons followed him in sacrifice. He had been pope for less than one year before he became a holy martyr, his courage bringing others to Jesus. If you listen carefully at Mass, you might hear the priest join his prayers with those of St. Sixtus II, along with other holy saints.

Pope St. Sixtus II, help me serve as an example of courage to others!

St. Dominic

August 8

St. Dominic

c. 1170–1221 • Spain

Bl. Joan of Aza had a dream that the baby in her womb was a dog carrying a torch in his mouth. The torch blazed so bright it illuminated the whole world. Soon, she gave birth to a baby boy and named him Dominic, and his words would shine so bright that they would illuminate the world, banishing the dark of falsehood.

Dominic grew up and studied at the university. His mind was sharp and his heart was kind. When famine struck the university town, he sold his books (which were very expensive because they had been copied by hand, word for word, which took many days) and his belongings to feed the poor. Soon after, he became a priest.

A heresy, which is a false teaching about the Catholic Faith, was spreading throughout Europe. Dominic knew he had to do everything he could to preach the truth so that he could save souls. But at first, when he preached from town to town, no one listened to him. Dominic's heart was heavy. He prayed to the Blessed Virgin for help. Tradition says that in answer to his prayers, the Blessed Virgin Mary appeared to Dominic and taught him how to pray the Rosary. She explained that praying the Rosary would bring sinners to Jesus. Dominic spread the devotion of the Rosary, and it is because of him that we have the Rosary today.

Strengthened by the graces of the Rosary, Dominic continued to preach the truth of the Catholic Faith. God granted him the power of miracles, too, so that others could see that God was with Dominic.

Dominic wrote a book about the truth of the Catholic Faith, and then he asked a heretic to give him a book about the heretic's false faith. Dominic summoned a crowd, and then he took both books and cast them into the fire. The heretic's book burned to ash. But not only was Dominic's book unharmed, it leapt from the fire to a safe place away from the flames. The crowd watched this miracle with astonishment. But that was not all: Dominic also healed the sick and even raised people from the dead through the power of Jesus. These miracles showed the power of God and the truth of Dominic's words, and so he won many souls back to the Catholic Faith.

Dominic formed an order of preachers to spread the light of the true Faith and banish the darkness of falsehood. Members of his order are called the Dominicans, and you can recognize them today by the white and black robes that they wear. Dominic preached the truth of Christ until he died a holy death.

St. Dominic, shine the light of the truth of Jesus in my soul!

St. Teresa Benedicta of the Cross (Edith Stein)
August 9

St. Teresa Benedicta of the Cross (Edith Stein)

1891–1942 • Germany

Edith was a Jewish girl in Germany, but she had left behind her Jewish faith because she did not know if God was real. Edith longed to learn what the truth was, and so she studied philosophy under the best masters in the university. She was a prized pupil and became a philosopher herself, writing many important works.

One day, she was inside a Catholic cathedral and saw a woman slip inside from the busy marketplace and kneel in silent prayer. Edith could not take her eyes away from the woman. She had never seen someone pray to God and speak to Him so closely, as if she and God were friends. This moment touched Edith's soul and made her wonder if maybe her desire for truth was really a desire for God.

Later, she was staying the night with some friends and was looking for something to read before going to sleep. She picked at random St. Teresa de Ávila's book about the story of her life. The book was so fascinating that Edith stayed up all night reading. When she had finished, she said, "This is the truth!" She realized that her longing for truth had been a prayer to God all along.

Edith became a Catholic and at the same time felt that she was Jewish again. She knew that Jesus was also a Jew, and that He was the promise of the Jewish religion. By becoming Catholic, she received the fullness of the faith that belonged to her blood. She wanted to become a Carmelite nun, but her spiritual advisers told her to remain at the university and teach. Edith agreed and through her teaching led others to God. But she did not remain a teacher for long.

Adolf Hitler and the Nazis were rising to power in Germany, and they wanted to hunt down and kill all the Jews. Edith was no longer allowed to teach at the university because of her Jewish blood. So she entered the Carmelite order and took the name Teresa Benedicta of the Cross. She knew the suffering of the Cross was her destiny and the destiny of the Jewish people. Soon, the Carmelite sisters snuck Edith out of Germany to a convent in the Netherlands because her life was in danger. Edith knew that her death was approaching, and she wrote down that she would willingly die if that was God's plan, offering her life for the salvation of Germany and the peace of the world.

The Nazis took over the Netherlands and hunted down the Jews and the Jewish Catholics. Edith was arrested and taken to the fearful concentration camp, Auschwitz, where she died offering her life up to God as she had said she would.

St. Teresa Benedicta of the Cross, help me offer up the crosses in my life to God!

St. Lawrence

August 10

St. Lawrence

d. 258 • Rome

Lawrence was a deacon in Rome who lived during the time of Emperor Valerian's persecution of Christians. His special job was to give the Church's money to the poor.

Having heard that Lawrence was in charge of the Church's riches, the chief Roman official summoned Lawrence and demanded that the deacon bring him all of the Church's treasure. Lawrence said that it was true that the Church had great treasure; in fact, the Church's riches were greater than anything the Roman emperor had in his treasure vault. He asked for a few days to gather all the riches to present to the Roman official.

The chief Roman official greedily rubbed his hands together. He could already imagine the Church's treasure—the silver cups and golden candlesticks. He would keep everything for himself! He let Lawrence go to gather the Church's treasure.

In a few days' time, Lawrence led the chief Roman official through the doors of his church. But instead of gold and silver, the official found men and women in rags, children with crutches, the ill, and the wounded, all crowded within the church. With a great sweep of his hands, Lawrence declared that these were the treasure of the Church: the poor and the sick. To God, these people were more valuable than gold and silver.

The chief Roman official was furious. He had no use for the poor and the sick. Lawrence had made a fool of him!

He ordered Lawrence's immediate arrest and torture. A large grid of iron was heated over a blazing fire. Lawrence was placed right on top. The flames licked his body, and the hot iron seared his flesh.

Despite his pain, Lawrence's spirit was not broken. After his body had been roasted on one side, Lawrence said to the guard, with a patient grin, "Turn me over. I've been grilled on this side long enough!" The soldier was astonished. Despite being tortured, Lawrence was making a joke, pretending he needed to be flipped over to be cooked properly!

Lawrence endured his pain bravely, offering his suffering to God in prayer. He died a glorious martyr for the Faith.

St. Lawrence, help me to endure my suffering with good humor!

St. Clare

August 11

St. Clare

1194–1253 • Italy

Eighteen-year-old Clare, in her fine dress and with perfectly combed hair, could not take her eyes away from the friar living like a beggar. The friar was St. Francis of Assisi, and he preached about how we can live as Jesus did, in poverty and humility.

St. Francis's words touched Clare's soul, and she went to Francis and told him that she, too, wanted to live as Jesus had lived and become a poor and humble nun. Both Francis and Clare knew that it would not be easy for her to become a nun. She was the oldest daughter of a noble family, and her parents would want her to marry a wealthy man. So Francis and Clare hatched a plan.

In the dead of night, Clare snuck out of her parents' home with her aunt to meet Francis in a small chapel. There, he and his friars were waiting for her, holding bright candles in the dark. Clare changed out of her rich dress into a poor robe and veil and made her vows to live in poverty and humility, like Jesus.

Clare's parents were furious and tried to drag her back home. But she bravely resisted them, and when they saw that nothing would change her mind, they let her remain a nun.

Clare and some other nuns lived in the poor church of San Damiano, the church that St. Francis had rebuilt with his own hands right outside of Assisi. Clare became the leader of the Franciscan nuns, who became known as the Poor Clares.

One day, when Clare was sick in bed, an army attacked Assisi. Hearing that soldiers were scaling the walls of San Damiano, Clare rose from her sickbed and took the monstrance containing the Eucharist from the chapel.

Clare knew that Jesus would protect Assisi.

She went to the walls and lifted the monstrance up high. A brilliant light shone from the monstrance, and the soldiers fell back and ran away in fright.

A new commander arrived with an even larger army to conquer the city. This time, Clare gathered her nuns, and they prayed for Assisi on their knees. A terrible storm broke out, and the winds uprooted the army tents and scattered the soldiers so that they, too, ran away. Assisi was saved, and the people celebrated with cheers that Clare and her nuns had defended the city.

Clare led the Poor Clares until she died a holy death. St. Clare, please help me to live in poverty and humility!

St. Jane Frances de Chantal
August 12

St. Jane Frances de Chantal

1572–1641 • France

A young noblewoman, Jane, married the Baron de Chantal and had four children. Christ was the center of their home, and her marriage was happy. But then the baron died in a hunting accident, and Jane de Chantal felt that her heart would break. With tears in her eyes, she spent hours praying before the Blessed Sacrament. She felt that God was calling her to make a great sacrifice of her life, but she did not know what He wanted of her yet.

One day, when Jane was out riding in the woods, she spied a man—dressed as a bishop and with a kind and holy face—ahead of her in the trees. A voice in her heart told her that she should go to this man for spiritual advice. But when she reached the spot in the woods where he had been, the man had disappeared. Jane realized that she had received a vision from God.

Not long after, Jane and her children went to live with her father-in-law, who was cranky and proud. He and his servants made life even more difficult for the sorrowing Jane. But she bore her father-in-law's bad humor with patience and gentleness.

One Lent, when Jane was visiting her elderly father, she went to the local church to hear the bishop preach. Her heart skipped a beat when she recognized the bishop's kind and holy face: he was the man from her vision! The bishop's name was Francis de Sales, and he, too, would one day become a saint.

Francis de Sales became Jane's spiritual adviser. Through his letters and wise words, she grew in holiness. She set aside special times in her day for prayer in the morning and evening, and she always took care to accomplish her duties in the home and raise her children in the Catholic Faith.

Jane realized that God was calling her to be a nun and give her life completely to Him. She told Francis de Sales about God's call for her, and together they started a new order of nuns called the Order of the Visitation. Most nuns lived hard lives that prevented those with weaker health from joining them. But the nuns of the Order of the Visitation would offer small sacrifices continuously to God to grow in holiness. That way, any woman could answer God's call! Jane led the order until she died a holy death. St. Jane Frances de Chantal, help me to discover God's call for me!

Sts. Pontian and Hippolytus

August 13

Sts. Pontian and Hippolytus

d. 235 • Italy

Pontian and Hippolytus were enemies. They lived during the Roman persecution of Christians, a time when many Christians gave up their faith in Jesus out of weakness and fear. Pontian was the pope and taught that if sinners who had left the Faith were sorry for what they had done, then Jesus would forgive them and welcome them back to His Church. Hippolytus was a priest who thought that the pope was being too kind and forgiving. He said that if Christians denied Christ, then they could not come back to the Church. Hippolytus was so angry with the pope that he set himself up as the pope's rival.

Hippolytus's rebellion against the pope was cut short when Emperor Maximinus arrested him for being a Christian. But he did not only arrest Hippolytus—he arrested Pope Pontian too! Pontian resigned the papacy so the Church could elect a new pope. That way, the Church could still have a leader while he was imprisoned. The emperor sentenced Pontian and Hippolytus to work in the mines for the rest of their lives because they were Christians.

Together, Pontian and Hippolytus labored in the hard, cruel mines. In the dark underground, the days were long, the air dank, and the food scanty and poor. Pontian's and Hippolytus's bodies grew weaker as time went by, but their faith grew stronger. Hippolytus realized that he was a sinner, that he should never have set himself up against Jesus' Church and His pope. He fell on his knees to beg Pontian's forgiveness and asked if they could become friends.

Pontian forgave Hippolytus with all his heart and welcomed him back into the Church. He rejoiced that the grace of God had allowed them to suffer together so that they would no longer be enemies but could become friends. Both Pontian and Hippolytus died in the mines, their friendship in God strengthening them until they became glorious martyrs for Jesus.

Sts. Pontian and Hippolytus, help me bring my friends to Jesus!

St. Maximilian Kolbe
August 14

St. Maximilian Kolbe

1894–1941 • Poland

When Maximilian was twelve years old, the most beautiful woman appeared to him in a vision. It was the Blessed Virgin Mary, and she held in her hands two crowns, one red and the other white. She explained that the red crown was the crown of martyrdom and that the white crown was the crown of purity. Then she gazed into his eyes and asked him if he would accept one of the crowns. Even though Maximilian was young, he knew that both of the crowns were treasures and that both would lead him to Jesus. He told the Blessed Virgin Mary that he would accept both crowns.

Maximilian grew up to become a priest especially dedicated to Our Lady. Through his life of priestly purity, he received the white crown that Our Lady had offered him. He started a radio program and a magazine called the *Knight of the Immaculata* to win the world to Christ with the help of Our Lady. He traveled to Japan and India, where he published his magazine in different languages, so that he could spread Jesus' message throughout the world. But then he had to return to his home country of Poland because of ill health.

Suffering and tragedy struck when the Nazis took over Poland. The Nazis specifically persecuted the Jewish people, but they also killed Catholics and outlawed priests. They arrested Maximilian and sent him to Auschwitz, a terrible concentration camp where few survived.

One day, a prisoner escaped Auschwitz, and to punish the rest of the prisoners, the guards chose ten other men to die in the escapee's place. One of the doomed prisoners was a man named Franciszek Gajowniczek. Franciszek begged for mercy because he had a wife and children and wanted to live.

Maximilian's heart leapt with pity for Franciszek. He bravely stepped forward and offered to die in his place. In this he imitated Jesus, who died for you and me. The guards accepted his sacrifice, and Maximilian and the nine other men were locked in a cell to starve to death. There in the cell, Maximilian led the other men in songs and prayer, and gave them peace and courage for their deaths. After two weeks of starvation, Maximilian was still alive, so the Nazis put him to death. He received the red crown offered to him by Our Lady and became a glorious martyr for the Faith.

Franciszek Gajowniczek survived the concentration camp because of Maximilian Kolbe's sacrifice. He was present at Maximilian's canonization, when the pope declared Maximilian Kolbe a saint, and he lived to be ninety-three.

St. Maximilian Kolbe, help me to offer sacrifices out of love for others!

The Assumption

August 15

The Assumption

Marian Feast Day

With sadness in their hearts, the Apostles went to visit the Blessed Virgin Mary's tomb to say their final goodbyes.

She had looked so peaceful in death. It was as if she had only been sleeping! They knew that she was now reunited with her Son, but they would miss her love, her wisdom, and all of her stories about Jesus.

But when the Apostles entered the tomb, Mary's body was nowhere to be found, and the tomb was filled with the most exquisite and fragrant of flowers.

The Apostles fell on their knees, their hearts rejoicing.

Jesus had raised His Mother from the dead, both body and soul, and now she was with Him forever in heaven.

God the Father had saved Mary from the stain of Original Sin because she was to be the Mother of His Beloved Son. She never committed a sin, and she was pure and full of grace! When she died, Jesus honored His Mother by assuming her body and soul into heaven to reign as queen at His side. Mary is Queen of the Angels, Queen of the Saints, and Queen of Heaven and Earth.

Mary shows us what will happen if we live the way that she did, saying to God in everything great and small, "Let it be done to me according to your will." If we love Jesus the way that Mary loved Him, then our souls, too, will go to heaven when we die.

At the end of days, God will also raise our bodies from the dead, and they will be reunited with our souls.

The Blessed Virgin Mary's Assumption is a promise of what is to come!

Dear Mary, assumed into heaven body and soul, help me to love Jesus the way you did!

St. Stephen of Hungary
August 16

St. Stephen of Hungary

c. 969–1038 • Hungary

It was a joyful day when a son was born to the pagan chief Géza of Hungary. Géza and his wife, Sarolta, named their baby boy Vaik. Sarolta was a Christian, and she invited the bishop St. Adalbert to the Hungarian court as a teacher for her growing son. St. Adalbert was such a good teacher that both father and son were baptized into the Christian Faith together, and Vaik took the Christian name of Stephen.

When Géza died, Stephen took the throne. He sent a message to Pope Sylvester II, asking his help in spreading the Christian Faith throughout Hungary. The pope granted Stephen his help, sending back to the king a royal crown, and so Stephen was crowned the Christian king of Hungary.

Stephen desired that Hungary give up its pagan ways and become a Catholic country. He sent priests and monks to preach throughout his kingdom, and he even preached to the crowds himself about the glory of Christianity. He routed the pagans in the kingdom with his army, passed just laws, and especially took care of the poor. He would even go about the kingdom in disguise to give out alms, and he never refused alms to a poor person who asked him for help. Because of King Stephen, all of Hungary became Catholic.

King Stephen was married to Bl. Gisela, sister of the Holy Roman emperor, and they had a son, Emeric. Together, they raised their son to love Jesus and the Faith. As he grew into manhood, Emeric became known for his holiness. King Stephen planned to pass on his kingdom to his son and retire to a monastery where he could end his life in prayer. But this was not to be.

One sorrowful day, Emeric died in a hunting accident. The grieving king offered this great loss to God and continued to rule over his kingdom faithfully. On his deathbed, he dedicated the Kingdom of Hungary to Mary, the Mother of God. He died on the Feast of the Assumption, when the Church celebrates that Mary was assumed by God into heaven both in body and in soul.

St. Stephen of Hungary, help me to dedicate my work to the Great Mother of God!

St. Hyacinth
August 17

St. Hyacinth

1185–1257 • modern-day Poland

Hyacinth was saying Mass when a cry of alarm sounded through the city. The non-Christian Mongols were attacking the capital city of Kiev! The Dominican priest did not let the tumult disturb him, but devoutly finished the Mass. After he said the final blessing, Hyacinth knew he must escape the city and take with him the city's most precious treasure: the Most Sacred Body of Jesus in the Eucharist.

Without taking off his priestly robes, he took the golden ciborium—the sacred vessel that holds the Eucharist—from the tabernacle and called his fellow priests to follow him. With great haste, he made to depart from the church. But as he passed the statue of Our Lady, before which he often said his prayers, Mary's statue called out to him in reproach, "My son Hyacinth, will you leave me here to be at the mercy of my enemies?"

Her voice brought tears to Hyacinth's eyes. He had to leave her behind, Hyacinth explained in a brokenhearted voice. Mary's statue was of solid alabaster, and Hyacinth explained that the statue was much too heavy to carry. "Try," was Mary's calm command. "My Son will help you carry me without difficulty." And so Hyacinth wrapped his one free arm around the statue, and, wonder of wonders, he discovered that he could just lift the statue and carry it away.

With the ciborium in one hand and Mary's statue in the other, Hyacinth and his priests dodged through the flames of the city under attack. God protected them from their enemies, and they passed through the city gate and reached the river Dnieper without meeting a single soldier. But now the river blocked their path, and there was no bridge to cross it.

Hyacinth knew that he was being watched over by Jesus and Mary. He firmly stepped upon the Dnieper River and did not sink, and so he carried the Eucharist and Mary's statue safely across the river without getting wet. The priests with him marveled at so great a miracle.

After this attack, Hyacinth returned to his home country of Poland to preach and look after the Dominican monasteries he had founded there. Hyacinth had been received into the Dominican order by its holy founder, St. Dominic, himself. As a missionary priest, Hyacinth preached and worked miracles all throughout Poland, eastern Europe, and Russia.

When he was seventy-two years old, God revealed to Hyacinth that he would die on the Feast of the Assumption of the Blessed Virgin Mary. On that great feast of Mary, Hyacinth assisted at Mass, received the final sacraments, and died a holy death.

St. Hyacinth, help me to remember that Jesus and Mary are always watching over me!

St. Helena

August 18

St. Helena

c. 248–c. 328 • Modern-day Turkey

The empress Helena had traveled to the Holy Land to find the true Cross of Jesus Christ. It was to the Sign of the Cross that Helena owed her faith.

Helena thought back on when her son, Constantine the Great, was newly crowned emperor of Rome. He had had to defend his title against the much larger forces of the usurper Maxentius. On the march with his army, Constantine had looked up at the sun above and seen a cross of light with the words "In this sign, you will conquer." Bewildered, Constantine did not know what this sign meant.

That night, Jesus Himself appeared to Constantine and explained that he must use this sign as protection against his enemies. And so Constantine had the Sign of the Cross, with Jesus' initials, placed on the flag leading his army into battle. Constantine's army defeated Maxentius's men at the Milvian Bridge across Rome's Tiber River. Constantine made Christianity legal throughout his empire, and, through her son, Helena had learned all about Jesus.

Now, after much searching, Helena had uncovered three crosses buried in a great mound on top of Jesus' tomb. Two of the crosses belonged to the good and bad thieves crucified beside Jesus, and one of the crosses was Jesus' true Cross. But there was no way to tell which was which!

The bishop Macarius, leader of the Church in Jerusalem, had a wonderful idea. He knew a woman who was dying from a terrible illness. He had her touch each of the three crosses. When the woman touched the true Cross on which Jesus had died, she was miraculously healed! The true Cross of Jesus had been found! No one rejoiced more than Empress Helena.

Macarius climbed the pulpit of his great church and lifted high the true Cross so that everyone could see it! The people cried, "Lord, have mercy!" when they saw Jesus' Cross.

Helena left the Cross in the great Church of the Holy Sepulchre, which was constructed around Jesus' tomb. But she also brought pieces of the true Cross back home with her to Rome, so that Christians from all over the world could venerate Jesus' true Cross. Soon after she returned to Rome, Empress Helena died a holy death.

St. Helena, help me to love the Cross of Jesus!

St. John Eudes

August 19

St. John Eudes

1601–1680 • France

From a young age, John Eudes knew that he wanted to give his entire life to Jesus and Mary. At the age of fourteen, he promised Jesus that he would never marry, and he became a priest at the age of twenty-four.

Soon after he became a priest, a terrible plague struck Normandy. The young priest took care of many sick and dying villagers no one would care for, out of fear of the disease. Because John was constantly exposed to the terrible sickness, he himself was afraid that he might pass on the plague to his fellow priests.

Then he had an idea.

When he was not taking care of the sick, he would live in a large barrel turned on its side in the middle of a field. That way, he would not pass on the plague to anyone else!

For the next six years, John Eudes cared for the plague victims. All throughout, he prayed to Jesus and Mary to give him strength, and they protected him.

When the plague had passed, John wanted to do whatever he could to share his love for Jesus and Mary with others. John began a mission to preach and hear confessions all throughout France.

Because he knew how important it is to have good priests, he started the Congregation of Jesus and Mary, dedicated to educating priests and to missionary work. He also founded the Order of the Sisters of Our Lady of Charity to care for unfortunate women with nowhere else to go.

John Eudes wrote books about how praying to Mary brings us closer to her Son, Jesus. He even composed the prayers for the Masses celebrating the Feasts of the Immaculate Heart of Mary and the Sacred Heart of Jesus. John Eudes continued preaching and writing until the end of his life. He died saying the names of Jesus and Mary on his deathbed.

St. John Eudes, bring me closer to the Hearts of Jesus and Mary!

St. Bernard of Clairvaux
August 20

St. Bernard of Clairvaux

1090–1153 • France

Every morning, Bernard would ask himself one question.

Why am I here?

Every day, he came up with the same answer.

I am here to lead a holy life.

Bernard had joined the monastery at a young age. And his love for a life of prayer and holiness had brought him, along with his entire family, to the monastery: all five of his brothers and his widowed father joined him there, and his sister entered a convent.

Ever since Bernard could remember, he had a deep love for Jesus and Mary. Now, at the young age of twenty-five, he was the founder and leader of the Abbey of Clairvaux, a position usually given to older men. But even though Bernard was young, he was also wise and, more importantly, holy. And so, every morning, Bernard would kneel on the cold, stone floor and remind himself that he was at the monastery to lead a holy life. He was here to help the monks under his care lead holy lives too.

Bernard wrote many books about the Blessed Virgin Mary. He wrote about how she is the Mother of the Church. She loves us so much that she wants nothing more than to bring us to her beloved Son, Jesus! One day, when Bernard was praying to the Blessed Virgin Mary, he said aloud to her picture, "I greet thee, O Queen of Heaven." And the image of Mary from the picture responded, "I greet thee, Bernard."

Bernard was also a preacher and miracle-worker. Everywhere Bernard went, people followed him to enter religious life. In addition to his abbey, Bernard helped establish the Knights Templar, an order of religious knights and monks who renounced earthly possessions and fought in the Holy Land. He cured the blind, the lame, and the deaf through the name of Jesus. Near the end of his life, he spent his days and nights in his little monk's cell in prayer, until he died a holy death.

St. Bernard of Clairvaux, help me to lead a holy life!

Pope St. Pius X
August 21

Pope St. Pius X

1835–1914 • Italy

Young Giuseppe Sarto was the oldest of eight children born to a poor postman and a seamstress. Every day, he walked almost four miles to go to school—often barefoot and carrying his shoes so they would not wear out. Giuseppe worked hard at his studies because he knew that Jesus was calling him to become a priest. Little did he know that Jesus was also calling him to become His representative on earth: the pope!

Giuseppe was ordained a priest at the age of twenty-three, and for many years he served God, first as a priest, later as a bishop, and then as a cardinal. Finally, he was elected pope at the age of sixty-eight, taking the name Pius X.

Pope Pius X had a deep love for Jesus in the Eucharist. Whenever he talked about the Eucharist, his eyes would shine with love and joy. He knew that Jesus wants us to receive Him and that when we do, we receive an unimaginable number of graces because we hold Jesus inside of us.

At that time, children did not receive Holy Communion until they were twelve or even fourteen years old. But the pope did not believe that Jesus would want children to wait so long to receive Him. After all, did not Jesus tell His Apostles, "Let the children come to me" (Matt. 19:14)? So instead, he lowered the age to receive Holy Communion to around seven years. That was old enough, he thought, for children to understand fully that they were receiving Jesus' Body, Blood, Soul, and Divinity in Holy Communion. (If you are under twelve years old and have received your First Communion, you have Pope St. Pius X to thank for this great gift!)

Even though he was pope, he never forgot that he was born poor and that he owed everything he had to God. He wrote in his will, "I was born poor, I have lived poor, and I wish to die poor," before he died a holy death.

Pope St. Pius X, help me receive Jesus in Holy Communion with love and joy in my heart!

The Queenship of the Blessed Virgin Mary

August 22

The Queenship of the Blessed Virgin Mary

Marian Feast Day

Mary is crowned Queen of Heaven and Earth. She is queen over the angels. She is queen over the saints. She is queen over all people.

She is queen over you and me.

When the Father assumed Mary into heaven, both body and soul, He crowned her queen to honor how she is the Mother of His Son and the holiest of the saints. She is the Mother of Jesus, who is the great King of all. He rules the earth and the heavens with power. He brings us justice, mercy, and peace.

As queen, Mary watches especially over you and over me.

We can go to her with all of our troubles, our sorrows, hurts, and needs.

We can go to her with all of our joys, our laughter, and our hearts bursting with song.

Mary takes everything we bring to her and lays it before the mighty throne of the King, her Son, Jesus.

Jesus loves His Mother. When He sees all of our troubles and our joys gathered in her gentle hands, His heart moves with pity and mercy. He grants Mary whatever she wishes. Mary wishes to bring us closer to her Son.

Remember that you have a Mother in heaven and that she is loving and kind.

Remember that she is a gracious queen, and she rules with gentleness next to the throne of her Son.

Dear Mary, may you always be the queen of my heart!

St. Rose of Lima
August 23

St. Rose of Lima

1586–1617 • Peru

The baby slept in her cradle with a peaceful smile on her face. On her cheek was a delicate red mark shaped like a rose. Her mother tenderly caressed the mark on the tiny cheek, and from that day on she called her little baby Rose.

From a very early age, Rose gave signs that God had touched her soul in a special way. When little children are hurt, they usually cry. But Rose would not cry; she would offer up her pain to God. She stopped eating all fruit, meat, and candy as a sacrifice to God. When she was only five, Rose promised that she would never marry because she wanted to give herself completely to God.

Her favorite place to pray was a little shed in the garden. It was small, dark, and quiet. But there was one problem.

The shed was full of mosquitos—mosquitos that buzzed and pricked, flying to and fro! Who could concentrate in prayer among such pests? But when Rose entered, the mosquitos fell silent and let her pray. If others tried to disturb her prayer, the mosquitos drove them away, and Rose left her flying friends in peace.

Rose grew into a beautiful young woman, and her parents wished her to marry. But Rose cut off her hair and took the Dominican veil, and so her parents let her keep her vow to God.

The garden was still Rose's favorite place to pray, and she placed little crosses among the green plants and flowers. A small hut was built to replace the little shed, and there she spent her days praying, making sacrifices, and sewing fine embroidery to help support her family.

Rose never committed a mortal sin in all her life. She watched over her words so that she never said anything unkind. She wore an uncomfortable silver band on her head to remind her of Jesus' crown of thorns. Jesus appeared to Rose in visions. Her greatest joy was when Jesus called her His bride.

At the age of thirty-one, she received a vision from God showing her that she would soon die with great suffering. Rose accepted her suffering without fear and soon became terribly ill. She endured the pain peacefully and received the last sacraments with great joy before she died a holy death.

St. Rose of Lima, help me not to become distracted in prayer!

St. Bartholomew

August 24

St. Bartholomew

Biblical figure

The day was hot, and a man was resting under the shade of a fig tree, lost in his thoughts.

Someone called out the man's name: "Bartholomew!" Startled, Bartholomew saw that it was his friend Philip calling.

"We have found Him!" Philip exclaimed. With growing excitement, Philip explained that he had found the man that Moses and the prophets had promised would come to save the Jewish people. The man's name was Jesus, and He was from Nazareth.

Bartholomew snorted and asked, "Can anything good come from Nazareth?" Nazareth was a little village in the middle of nowhere. Surely nobody important could come from Nazareth.

All that Philip said in response was, "Come and see."

And so Bartholomew rose and followed his friend, who led him to the man named Jesus. When Jesus saw Bartholomew coming, He declared, "Here is a true Israelite." And Jesus explained that Bartholomew was an honest man: there was no trickery or falsehood in him.

Bartholomew was amazed. It was as if Jesus had just looked into his heart. "How do you know me?" he asked.

"Before Philip called you, I saw you under the fig tree," Jesus responded.

Bartholomew felt even greater astonishment. How could Jesus have known that he had been under a fig tree? It was a miracle! Bartholomew realized that everything that Philip had said about Jesus was true. He exclaimed that Jesus was the Son of God and the King of Israel.

Jesus gently smiled at Bartholomew. "Do you believe because I told you that I saw you under the fig tree? You will see greater things than this."

And Bartholomew did.

He became one of Jesus' Twelve Apostles. He saw Jesus heal the blind, the lame, and the deaf. He saw Jesus raise Lazarus from his tomb. He saw Jesus risen from the dead.

Bartholomew preached the Good News that Jesus rose from the dead, and he became a glorious martyr for the Master whom he loved.

St. Bartholomew, help me to listen to those who call me to Jesus!

St. Louis IX

August 25

St. Louis IX

1214–1270 • France

Louis became the king of France when he was only twelve years old. His mother helped him rule until he was twenty-two, and she taught the young king that it was better to die than to commit a mortal sin. As he grew into manhood, Louis declared that it was a higher honor to be a Christian than to be a king. More than anything, he desired to be both a king and a saint.

King Louis knew that being king did not mean seizing all the wealth and power that he wanted. Being king meant that he must protect and serve his people the way that Jesus served His Church. Every Saturday, King Louis washed the feet of the poor, and every day he fed over one hundred of the hungry at his castle. Twice a week, he would sit in the garden or under a tree to give his royal judgment. Rich and poor alike could come to him, and he would settle their disputes in mercy and justice.

The emperor gave King Louis the wondrous relic of the crown of thorns that Jesus wore on His head during His Passion. When the relic reached France, King Louis greeted it in a great procession and marched barefoot with the relic to Paris. To house the relic, he built the glorious Sainte-Chappelle, with walls soaring with brilliant stained-glass and a ceiling spangled with stars.

In the eighteenth year of his reign, King Louis fell so ill that his attendants despaired of his life. They brought a relic of the true Cross to his bedside, and soon the king recovered. In thanksgiving for his healing, the king promised to go on crusade. For King Louis, the Crusades were a way of protecting Christians in the Holy Land.

The king set off on crusade, prevailing in many hard-won battles, but he was then captured by the enemy. A great ransom was paid, and he returned home to govern his kingdom. But when he heard that Christians were still being persecuted in the Holy Land, he set off on a second crusade. A terrible fever raged through his army, and King Louis caught the fever and knew he was soon to die. So he passed on his advice to his son, the crown prince, on how to be a holy and just king. On his deathbed, he received the sacraments and kissed the crucifix. His last words were a prayer from the Psalms.

St. Louis IX, help me to know that there is no higher honor in the world than to be a good Christian!

St. Melchizedek
August 26

St. Melchizedek

Biblical figure

Abraham lived almost two thousand years before Jesus was born. God called Abraham out of Haran and into the wilderness to find the Promised Land. Abraham left behind his home and all the lands he had ever known to listen to God's call. He is known as the "Father of Faith" to both the Jewish people and to Christians.

After Abraham had won a great battle against his enemies, he was greeted by Melchizedek, a priest and the king of Salem. Melchizedek's name means "king of righteousness," and the name of his city, Salem, means "peace." Later, Salem would have a new name: Jerusalem, that holy city where Jesus would one day die to bring peace between God and man.

The priest Melchizedek served God Most High. He brought out an offering of bread and wine, and with them he blessed Abraham and gave thanks to God for Abraham's victory. In return, Abraham gave Melchizedek a tenth of everything he had, including the treasures of the enemies he had defeated.

Almost two thousand years later, Jesus would also make an offering of bread and wine at the Last Supper, giving thanks to God. Jesus transformed bread and wine into His Body and Blood. Jesus became both priest and sacrifice, offering His own Body and Blood as a sacrifice on the Cross for the forgiveness of our sins. This is why the Bible says, "You are a priest forever according to the order of Melchizedek" (Heb. 5:6).

Today at Mass the priest offers bread and wine to God, just as the priest Melchizedek did many years ago.

St. Melchizedek, please bring peace and blessing to my home!

St. Monica
August 27

St. Monica

322–387 • North Africa

Monica was a Christian woman from Roman North Africa and was married to a man named Patricius. Patricius was a pagan, and he thought Monica's Christian care for the poor and love of God were a waste of time. Monica prayed and worked hard to be a good wife. She was gentle, faithful, and kind, even when Patricius lost his temper. Because of this, Patricius was kind to Monica too.

She and Patricius had a son named Augustine. Augustine was raised a Christian but lost his faith and lived a wild life that gave his mother sorrow.

Monica wept and prayed to God that her husband and her son would become Christians. The years went by, and it seemed that God did not hear her prayers. But Monica did not stop sending her prayers and tears to God. Finally, Patricius was baptized and spent the end of his life as a Christian.

But Monica's beloved son Augustine did not want to be a Christian. He had become a brilliant scholar and speaker, but for all his brilliance, he still enjoyed living a sinful life. Monica loved her son and was willing to do anything to bring him to God. She left her home in Africa and followed him to Rome, and later to Milan, so that she could share the Faith with him and bring him to God.

Still, Augustine did not listen. And so Monica went down on her knees, wept, and sent her prayers to God. She prayed and prayed, trusting that God would hear her.

In the middle of Monica's tearful prayer, the Blessed Virgin Mary appeared to her. She spoke gentle words of comfort to Monica. Then the Blessed Virgin took off her belt and gave it to Monica, telling her to wear it so that she would remember that Mary would always be with her.

After many years of resisting his mother's faith, Augustine finally realized his mother was right and became a Christian. Monica told her son about her vision of Mary, and he, too, wore a black belt around his waist to remember the Blessed Virgin Mary always. Because of Monica's patience and tireless prayer, her son became one of the greatest teachers of the Faith, St. Augustine. To this day, the Augustinian monks wear a black belt around their robes in memory of the belt that the Blessed Virgin Mary gave to Monica.

Shortly after her son's conversion, Monica died on her way home to Africa. She died a holy death with the joy of knowing that God had heard her prayers.

St. Monica, help me to never give up praying to God!

St. Augustine of Hippo
August 28

St. Augustine of Hippo

354–430 • North Africa

Augustine was a wild and restless youth, and he caused his mother, Monica, much worry. Monica had raised him as a Christian, but Augustine lost his faith and lived a sinful life. He was a brilliant scholar and speaker, and he left his home in North Africa to teach speech-making in Italy. His mother followed him, and through her prayers and the teachings of the holy bishop St. Ambrose, Augustine returned to the Faith and was baptized on Easter.

He and his mother made preparations to return home to Africa. But to his great sorrow, Monica passed away before they could make their journey. Augustine returned to his home, gave his money to the poor, and lived a life of prayer. In prayer, Augustine found peace. He realized that because God had made each and every one of us to love Him more than anything, only in God could our restless hearts find rest.

When the bishop of the city of Hippo died, Augustine (who had already been ordained a priest) was consecrated bishop. He gave eloquent speeches and wrote letters and books in defense of the Faith.

One day, Augustine was walking by the seashore, lost in thought. He was trying to understand the mystery of the Trinity, how there could be three Persons in one God. His thoughts were interrupted when he noticed a child on the shore in front of him doing a curious thing. The child had dug a small hole in the sand and was using a seashell to pour in water from the sea.

Augustine asked the child what he was trying to do.

The child explained that he was trying to pour the entire sea into his hole in the sand.

"Impossible!" Augustine exclaimed. The sea was too great and vast to be poured into a small hole dug in the sand.

"It is easier for me to pour all of the sea into this hole," the child explained, "than for you to understand the Trinity." Then the child disappeared. Now Augustine understood that the child had been sent by God to tell him that the mystery of the Trinity was too great and vast for him to understand.

Augustine served as bishop of Hippo until he died a holy death. St. Augustine, help my heart to rest in God!

The Martyrdom
of St. John
the Baptist
August 29

The Martyrdom of St. John the Baptist

Biblical figure

John the Baptist was the last and greatest prophet. He was Jesus' cousin; he had prepared the way for Jesus and had baptized Him in the river Jordan. He called people to repent for their sins because God's Kingdom was at hand!

Because he was a prophet, John the Baptist always spoke the truth. He told Herod, the ruler of Jerusalem, that he was committing a sin because he had stolen and married his brother's wife. Herod was furious. He was the ruler! To him, that meant he could do whatever he wanted, even breaking God's Law. He ordered John the Baptist's arrest and threw him in prison. But he did not kill John the Baptist because he knew the people loved the prophet, and he did not want them to rise up in anger.

But this was not enough for Herodias, Herod's wife. She plotted a way to take John the Baptist's life. She had a beautiful daughter named Salome and decided she would use her daughter to get her revenge. And so Herodias told Salome to dance at Herod's birthday party.

Salome did as her mother asked, and she danced so beautifully before Herod that the king was delighted. In front of all his guests, Herod promised he would give Salome anything she wanted as a reward for her dance.

Salome went to her mother, who whispered in her ear. Salome returned to King Herod and asked for the reward her mother had whispered to her: the head of John the Baptist on a platter.

Herod turned pale, and a loud groan burst from his lips. He was afraid because he did not want to murder God's prophet. But he had made a foolish promise in front of his guests, who would mock him if he refused now.

Herod felt trapped. But in the end, he cared more about what other people thought about him than what God thought about him. And so he ordered John the Baptist's death. John the Baptist died a glorious martyr because he stood up for the truth of God's Law. He died as a prophet of God, preparing the way for Jesus, who is the Way, the Truth, and the Life.

St. John the Baptist, please help me always to stand up for the truth of God's Law!

St. Margaret Ward

August 30

St. Margaret Ward

d. 1588 • England

The loud clank of the turning key resounded throughout the prison. Margaret Ward's fingers brushed against the rough fibers of the rope hidden under her cloak as she waited for the jailer to let her into the priest's cell.

Queen Elizabeth I of England had outlawed Catholicism, and so Fr. Richard Watson had been imprisoned for secretly saying Mass for English Catholics. Margaret Ward was one of the faithful English Catholics, and when she had heard that Fr. Watson was in prison, she had begun to visit him.

At first, the jailer had searched Margaret carefully before letting her into the priest's cell. But Margaret had noticed that he was growing more and more careless with each visit. The last time, he had not searched her at all! Now Margaret held her breath as the jailer let her into Fr. Watson's cell. The lazy guard never bothered to look and see what was under her cloak! After the guard left, Margaret hastily handed Fr. Watson the rope, and he bestowed on her his grateful blessing. Together, they made plans for escape.

Under cover of darkness, Fr. Watson lowered himself from the prison's high window. But the rope was not long enough! With a prayer to God, he let go and landed with a loud crack. Two boatmen waiting to rescue him hurried over and carried him to their boat. One boatman—John Roche, Margaret's servant and friend—swapped clothes with Fr. Watson to help disguise him. The boatmen rowed the priest to safety.

The jailer rushed out in alarm, found the rope, and knew that Fr. Watson had escaped. He also knew that Margaret Ward was the only one who could have given him the rope. He sent the constables to arrest Margaret. They captured John, too, because he was found dressed in the priest's clothes.

In prison, Margaret Ward was promised freedom if she gave up the Catholic Faith. But Margaret refused. She knew that the Catholic Church was the true Church Jesus had founded on earth, and that to deny her Faith would be to deny Jesus. If she died for Jesus, Margaret knew that she would soon be with Him forever in heaven. And so Margaret Ward, along with the boatman John Roche, was executed and became a glorious martyr for the Faith.

St. Margaret Ward, help me always to remain true to Jesus!

St. Aidan of Lindisfarne
August 31

St. Aidan of Lindisfarne

d. 651 • Ireland

On a small island off the coast of Scotland lived a group of monks. A king in England sent a messenger to them, asking the monks to send someone to his people and teach them about the Faith.

The first monk sent to preach to the English returned unexpectedly. He had given up because he said that the English were too wild and did not follow the rules of the Church. An Irish monk who was listening suggested that the complaining monk had perhaps been too hard on the English. They must first learn the easy rules. Later, they would grow strong enough to follow the hard rules out of love for God. This was what the Apostles did when they first preached to the pagans, he explained. The other monks agreed, and decided that the Irish monk, Aidan, should be the one to go and preach to the English.

Aidan journeyed to England and became the bishop of Lindisfarne, an island off the northernmost coast of England. There, he founded a monastery and walked all across the country, preaching about Jesus to anyone he met: poor and rich, believer and unbeliever alike.

The king noticed that Aidan traveled throughout his kingdom by foot. And so he gave Bishop Aidan a magnificent steed as a gift befitting a bishop. But as Bishop Aidan rode his horse on the road, he met a beggar who asked him for alms. Immediately, he dismounted and gave the beggar the royal horse.

The king was offended that Aidan had given away his gift, and the next time he saw Bishop Aidan, he asked him why he had done this. Aidan answered, "Is a horse worth more to you than a son of God?" The king was humbled by this and promised to let the bishop give away as much money as he wanted to the poor, who were sons and daughters of God.

Bishop Aidan also worked miracles through the power of God. One day, a pagan king attacked the royal city. The enemy forces gathered wood, straw, and thatch and piled it around the city walls. Then they set the kindling on fire so that they could burn the city down!

Bishop Aidan was praying on the island of Lindisfarne, some miles away, when he saw the smoke rise up from the royal city. He prayed that God would save the city, and God answered his prayer. The winds shifted and blew the fire away from the city and onto the enemies! The enemy warriors fled, and the city was saved. Bishop Aidan served as bishop of Lindisfarne until he died a holy death. St. Aidan, help me to treat everyone as a child of God!

St. Beatrice da Silva

September 1

St. Beatrice da Silva

1424–1492 • Portugal

The young and fair Beatrice was the lady-in-waiting for the queen of Spain. Beatrice was different from the other women at court. Not only was she beautiful and graceful, but she was also virtuous and modest.

Beatrice's beauty and virtue attracted many admirers at court—so many, in fact, that the queen grew jealous. The queen's jealousy poisoned her heart. In a fit of cruelty, she locked up Beatrice all alone in a room in her castle! For three days, Beatrice remained locked in her room without food or water. She was trapped and afraid.

Then, a beautiful woman miraculously appeared in Beatrice's room. The woman wore a habit of blue and white, and her presence filled Beatrice with peace and comfort. The beautiful woman was the Blessed Virgin Mary. She asked Beatrice to start an order of nuns dedicated to her Immaculate Conception. These nuns should wear a blue and white habit, just like the one that she was wearing.

When Mary left, her peaceful presence remained in Beatrice's heart. She knew that Mary was watching over her. Not long after Mary's visit, Beatrice's uncle came to the castle and rescued Beatrice from the locked room. Beatrice knew that she must leave the Spanish court and dedicate herself to prayer so that she could one day start the order of nuns as Mary had asked.

For thirty years, Beatrice lived in a convent in the great walled city of Toledo. She spent her days in prayer, waiting for Mary to show her when the time had come to start her new order. When Mary again appeared to her, Beatrice knew the right time had come.

By now, the queen's daughter had grown up and been crowned queen of Spain. She became known as "Isabella the Catholic" for her great dedication to bringing her country to God. Queen Isabella met with Beatrice in the convent. She helped Beatrice found her new order: the Order of the Immaculate Conception of the Blessed Virgin Mary. The nuns of the new order wore the blue and white habit that Mary had worn when she first appeared to Beatrice.

Beatrice was the abbess of her order until her death. As her final hour arrived and she lay in bed, Beatrice lifted the veil she always wore, and the nuns were astonished to see on her forehead a dazzling star of gold, which shone even after her death for ten days. The star was a sign to the world of the beauty and virtue of Beatrice's soul.

St. Beatrice da Silva, help my soul be beautiful and virtuous!

St. Agricola of Avignon

September 2

St. Agricola of Avignon

c. 625–c. 700 • France

Fourteen-year-old Agricola paused at the gates of the monastery. Agricola's mother had died when he was young, and so his father, a man named Magnus, had renounced the world to become a monk. Later, Magnus was appointed bishop of the French city of Avignon. Agricola's father was a holy man and would become a saint, and Agricola wanted to live a holy life like his father's.

Agricola entered the monastery and became a monk. He grew in wisdom and holiness, and so his father, Bishop Magnus, called Agricola to Avignon to be his helper. When his father died, Agricola became the next bishop of Avignon.

The poor and the sick were Bishop Agricola's special care, and he built a church and convent in Avignon. The people of the city greatly loved their holy bishop.

There is a tradition that a flock of storks invaded the city. The storks' great wings beat the air overhead. In their beaks, they carried deadly snakes. The citizens of Avignon were terrified as snakes rained down from the sky, dropped from the storks' beaks.

Agricola heard the frightened shouts of his people. He fell on his knees and pleaded with Jesus to save the city and send the storks with their serpents away. Then, rising, he stood tall and with the Sign of the Cross banished the storks from the city. The storks flew away with the snakes, and the people rejoiced that God had heard their holy bishop's prayers. Because of this miracle, artists often portray Bishop Agricola with a stork standing beside him.

Agricola served the people of Avignon until he died a holy death.

St. Agricola of Avignon, help me always turn to Jesus for protection!

St. Gregory the Great
September 3

St. Gregory the Great

540–604 • Italy

Bishop Gregory was the chief adviser to the pope in Rome. One day, he went to the busy and noisy marketplace, where he noticed some unusual strangers. They were tall for their age and had shining, beautiful hair, which was very different from the dark, Italian hair Bishop Gregory was used to seeing. Then his heart grew heavy when he saw that they were in chains. This meant that the strangers were slaves.

Bishop Gregory asked where the slaves were from, and he was told that they were Angles, who are people from England. "Not Angles," Gregory exclaimed, marveling at their beauty, "but angels!" For Gregory, the Angles were as beautiful as angels. When Gregory heard that the Angles were pagans and had never heard about Jesus, Gregory vowed in his heart to help them. He went to the pope and received permission to become a missionary in England so he could teach the Angles all about Jesus' love for them.

After Bishop Gregory left Rome, the people of Rome complained to the pope. Gregory was very wise and important, and they did not want to lose him! And so the pope was forced to send his messengers to go after Gregory. When the messengers reached him on the third day with the pope's summons, Gregory saw that it was not God's will for him to leave Rome.

Floods and a terrible plague struck all of Italy, and the pope died. Gregory was unanimously elected pope, to his great dismay. Gregory knew that being pope would be hard and would involve much suffering. He was so upset that he even thought about running away! But in the end, he followed God's will and became the next successor to St. Peter.

After Gregory became pope, he did not forget the English people. He knew that, as pope, he could not go to England. But he could send one of his bishops instead! He sent Augustine, who became the bishop of Canterbury, to the shores of England to spread the Christian Faith. Through Pope Gregory and Augustine of Canterbury, the Faith came to England.

Throughout his papacy, Gregory suffered from fevers and illness. But he did not let his pain stop him! He wrote important works about the Mass and promoted the clear and beautiful chanting that became known as Gregorian chant. After fourteen years as pope, Gregory died a holy death.

St. Gregory the Great, help me to share God's Word with all people!

St. Rosalia
September 4

St. Rosalia

c. 1130–c. 1160 • Italy

Two angels led the young maiden Rosalia to a small cave on the side of the mountain. Above the cave's entrance, she wrote, "I, Rosalia, daughter of Sinibald, Lord of Quisquina and Roses, have resolved to live in this cavern out of love for my Lord, Jesus Christ."

The cave was just outside of her family's grand estate in the Italian city of Palermo, where Rosalia had been born into a life of wealth and luxury. But Rosalia's soul longed for God alone, and nothing on this earth could satisfy her. And so she gave up all the dances at court, her precious jewels, and the rich suitors seeking marriage to live in this poor cave, where she could give herself to God.

For the rest of her life, Rosalia lived a life of prayer and sacrifice, hiding deep inside the cave whenever she heard another person approach. But Rosalia was not lonely in her solitude. Jesus, Mary, the angels, and saints would come and visit her. Sometimes an angel would give her Holy Communion, so Rosalia could feed her body and her soul with the Body of Christ. She died a holy death, and finally her soul was united to God in heaven, just as she had longed for so deeply when she was on earth.

Nearly five hundred years after her death, a terrible plague struck Palermo. Rosalia appeared to a hunter and instructed him to find her remains inside of her secret cave and to hold a procession with her remains around the city. The hunter found her remains just where she had told him they would be. He brought them to the church. Three times, her remains were processed around the city. And just as mist vanishes in the morning sun, so the plague disappeared from joyous Palermo at the appearance of St. Rosalia's relics. God had heard Rosalia's prayers on behalf of the people in Palermo and healed the city! From then on, Rosalia became the special patroness of the people of Palermo.

St. Rosalia, help me to live my life for the love of Jesus!

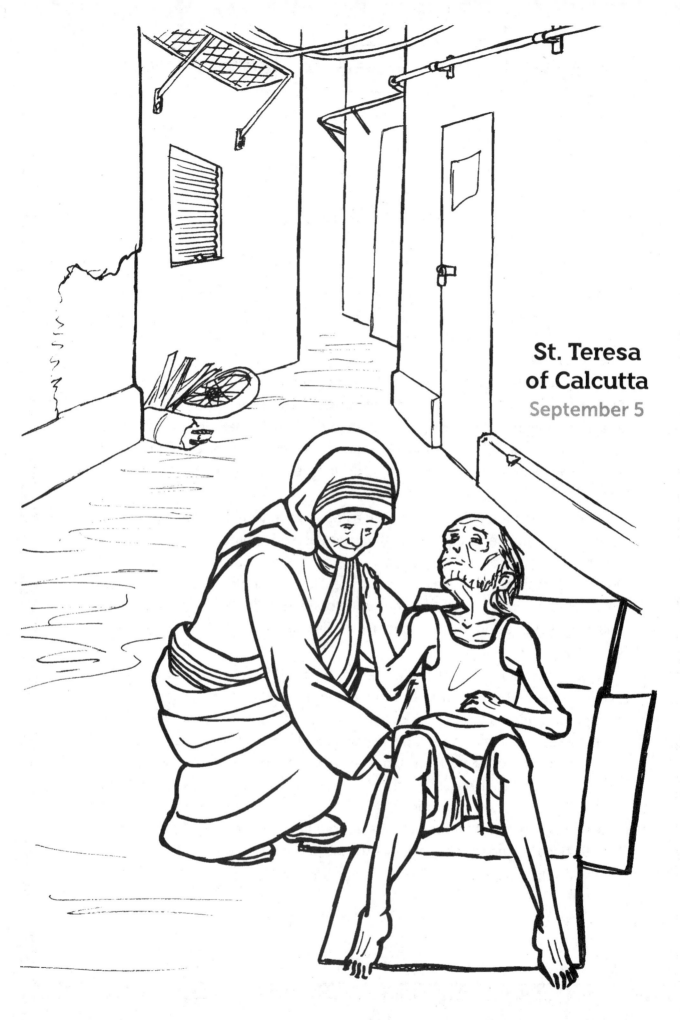

St. Teresa
of Calcutta
September 5

St. Teresa of Calcutta

1910–1997 • Albania

Mother Teresa was riding on the crowded train from Calcutta to Darjeeling to attend a prayer retreat. A voice called to her deep in her heart. It was Jesus' voice, and He was calling her to bring His love to the poor.

Born in Albania, Teresa had felt a deep love for God in her heart ever since she received her First Holy Communion. She became a missionary sister at the age of eighteen and had spent the past twenty years as a teacher in a girl's school in India. But now Jesus was giving Mother Teresa a call within a call. He was calling her to be His feet and hands in loving care for the poor. "Come be My light," Jesus begged Mother Teresa. "I cannot go alone." Mother Teresa's soul was filled with the same thirst for the poor that Jesus had felt when He had thirsted on the Cross. Mother Teresa knew that she must answer Jesus' call and give her life to loving His poor.

Mother Teresa of Calcutta went to the bishop and told him of Jesus' call for her. It took the bishop two years to grant his approval for her new order, the Sisters of Charity. But when he did, Mother Teresa donned her new habit, a white sari hemmed with blue, and went out to the slums to care for Calcutta's poor.

And Calcutta's poor were poor indeed. Abandoned and neglected "untouchables," the poor and sick lay down to die on the streets. Mother Teresa knelt down beside a sick man, his weak body festering with sores. She gathered him into her arms and bathed his wounds. With tears of thanks in his eyes, he told her, "All my life I have lived like an animal in the streets, but here I am dying like an angel, because I am loved and cared for."

Mother Teresa started a hospital and home for the dying. She told the sick and the poor that God was a God of love. More and more women joined the Sisters of Charity, and Mother Teresa sent her sisters to serve the poor throughout all of India, and then throughout the world.

Mother Teresa remained true to Jesus' call even when she experienced a "dark night of the soul," which means she stopped feeling Jesus' presence in her heart. Sometimes the greatest saints suffer a dark night of the soul so that Jesus can strengthen their love and trust in Him. And so Teresa learned to trust in Jesus completely and remained faithful to Jesus' call to her on the train. Mother Teresa never stopped bringing God's love to the poor until she died a holy death, having touched the lives of millions and inspired works of mercy and charity around the world.

St. Teresa of Calcutta, help me bring Jesus' light to the poor!

St. Bega
September 6

St. Bega

d. 681 • Ireland

Bega was a beautiful Irish princess who wished to give her love to God alone. But her father, the king, wished Bega to marry a prince. So on the eve of her wedding, as the din of a great feast echoed through the halls, Bega snuck out of her father's castle under the cover of darkness.

Wrapping her cloak tightly around her shoulders, Bega climbed into a little boat and cast off into the dark waters for the Kingdom of Northumbria on the opposite shore. Even though she was all alone, she was unafraid, because she put her trust in God. Her boat reached the shore, and Bega knew that she was safe because God was watching over her.

Deep in the woods, Bega found a little grotto and built a hut of sticks, which she covered with the forest leaves. There, she remained in solitude to offer her life in prayer to God, whom she loved with all her heart. The stillness of the forest helped her pray, and for company, she could hear the seagull's cry just beyond the wood by the shore.

God watched over Bega in the wood. He sent the seagulls and birds to bring Bega food, and there she stayed in joy and peace, offering her prayers to God.

One day, the king of Northumbria, the good Oswald (who would one day be known as a saint), was hunting down ruffians in the forest. With surprise, he happened upon Bega in the wood. He saw that Bega was a holy virgin, and he advised her to join a convent. Bega saw that through King Oswald, God had revealed His will for her to live as a nun. And so King Oswald brought her to St. Aidan, the bishop of Lindisfarne, who gave Bega the veil, and she became a nun.

Bega founded a nunnery and helped the poor and those in need nearby. A village grew around her nunnery, and after Bega died a holy death, her burial place became a destination for pilgrims.

St. Bega, help me to love God with all my heart!

Bl. Florent Dumontet de Cardaillac

September 7

Bl. Florent Dumontet de Cardaillac

1749–1794 • France

Fr. Florent Dumontet de Cardaillac was a priest during the French Revolution. While the revolution started as an uprising of the poor people of France seeking a better life for themselves, it quickly turned into terrible violence not only against the upper classes but also against the Catholic Church.

The revolutionary authorities passed a law that not only required the French priests to swear loyalty to the new state, but also to reject the pope in Rome. Florent knew that he could not swear that oath because to reject the pope would be to reject the Catholic Faith, and to reject the Catholic Faith would be to reject Jesus. Refusing to swear the oath would mean prison or even death. But Florent was not afraid. He knew he was ready to suffer and die for Jesus so he could be with Him forever in heaven.

With great peace in his heart, Florent refused to swear the evil oath. The revolutionary guards seized Florent and threw him into a prison hulk in the port of the French town of Rochefort. Now, prison hulks were large wooden ships that were too old to be seaworthy, and so the revolutionaries used them as makeshift prisons. Over eight hundred faithful priests and religious who refused to swear the evil oath were thrown into the belly of the prison hulks in Rochefort and became prisoners for Jesus.

Once in the ships, the faithful priests and religious were cruelly ignored. They were given very little food and water. No one cleaned up after them or gave them medicine when they were sick.

Florent did all that he could to care for his fellow prisoners for Jesus. Tending to all who were sick, he spoke words of hope. As his eyes shone with the fire of his love for Jesus, he reminded them that they were soon to see Jesus in heaven.

Florent cared for others and spared no thought for himself until he grew weak and sick. He died a holy death, a glorious martyr for the Faith. Over five hundred priests and religious died on the hulk ships, and all together they are called the Martyrs of the Prison Hulks of Rochefort.

Bl. Florent Dumontet de Cardaillac, help me to remain ever faithful to Jesus!

The Nativity of Mary
September 8

The Nativity of Mary

Marian Feast Day

Mary's parents were Joachim and Anne, a Jewish couple who loved God.

Early Church tradition says that Joachim and Anne were sad because they did not have any children. Anne shed many tears and begged God on her knees for a little baby she could hold in her arms and love with all her heart. Joachim would go to the Temple and pray to God to bless them with a child.

One day, in the middle of their prayers, a bright angel appeared to Joachim and Anne and announced that God would bless them with a child. They were overjoyed!

When the time came, Anne gave birth to a girl. She was the most beautiful and sweetest baby Anne had ever seen. Joachim and Anne named their daughter Mary.

Anne's heart was full of love as she held her little girl tenderly to her heart. She knew that Mary was a special blessing from God.

But even she did not know how special Mary was.

Mary would be the Mother of Jesus, the Son of God.

Someday, Mary would become everyone's Mother.

We celebrate Mary's birthday to honor Mary as the Mother of God. Her birthday is an important event in the life of Jesus, because through Mary, Jesus came into the world.

Dear Mary, help me to be especially kind to others on your birthday!

St. Peter Claver
September 9

St. Peter Claver

1581–1654 • Spain

Peter Claver bravely entered the hold of the ship, carrying medicine, food, and wash towels. His heart wept at what he saw there. Slaves, chained and fettered, were so packed together they could barely move. The hull was dark and the air heavy with sweat and disease. He knelt among the slaves, washing and applying medicine to their wounds. His touch was gentle. His words in the Kongo language were kind. His lips formed a silent prayer.

Peter was a priest. He had left Spain to become a missionary in Cartagena, the great harbor city of Colombia. Ten thousand African slaves arrived at the port each year, where they were bought and sold. Peter did not know how men could treat other men so. Slavery was evil. The way his white, Spanish brethren treated the Africans was a terrible sin. He would do everything he could to care for the slaves and bring them to Jesus. He called himself the "slave of slaves."

When the slaves left the ship, Peter Claver would wrap the sick and injured in his cloak and carry them to the hospital. Sometimes, his very touch healed the sick.

To the healthy, Peter spoke about Jesus and how Jesus had died for them. He told them that they were children of God who had great worth and dignity, no matter what others told them. Peter baptized three hundred thousand African slaves. Black and white alike he invited to his church, ignoring anyone who complained about the African slaves.

Peter's face was always sad. He knew that when people rejected the slaves, they rejected God. He cared for, taught, and baptized slaves until he turned seventy and caught the plague. He did not die, but he had to stay in bed for the last four years of his life. He offered all of his suffering to God before he died a holy death.

St. Peter Claver, help me to treat everyone like a child of God!

St. Pulcheria
September 10

St. Pulcheria

399–453 • Modern-day Turkey

The emperor of Constantinople had just died. His two children, Pulcheria and Theodosius, fought back tears as they said prayers for his soul at the funeral. Seven-year-old Theodosius was now emperor, and at first, his guardian ruled the empire in his place. But when Pulcheria came of age at fifteen years old, the Byzantine Senate declared Pulcheria the empress regent until Theodosius came of age.

A wise and good guardian of the empire, Pulcheria tenderly cared for the poor. Her love for God was so great that she made a vow to dedicate herself to God. She did not live in luxury, but in prayer, chanting the Scriptures in the morning and the evening.

Pulcheria watched over her brother, training him in all he needed to know to be emperor. She taught him how to sit on his throne, how to walk and talk with great dignity. But most importantly, she showed him how to teach and protect the true Faith throughout the Eastern Roman Empire. Even when Theodosius came of age and ruled as emperor, he relied on Pulcheria for her wise advice, and she helped Theodosius govern the empire.

False teachings about Jesus and Mary were spreading throughout the Church. Some people did not believe that Jesus was fully God and fully man, and some people did not believe that Mary was the Mother of God. Pulcheria did everything in her power to defend the true Faith. She attended and supported a Church council and built three beautiful churches dedicated to Mary, the Mother of God. Pope Leo I wrote a letter to Pulcheria declaring that the false teachings had ended largely because of her help.

When her brother died in a hunting accident, Pulcheria became the empress. But the law did not allow her to rule long without a husband. She married a military officer named Marcian. But before their marriage, she made him swear an oath to respect her vow to God. This Marcian did, and he became the emperor. Together, they ruled justly and defended the Faith throughout the empire. Pulcheria died a holy death and left all her great wealth to be distributed to the poor of her empire.

St. Pulcheria, help me to do everything in my power to defend the true Faith!

Sts. Protus and Hyacinth
September 11

Sts. Protus and Hyacinth

d. c. 257 • Rome

Protus and Hyacinth were brothers who served a noble lady in Rome. Both were faithful to Christ even though they lived during a time when it was of great danger to be Christian. The Roman emperors arrested and put to death all who proclaimed their belief in Jesus instead of offering worship to the emperor.

But Protus and Hyacinth were not afraid to live and preach the Faith. When the brothers were discovered, Roman soldiers seized them and dragged them to prison.

First, they tortured Hyacinth, trying to force him to give up his faith. But Hyacinth would never deny Jesus, whom he loved more than his own life.

Protus stood as strong as his brother, and he, too, proclaimed his love for Christ.

Both brothers put their trust in Jesus. They knew that their suffering would last only for a moment, and that Jesus would raise them from the dead, as He had promised, and so they would be with Jesus in heaven as His faithful servants forever.

When the time came, they were put to death by fire. Protus was the first to enter the flames, followed by his brother. Together, they became glorious martyrs for Jesus, and their souls reunited in heaven, where they are rejoicing forever with Jesus.

The Christians gathered the ashes of the two brothers and placed them in a tomb. One hundred years later, Pope St. Damasus wrote this inscription over their graves, where he gives them the palm and crown, both symbols of victory and martyrdom.

Heaven better preserves you for itself, Protus.
With purple blood you follow, Hyacinth, the esteemed.
True brothers and extraordinary souls, both.
The latter victor deserved the palm, the former likewise his crown.

Sts. Protus and Hyacinth, help me to be Jesus' faithful servant!

St. Franciscus Ch'oe Kyong-hwan
September 12

St. Franciscus Ch'oe Kyong-hwan

1805–1839 • Korea

In the dark of night, Franciscus and his wife, Maria, buried the sacred objects of the Faith: the crosses, rosaries, and statues that helped them pray to God in heaven. They knew the time of persecution was coming, and so they gathered all of the holy objects in their village so that the soldiers would not dishonor and destroy them.

Franciscus, Maria, and their children had left behind wealth and prosperity to move to a small village because it was hard for them to live as Catholics in a large pagan city. They became tobacco farmers, and soon, other Catholic families came to the village to join them. Franciscus had brought precious books about the Catholic Faith and taught his fellow villagers about Jesus and the commandments. A missionary priest told Franciscus and Maria that God was calling their eldest son to be a priest. They rejoiced that God was giving such a great blessing to their family, and they sent their son overseas, where he could safely study for the priesthood.

The time was coming, Franciscus warned the people of his village, when they would face persecution and be asked to die for Jesus. And so here he was, with his wife Maria, burying their crosses, statues, and rosaries. Franciscus prayed in his heart that someday these sacred objects would be found and that the Korean people would be free to practice the Faith.

Soon, the soldiers pounded on Franciscus's door. He welcomed the soldiers into his home and treated them with warmth and kindness. He invited them to eat at his table and rest for the night. He even gave one soldier some clean clothes to replace his tattered ones. The soldiers were amazed at Franciscus's kindness in the face of danger.

In the morning, the soldiers rounded up the entire village and forced them on a long and cruel march to the capital, under orders from the queen. There, the Catholic villagers were thrown into prison. Out of fear, many of them denied their faith. But Franciscus refused to deny Jesus. He was ready to die for Christ so that he could be with Him forever in heaven. For more than forty days he was mercilessly beaten, but he withstood all of his suffering and achieved the glorious crown of martyrdom.

At the death of her husband, Maria broke down and denied her faith. But then, through God's grace, she was sorry for her sin, proclaimed her faith in Jesus, and died for her Lord. Franciscus and Maria's son returned as a missionary priest to Korea and wrote about the glorious martyrs of Korea who bravely gave their lives for Jesus.

St. Franciscus Ch'oe Kyong-hwan, help me to support other Christians in the Faith!

St. John
Chrysostom
September 13

St. John Chrysostom

347–407 • Syria

John Chrysostom was the archbishop of Constantinople, known for his inspiring sermons and his love for the poor. In fact, "Chrysostom" means "golden-mouthed" in Greek, and he was called John Chrysostom because his words were so beautiful as to be golden.

Archbishop John Chrysostom especially spoke out against the rich, who were living in too much vanity and luxury. Many women of the noble court became angry at John Chrysostom for his preaching. They liked their parties, their fancy dresses, and their wasteful pastimes, and they did not give a second thought to the poor.

One of the ladies whom John offended was the empress of Constantinople herself. The empress became so angry that she asked the emperor to banish John Chrysostom from the city. But shortly after his exile, a great earthquake shook the city. The empress became afraid. She did not want to rouse God's anger because she had acted against His holy archbishop. She also knew that the people of Constantinople loved their archbishop, and she did not want the people to rise up against her. And so the empress called the archbishop back to Constantinople.

Things were quiet between the empress and the archbishop for a time. But then the empress erected a great silver statue of herself right outside of the great church of Hagia Sophia. Wild and immodest celebrations honoring the empress's statue interrupted the archbishop and his priests at their prayers. John Chrysostom spoke loudly against these madcap celebrations. The empress was insulted by the archbishop's words because she believed they were spoken against her. Once again, she asked the emperor to send John Chrysostom from Constantinople.

The emperor ordered soldiers to banish John Chrysostom from the city. But when John Chrysostom arrived at his place of banishment, the people there welcomed him with friendship, kindness, and honor. John Chrysostom's enemies could not stand to see the archbishop treated with such kindness. They wrote to the emperor and asked him to get rid of the archbishop once and for all. And so the emperor sent soldiers to force the holy archbishop out on a long and cruel march.

The hot sun beat down upon John Chrysostom's head, and the cold night chilled his bones. He had very little to eat and drink and became weak and feverish. Finally, the soldiers saw that John Chrysostom would not last much longer, and so they took him to a chapel. There, John Chrysostom received Jesus in the Eucharist, said his final prayers, and offered his last breath to God.

St. John Chrysostom, help me to live with modesty and virtue!

The Exaltation of the Holy Cross
September 14

The Exaltation of the Holy Cross

629 • Feast of Jesus

The Persian king Chosroes sacked Jerusalem and carried away its most precious treasure: the true Cross, which had been discovered by St. Helena and placed in the Church of the Holy Sepulchre, the great church over the spot where Jesus had died on the Cross and been buried in the unused tomb. The newly crowned Byzantine emperor Heraclius offered great prayers, fasted, and raised an army to reclaim all the cities that Chosroes had stolen and to regain the true Cross. God favored Heraclius, and the Byzantine emperor defeated his enemy and recovered Jesus' true Cross. The emperor and the people rejoiced that they would be able to return Jesus' Cross to Jerusalem, where it belonged.

Heraclius triumphantly marched back to Jerusalem in magnificence and splendor. He wore his golden crown and his robe of royal purple. To give thanks to God for his victory, he decided he would carry the true Cross through the gates and the streets of Jerusalem, just as Jesus had carried His Cross to His Crucifixion.

Heraclius bore the true Cross on his shoulder, but when he came to the gates of Jerusalem, he found himself blocked as if by some invisible force. He could not move forward through the gates!

Patriarch Zachary of Jerusalem explained to the emperor that he could not go forward because he desired to carry the Cross through Jerusalem dressed as an earthly king, in glory and riches. But Jesus, the King of Heaven and Earth, had humbled Himself to carry His Cross. Instead of splendid robes, Jesus had worn poor garments. Instead of a golden crown on His head, Jesus had worn a crown of thorns. Instead of wearing kingly shoes, Jesus had walked barefoot through Jerusalem's streets.

At Patriarch Zachary's words, the emperor laid aside his royal purple robe and his golden crown. He put on poor clothes and dressed his heart in humility. Once again, he bore the true Cross on his shoulder, and this time he was able to walk through the gates of Jerusalem bearing the true Cross of Jesus. With prayer and ceremony, Heraclius placed the Cross in the Church of the Holy Sepulchre, where it belonged.

Like Heraclius and Patriarch Zachary, we must always remember to treat the Cross of Jesus with honor and humility. The Cross reminds us of Jesus' great sacrifice for us, and that is why it is an important symbol of our faith in Jesus. We make the Sign of the Cross before we pray, and we place crosses in our churches and our homes.

Dear Jesus, who died on the Cross for our sins, have mercy on us!

Our Lady of Sorrows
September 15

Our Lady of Sorrows

Marian Feast Day

When Jesus suffers, Mary suffers too. That is why she is called "Our Lady of Sorrows."

Joseph and Mary took Jesus to the Temple when He was a baby. There, the holy and just Simeon told Mary that her soul would be pierced by a sword: the sword of sorrow. This meant that Mary's heart would go through so much sadness and pain it would feel as if a sword were piercing her heart.

Sorrow soon pierced Mary's heart when Herod tried to kill baby Jesus. She had to flee to Egypt with Joseph to protect Jesus from Herod's soldiers.

Later, her heart beat fast with fear and pain as she frantically searched for Jesus in Jerusalem for three days, until she and Joseph found Him in the Temple.

But Mary suffered no greater sorrow than when she met her Son's eyes as He carried His Cross on His way to be crucified.

She watched Him suffer and die on the Cross to save us from our sins. Mary took Jesus' body in her arms as He was lowered from the Cross, and she laid His head close to her sorrowful heart.

When they buried Jesus in His tomb, Mary felt as though her heart were being buried too.

Because Mary loves Jesus more than she loves anyone else, she takes part in His sorrows. But that also means that she takes part in His joy! When Jesus rose from the dead, Mary was radiant with happiness.

We should remember to turn to Jesus and Mary when we are sad, because they will give us joyful hearts.

Our Lady of Sorrows, comfort me when I am sad!

Sts. Cornelius and Cyprian

d. 253 and d. 258 • Italy and North Africa

For the first three hundred years after Jesus' death and Resurrection, it was very dangerous to be a Christian. Rulers from all different countries persecuted Christians for worshiping the one true God instead of pagan gods.

So when a bishop named Cornelius became the pope in Rome, he knew that he would not be pope long. The popes before him had died for their faith in Jesus and had become saints in heaven. At first, Cornelius was afraid and did not want to be pope. But once the other bishops chose him as pope, Cornelius was ready to give his life to protect and guide the Church.

Because it was a time of terrible persecution, there were many Christians who denied Jesus out of fear of pain and death. Many of these Christians were sorry for this terrible sin and asked for forgiveness. Pope Cornelius declared that these Christians could be forgiven and come back to the Church, as long as they were deeply and truly sorry.

But not everyone agreed with Pope Cornelius.

A man named Novatian said that Christians who had denied Jesus had committed too big a sin to be forgiven. Novatian was wrong, but he set himself up as a false pope and declared that the bishops should follow him instead of Pope Cornelius. Because of this, many bishops did not know whether Cornelius or Novatian was pope.

Cyprian, the bishop of Carthage (in North Africa), called for a meeting to learn the truth and found out that Cornelius, not Novatian, had been elected pope. Cyprian supported the true pope, and by his example, all the bishops of Africa and eventually everyone in the Church followed Cornelius as well.

Then came the day that Cornelius had been waiting for: the day he would suffer for Jesus. The Roman emperor arrested Pope Cornelius and exiled him from Rome with very little to eat and not enough to keep warm at night. Bishop Cyprian sent Pope Cornelius a letter to comfort him and remind him that his suffering was glorious, because he was suffering for Jesus. Soon, Pope Cornelius died in exile and became a saint in heaven.

Bishop Cyprian knew that Pope Cornelius would pray for him in heaven. And he was in need of St. Cornelius's prayers because Roman soldiers were coming for him too. In exile, Bishop Cyprian wrote letters to guide his people, as well as many holy books about the truths of the Christian Faith. Eventually, Cyprian was also arrested by soldiers and became a glorious martyr for Jesus.

Sts. Cornelius and Cyprian, help me always to trust in God's mercy!

St. Robert
Bellarmine
September 17

St. Robert Bellarmine

1542–1621 • Italy

Robert Bellarmine belonged to a noble but poor family. His father knew that Robert was intelligent, and he wanted his son to go to university and gain an important position to bring wealth back to the family. But Robert was not interested in money, because God had called him to something more important. God had called him to be a priest!

Robert Bellarmine lived during the Reformation, the time when many people were leaving the Catholic Church to become Protestants and make their own churches. After Robert Bellarmine became a priest, he wrote many important books explaining how the Catholic Church is Jesus' true Church. He suffered from terrible headaches and weakness. His health was so poor that, many times, his friends thought he was going to die! But he never let his headaches stop him from his important work of defending the Catholic Faith.

Robert Bellarmine's writings were so wise, and his preaching touched so many hearts, that the pope made him a cardinal, which is an important office in the Church, second only to the pope. Being a cardinal came with riches, and Cardinal Bellarmine also made money from selling his books. But instead of spending his wealth on himself, he gave all of his money to the poor.

Once, a thief stole a valuable stone from a cathedral and tried to sell it at a low price. He was caught and brought before Robert Bellarmine, who learned that the thief was a poor man. After telling the thief about the wickedness of stealing (from a church too!), Robert Bellarmine gave the sorrowful thief ten times the amount he had tried to sell the stone for. He also sent the thief money every month to make sure he was taken care of. Another time, Robert Bellarmine gave away all of the tapestries, curtains, and covers in his room to be turned into clothes for the poor. He said, "The walls won't feel cold, but the poor will!"

When Robert Bellarmine was in his early sixties, the pope appointed him to be the head of the great Vatican Library. There, Robert Bellarmine continued writing about and defending the truth of the Catholic Faith. When he was ill and close to death, he was often heard saying, "Dear Lord, I would gladly go home." Soon, the Lord granted his wish for a holy death.

St. Robert Bellarmine, help me remain faithful to Jesus' true Church!

St. Joseph of Cupertino
September 18

St. Joseph of Cupertino

1603–1663 • Italy

No one wanted Joseph in the village of Cupertino. His mother thought he was good for nothing. The boys at school made fun of him. Even though he worked for a shoemaker, Joseph never learned how to make a single shoe. When he went to join the Capuchin friars, they sent him back home after a little while because he never finished anything he started. Poor Joseph felt he could never get anything right.

But what no one understood was that Joseph was so clumsy because God spoke to his soul in a special way. Joseph would be doing his everyday work, when a sudden thought of God would so fill his heart that he could not think of anything else. If he thought about God while washing dishes, the plates would drop and shatter at his feet. Sometimes, people would walk by as Joseph stared straight into nothing, thinking only about God. They would poke him and pinch him, and Joseph would never notice. So full was his heart with love for God that nothing else could disturb him.

Joseph knew that he was meant to serve God. He went to the Franciscan friars near Cupertino and asked to be their stable boy. He was always cheerful, and soon, the Franciscans noticed the stable boy whose eyes shone with love for God. Even though Joseph could not read or write, he had more spiritual knowledge than many great thinkers and philosophers, so in touch was his soul with the things of heaven. And so Joseph became a friar and then a priest.

Joseph grew closer and closer to God. When he received Holy Communion, his love of God raised his soul so high that it even lifted his feet off the ground! The other priests and monks watched amazed as Joseph miraculously floated in the air. Sometimes, the sound of church bells would make his spirits soar, and up Joseph would go, floating into the sky!

But some were embarrassed by Joseph's floating. Even worse, others accused Joseph of practicing witchcraft. They called on the Church to investigate him, but the Church leaders found that Joseph was completely innocent and his soul full of the love and joy of God. But now the other friars would not let Joseph sing in the choir or go out in public, for fear that he would disturb others with his floating. Joseph took his banishment with all humility. For ten years, he dedicated himself to God in prayer until he died a holy death.

St. Joseph of Cupertino, let nothing disturb my love for God!

St. Januarius

d. c. 305 • Italy

St. Januarius was a miracle-worker. He was the bishop of Beneventum, a city in Italy, during the time of the cruel emperor Diocletian's heartless persecution of Christians. Diocletian persecuted the Christians because they refused to worship him as a god. Knowing that there was only one God, the brave Christian martyrs joyfully gave their lives for Jesus.

The Roman official in charge, Timotheus, arrested Januarius and sentenced him to death. But soon, Timotheus discovered that Januarius was very hard to kill!

First, Timotheus had Januarius cast into a fiery furnace, expecting him to be burned to a crisp. But the flames would not touch Januarius.

Next, Timotheus threw Januarius and his fellow Christian martyrs in an amphitheater full of savage beasts. The crowds of people watching expected the ferocious animals to tear the martyrs to pieces. But the beasts completely ignored Januarius and his companions!

Frustrated, Timotheus ordered Januarius's death by beheading. But before the execution, God struck Timotheus blind!

Knowing that the moment had come for him to give glory to God, Januarius healed Timotheus of his blindness. As the crowd of people watched Januarius perform this great miracle, they became awestruck by the power of God. Five thousand of them became Christians. But the miracle did not touch Timotheus's heart, and his soldiers carried out his wicked command. And so Januarius and his companions were beheaded, becoming glorious martyrs for Jesus.

Januarius's relics were taken to a church in Naples, and there the saint performed more great miracles from heaven. He stopped Mt. Vesuvius—the fearsome volcano—from erupting and destroying the city of Naples in fire and ash. To this day, in the cathedral in Naples, a relic of his dried blood regularly bubbles to liquid three times a year. All of Januarius's miracles witness to the greatness of God.

St. Januarius, help me never to forget God's greatness!

Sts. Paul Chong Ha-sang
and Andrew Kim Tae-gon
September 20

Sts. Paul Chong Ha-sang and Andrew Kim Tae-gon

d. 1839 and d. 1846 • Korea

The Catholic Church in Korea in the 1800s was small but strong. The kings and queens of Korea persecuted Catholics in their kingdom without mercy. Thousands upon thousands of men and women in Korea fearlessly gave their lives out of love for Jesus. Two of these brave martyrs were Paul Chong Ha-sang and Andrew Kim Tae-gon.

Paul Chong Ha-sang knew firsthand that being a Catholic was dangerous. In fact, his father and brother had died as martyrs for the Faith. But instead of scaring Paul Chong Ha-sang, his family's sacrifice made him treasure his Catholic Faith all the more. Paul Chong Ha-sang wanted to help the Catholic Church in Korea as much as he could.

At that time, there were no priests in Korea, because they had all been killed by the king. Paul Chong Ha-sang knew that the Catholics in Korea needed priests to teach them their Faith and give them the sacraments. So he traveled back and forth between Korea and China so that he could send out letters asking for priests to come to Korea. He even wrote a letter to the pope, begging him to recognize the Church in Korea and to send more priests.

The pope did as Paul Chong Ha-sang asked. Missionary priests traveled to Korea, risking their lives to serve the Korean people. Paul Chong Ha-sang himself went to seminary to study for the priesthood. But before he was ordained, Korean officials arrested him. Nothing they did could make Paul Chong Ha-sang give up his faith in Jesus. Finally, Paul Chong Ha-sang was tied to a cross inside a cart, where he became a glorious martyr for Jesus.

The first Korean man to become a priest was Andrew Kim Tae-gon. His father, like Paul Chong Ha-sang's, had been killed by the Korean king for the Faith. But Andrew Kim Tae-gon was not afraid to die for Jesus! He left Korea to become a priest, and when he returned, he secretly taught his people the truth about Jesus at night to avoid capture.

Then one day—as Andrew Kim Tae-gon tried to smuggle more priests into Korea—he was caught and arrested. At first, the king did not want to put Andrew Kim Tae-gon to death. Andrew Kim Tae-gon was so friendly and intelligent, the king thought it would be a shame for him to die. But no one could say anything to make the young priest give up his love for Jesus. So Andrew Kim Tae-gon was beheaded and became a glorious martyr for Christ. Sts. Paul Chong Ha-sang and Andrew Kim Tae-gon, help me never to be too scared to share my faith in Jesus!

St. Matthew

September 21

St. Matthew

Biblical figure

Matthew was a Jewish tax collector. The other Jews despised Matthew because of his job. Tax collectors collected money for the Romans, who oppressed the Jews. And so Matthew was an outcast.

But Jesus saw beyond Matthew's job. He saw into Matthew's heart. He knew that Matthew would become His disciple.

One day, when Matthew was sitting at his post at work, Jesus came to him. Jesus said two simple words: "Follow me."

Jesus' words reached straight into Matthew's soul. Immediately, Matthew rose from his seat and followed Jesus. His fellow tax collectors marveled to see him leave his well-paying job behind to follow a poor preacher.

Matthew's heart was so full at being called by Jesus that he had Jesus over for dinner at his house. Many tax collectors and other sinners sat next to Jesus and His disciples. The Pharisees —Jewish religious experts—were shocked. "Why does your teacher eat with tax collectors and sinners?" they asked Jesus' disciples.

Jesus overheard their words and said, "Those who are well do not need a physician, but the sick do." Jesus came to heal sinners, just as He had healed Matthew.

Matthew became one of Jesus' Twelve Apostles. He followed Jesus all throughout Galilee and saw how Jesus healed the blind and the sick. When Jesus would heal someone's body, He would also heal the person's soul, saying, "Your sins are forgiven." Matthew understood that healing the soul was the most important part.

After Jesus died on the Cross and rose from the dead, He told His disciples to tell all the world the Good News of the Kingdom of Heaven.

Again, Matthew followed Jesus' words. He wrote the Gospel of Matthew to tell the world all about Jesus. You can read this first Gospel in the Bible. Matthew starts off by telling us about Jesus' human family, all the way back to Abraham. In art, a winged man is usually shown next to Matthew, because Matthew wrote about how Jesus, the Son of God, belonged to a human family.

Matthew preached about Jesus' life to the Hebrews and then traveled as far as Persia to preach the Gospel. Tradition tells us that Matthew died a glorious martyr for Jesus.

St. Matthew, help us to follow Jesus!

St. Maurice and the Theban Legion
September 22

St. Maurice and the Theban Legion

d. c. 287 • Egypt

Maurice was the commander of a legion from Thebes of over six thousand soldiers. Maurice had met Christians when he was stationed at Jerusalem, and he, too, became a Christian. Soon, all of his soldiers were baptized and swore their allegiance to Christ. And so the Theban legion became a Christian legion in the Roman army.

The emperor called the Theban legion to help fight a revolt in Gaul. Before the battle, the emperor ordered his legions of soldiers to offer sacrifices to false gods in order to pray for victory.

Maurice gathered his legion and announced if they did not offer the false sacrifice, they would offend the emperor. But if they offered the sacrifice, they would offend the true God. It was much better to offend the emperor than to offend the true God. In one voice, Maurice's soldiers declared their support for Maurice's choice and their allegiance to the true God.

When the emperor noticed that the Theban legion was absent from the sacrifice, he sent a messenger to Maurice. Maurice declared that he and his soldiers were faithful to God and to the emperor. They would not betray God by offering sacrifice to false gods, but they were still loyal soldiers of the emperor and would fight for him at his command. Where their duties to God and the emperor conflicted, though, they would choose God first.

When the emperor heard this, he was furious. He did not want Maurice and the Theban legion to give their allegiance to anyone but him. He declared that if the soldiers in the Theban legion did not offer sacrifice to the gods, one-tenth of them would be put to death.

Maurice and his soldiers stood strong as one in ten soldiers was put to death. The Theban legion were soldiers for Christ, ready to lay down their lives for God.

Once again, the emperor ordered the soldiers to offer sacrifice to the gods. Again, the soldiers of the Theban legion stood strong. As another tenth was put to death by the sword without resistance, Maurice spoke ringing words of encouragement to his men. The victory was theirs! They were soldiers of Christ and would receive glory in heaven!

When the emperor saw that not a single soldier wavered in his allegiance to Christ, he ordered his army to destroy Maurice and his soldiers entirely. Every soldier in the Theban legion became a martyr for Christ and achieved glory with Him in heaven. St. Maurice, help me to be faithful to God above all!

St. Pius of Pietrelcina
September 23

St. Pius of Pietrelcina

1887–1968 • Italy

Pius of Pietrelcina, better known as Padre Pio, wanted to be a priest ever since he was five years old. His father was a poor farmer, but he worked extra hard so that his son could enter the seminary and become a priest.

As a young priest, Padre Pio struggled with his health. He was weak and often sick, but that never kept him from his prayers. The Friday after the Feast of the Stigmata of St. Francis of Assisi, Padre Pio was saying his usual prayers when a sharp pain stabbed through his hands and feet. The pain was so great that he fainted. When he woke up, he found that he, too, had been given the gift of the stigmata. That means that his hands and feet bore the same wounds that Jesus had suffered when He was nailed to the Cross.

Padre Pio's wounds never stopped bleeding, which is why he always wore fingerless gloves. When people saw Padre Pio's wounds, they remembered Jesus' suffering. Padre Pio was happy to suffer, since his pain made other people think of Jesus.

God also worked many miracles through Padre Pio. When people came to him for confession, he would remind them of sins they had forgotten. Once, a little blind girl came to him for her First Confession and First Holy Communion. Afterward, he rubbed her eyes, and she could see!

Padre Pio could also be in two places at the same time. Once, there was a concert at the monastery. A fellow monk noticed that during the intermission, Padre Pio remained seated in his chair and closed his eyes.

The next day, the monk visited a sick villager and discovered that the villager had been healed. The happy villager explained that Padre Pio had visited him the night before. The monk shook his head. That was impossible, the monk explained. Padre Pio had been at the concert. But when he asked the villager more questions, he discovered that Padre Pio had visited the sick man during the intermission. Padre Pio had miraculously visited the villager while remaining in his chair!

Fifty years after Padre Pio received the stigmata, the people in the church noticed something different about him as he said Mass. The wounds on his hands and feet had disappeared. The next day, Padre Pio died a holy death.

St. Padre Pio, help my suffering remind others of Jesus!

Our Lady of Walsingham
September 24

Our Lady of Walsingham

1061 • Marian Apparition

A noble widow, Lady Richeldis de Faverches, prayed to the Blessed Virgin Mary, asking Mary to show her how to do good for Mary's honor.

Mary heard Lady Richeldis's prayer and appeared to her. She showed the Lady Richeldis a vision of her small home in Nazareth, where Jesus had grown up with her and Joseph. She then asked the Lady Richeldis to build a small house like the one in Nazareth in the little country village of Walsingham in England.

The Lady Richeldis did as Mary asked.

She built a small wooden house with the exact same measurements as Mary's house in Nazareth. The holy house had the smallest of windows, but the darkness was banished by the light of many candles.

Inside the small house was a statue of Mary seated on a throne with Jesus on her lap, both wearing royal crowns. On the back of her throne was a rainbow. Under her foot is a toadstone, a symbol of evil for the English. The statue is called "Our Lady of Walsingham."

A great monastery with high columns and grand arches was built around the holy house. Many pilgrims came to pray and visit. Even many English kings came barefoot to offer their prayers.

Many hundreds of years later, King Henry VIII left the Catholic Church to make a rival church of his own, and he destroyed the monastery and the house. He had Mary's statue thrown into the fire. In the twentieth century, a new shrine and new statue were built. But sadly, Mary's little house is there no more.

Today, pilgrims flock to the shrine of Our Lady of Walsingham to pray just as they did long ago. They go to Our Lady of Walsingham to ask for help in doing what is good.

Our Lady of Walsingham, show me how to do good for your honor!

St. Cleopas
September 25

St. Cleopas

Biblical figure

Two men were on the road to Emmaus, a village about seven miles from Jerusalem. Their faces were sad and tired and their shoulders stooped, as if bearing a heavy burden.

One of the men, named Cleopas, talked with the other about the sorrowful death of Jesus. They both had hoped that Jesus would be God's promised Messiah. But their hopes had died three days before, when Jesus had died on the Cross. That morning, some women had visited Jesus' tomb and said He had risen from the dead. Though it was true that no one could find Jesus' body, Cleopas and his friend did not believe the women, and that was why they were leaving for Emmaus.

A stranger drew near Cleopas and his friend and walked with them on the road to Emmaus. The stranger asked them what they were talking about. The two men stopped walking, as if all of their strength had left them, and their sadness drew their faces downward. Cleopas asked how it was possible that the stranger had not heard what had happened to Jesus, and then he explained the terrible news.

Then, the stranger said, "Oh, how foolish you are! How slow of heart to believe all that the prophets spoke!" He explained all of the Scripture passages that showed how it was necessary for Jesus to die in order to fulfill everything the prophets had foretold about the Messiah. Cleopas's heart burned within him. Could this man be speaking the truth? Was Jesus' terrible suffering and death part of God's plan to save His people? Did that mean that Jesus still was the promised Messiah?

By now, they were approaching Emmaus, and the stranger made as if to continue on his journey. But Cleopas and his friend did not want the stranger to leave! His words spoke to their hearts, and they begged Him to stay. And so the man joined them where they were staying. They sat at the table for their meal, and the stranger took bread and, after saying the blessing, broke it and handed it to Cleopas and to his friend.

With the breaking of the bread, Cleopas recognized the stranger. He was Jesus! How had he not known Him before? At that instant, Jesus vanished from sight. Cleopas and his friend gazed at each other, astonishment and joy in their eyes. They said to each other, "Were not our hearts burning while he spoke to us on the way and opened the scriptures to us?" Immediately, they set off back toward Jerusalem, where they found the other disciples and joyfully proclaimed how Jesus had joined them on the road to Emmaus. St. Cleopas, help my heart always recognize Jesus!

Sts. Cosmas and Damian
September 26

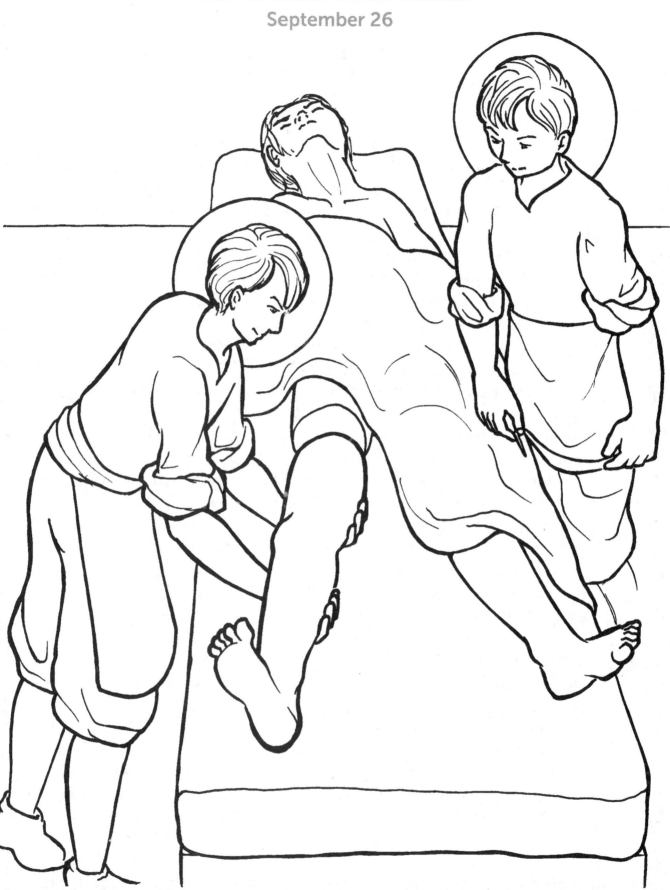

Sts. Cosmas and Damian

d. c. 303 • Jordan

Cosmas and Damian were twin brothers and Christian doctors. The pair took care of the sick as a way to share Jesus' love for others, and they refused to take the silver coins their patients tried to give as payment. Because of this charity, they were called "the silverless."

God worked healing miracles through the twin doctors. They would ask their patients about what was wrong. Then, they would make the Sign of the Cross over the sick and work their skills of healing with God's help, and in this way, many were cured who were thought beyond hope.

Cosmas and Damian healed both pagans and Christians alike. After their patients were healed, the twin brothers would teach them about Jesus. Many pagans' souls were healed, along with their bodies, when they became Christian because of the brothers' words.

The pagan governor of the area saw the brothers as enemies because they converted so many pagans to the Christian Faith. When the Roman emperor Diocletian declared his cruel persecution of the Christians, the twin brothers were among the first Christians that the governor arrested.

The governor accused the brothers of practicing magic to heal their patients. But Cosmas and Damian declared that they practiced science, not magic, and that they healed through the power of Christ. When the brothers proclaimed their faith in Jesus, the governor immediately ordered their deaths.

God would allow the two brothers the great glory of dying for Him so that they would go straight to heaven. But first, He would perform even more great miracles for the two brothers so that all who watched would see God's power and know that He was the true God.

And so, when the governor had Cosmas and Damian whipped and cast into the sea in chains, God sent an angel to rescue the brothers and bring them to the shore. When the governor ordered the brothers to be thrown into a fiery furnace, God shielded them so that the hot flames did not burn them. Furious, the governor ordered Cosmas and Damian to be stoned and shot with arrows, but God turned the stones and arrows around in the air, so that they fell instead on the persecutors, and the brothers were left unharmed. Many pagans watched these incredible miracles and became Christians because of God's great power. Finally, the governor ordered Cosmas and Damian to die by the sword, and God allowed them to die so that they would go straight to heaven.

Sts. Cosmas and Damian, please ask God to heal my body and my soul!

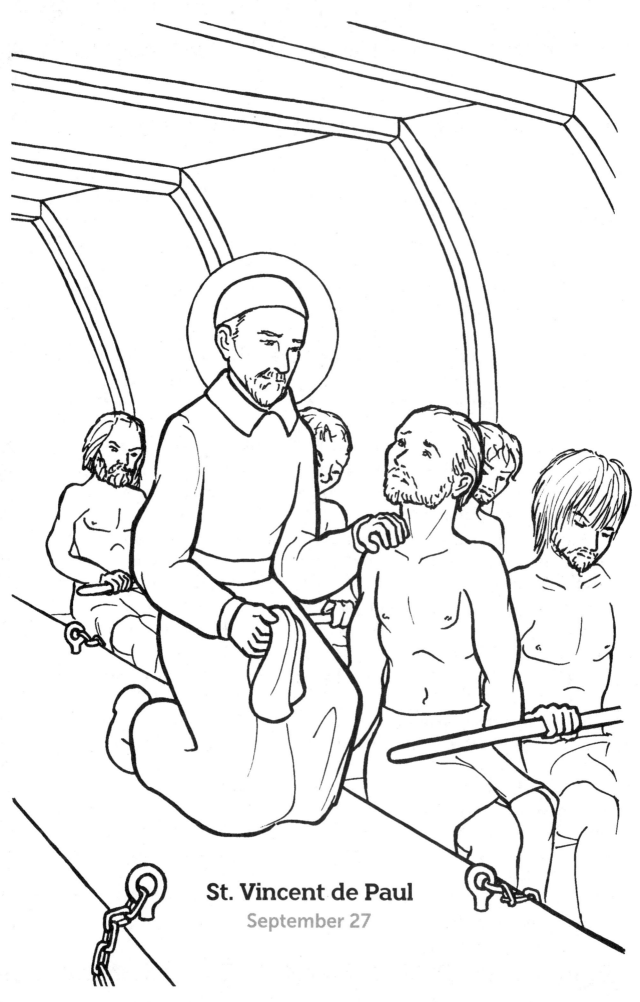

St. Vincent de Paul

September 27

St. Vincent de Paul

1581–1660 • France

A young priest, Vincent de Paul, was sailing home to his parish from Marseilles. Suddenly, one of the sailors cried out—pirates were attacking the ship! Vincent de Paul fell, wounded by an arrow. The pirates captured the young priest and sold him into slavery in North Africa.

Over the next two years, Vincent de Paul served three different masters. His final master was a Catholic who had left the Faith. When Vincent was working in his master's fields, his master's wife came out to watch him work.

She asked Vincent de Paul to sing her a song. In a clear voice, Vincent sang the "Hail, Holy Queen," a beautiful hymn in honor of the Blessed Virgin Mary.

The woman was enchanted.

She returned to her husband and asked how he could have given up a Faith that was so beautiful. In time, Vincent de Paul brought his master back to the Catholic Faith, and both escaped back to France. Now Vincent de Paul could return to serving the people of France as a priest.

He founded a congregation of priests and helped found an order of nuns, the Daughters of Charity, who looked after the poor and the sick. One snowy night, he discovered a little child abandoned in the streets. Sadly, this practice was common for poor, unwanted babies. He brought the child to a home to look after him. His heart went out to the babies of Paris, and he and a group of kind ladies started a home for abandoned children.

The king assigned Vincent de Paul to look after the galley slaves, prisoners who did the backbreaking rowing of the king's ships. The prisoners in the galley ships must have reminded Vincent de Paul of his time as a slave. He visited the galley slaves every day, reminding them that Christ still loved them and preparing them for the sacraments.

St. Vincent de Paul did many such good works, caring for the poor, the sick, and the abandoned. He served God and others with love until he died a holy death in his old age.

St. Vincent de Paul, help me to care for the poor, the sick, and the abandoned!

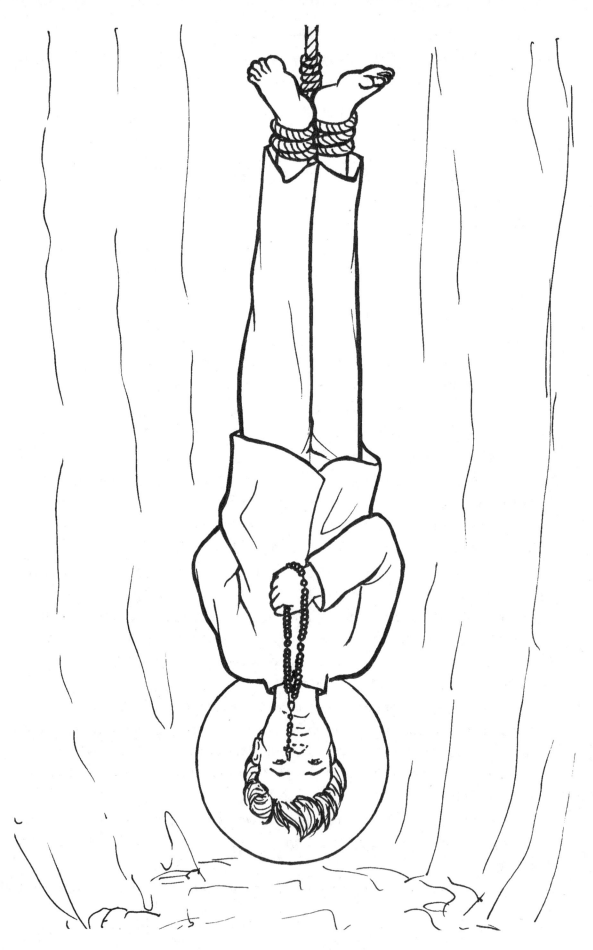

St. Lorenzo Ruiz
September 28

St. Lorenzo Ruiz

c. 1600–1637 • Philippines

Lorenzo Ruiz could just spot the Japanese shore from where he was standing on the ship's deck. He was very far from his home in the Philippines.

He missed his home, his wife, and his children.

He had not wanted to leave them. But he had had no choice. He had been falsely accused of murder, and his friends, the Dominican priests, had taken him aboard their ship to save his life.

Lorenzo Ruiz had been friends with the Dominican priests for a very long time. He had been born in the Philippines to a Chinese father and a Filipina mother, and he had grown up serving the Dominicans as an altar boy and a clerk for his church. He was strong in his faith in Jesus and was especially dedicated to praying the Holy Rosary.

Now that he was in trouble, the Dominican priests did the best they could to help him, and that was why Lorenzo Ruiz had joined the priests on the ship leaving the Philippines to do missionary work in Japan. At that time, the Japanese government persecuted Catholics, so Lorenzo knew that he would be in danger in Japan too.

Not long after Lorenzo Ruiz and the priests landed in Japan, they were arrested and taken to Nagasaki, where the first Japanese martyrs had bravely gone to their deaths because they refused to deny Jesus. Lorenzo knew that he would die, too, if he did not give up his faith. But even though Lorenzo had left home to save his life, that did not mean his life was more important to him than his love for Jesus.

The Japanese officials cruelly tortured Lorenzo Ruiz and the priests. At first, Lorenzo did not know if he was ready to die for Jesus. He wondered if he should give up his faith and save his life.

But then God's grace made Lorenzo strong.

Lorenzo knew that if he kept his faith, he would be with Jesus forever in heaven. He declared to the government officials that he was a Christian. He cried out that he would rather die a thousand times over than give up his faith. Then, the government officials hung him upside down in a pit for three days. Lorenzo Ruiz and his Dominican companions became glorious martyrs for Jesus.

St. Lorenzo Ruiz, help me to be strong in the face of unexpected trials!

Sts. Michael, Gabriel, and Raphael

September 29

Sts. Michael, Gabriel, and Raphael

Biblical figures

St. Michael, St. Gabriel, and St. Raphael are the three archangels named in the Bible. They praise and worship God before His throne and take special care of God's people.

The Archangel Michael is the prince of the angels. The name "Michael" means "Who is like God?" (because no one is equal to God). The Archangel Michael led the good angels in the great battle against the Devil and the fallen angels. All the good angels cried out, "Who is like God?" as Michael defeated the Devil and cast all the fallen angels out of heaven. He defends the Church against the Devil and all evil spirits.

We can turn to the Archangel Michael as our protector.

The Archangel Gabriel is God's messenger from heaven. The name "Gabriel" means "God is my strength." The Archangel Gabriel appeared to Zechariah to announce the birth of John the Baptist. He appeared to the Blessed Virgin Mary with the greeting "Hail, full of grace." He announced to Mary that she was to be the Mother of God.

We can ask the Archangel Gabriel to help us listen to God's Word.

The Archangel Raphael is God's healer. The name "Raphael" means "God has healed." The Archangel Raphael appeared to a young man named Tobias and led him to his future wife, named Sara. He healed Sara from an attack of an evil spirit. He also ordered Tobias to catch a fish and to make medicine from it. Then, he commanded Tobias to smear the medicine onto his blind father's eyes. Tobias's father's name was Tobit, and Tobit was a good man faithful to God. When Tobias did as the Archangel Raphael ordered him, his father Tobit was healed and could see!

We can ask the Archangel Raphael for God's healing of our bodies and souls.

Sts. Michael, Gabriel, and Raphael, please pray for me before the throne of God!

St. Jerome
September 30

St. Jerome

347–419 • Dalmatia

Jerome was a brilliant scholar from a young age, and he went to Rome to pursue his studies. At this time, Jerome did not put God first in his life, even though he had been brought up in the Christian Faith.

But then he had a dream that changed him forever.

In his dream, Jesus appeared to Jerome and said, "You are a Ciceronian, not a Christian." (Cicero was a famous Roman writer.) When he woke, Jerome knew that Jesus was telling him that he loved his Roman and Greek studies more than he loved God. For penance, he spent four years as a hermit in the desert and learned Hebrew so he could study Scripture.

Jerome returned to Rome and, because of his great learning, he became Pope Damasus's secretary. But Jerome had a bad temper! He harshly criticized the people who lived sinful lives in Rome. When the pope died, all the enemies Jerome had made because of his bad temper spread lies and gossip about him.

So Jerome left Rome. He traveled to Bethlehem and wrote in a cave near where Jesus was born. Legend says that he made friends with a lion while he was staying at the cave in Bethlehem.

Jerome's writings are very important. He wrote in defense of the Faith, even though many of his letters are cranky. He got into arguments with many other theologians, even St. Augustine, though they became friends later.

In Bethlehem, Jerome completed his most famous work. He translated the Bible from Hebrew and Greek into Latin. This took Jerome fifteen years! Up to that point, there was no good translation of the whole Bible into Latin, the language many people spoke. Because Jerome knew Hebrew, he could read the original books of the Bible, and so his translations were the best! Jerome's translation of the Bible is called the Vulgate, which comes from the Latin word vulgus (which means "common people"). Because of Jerome, many more people could read the Bible!

St. Jerome died a holy death, and he reminds us that even saints are not perfect. His life was holy, even though he had a bad temper!

St. Jerome, help me to learn to love Jesus through reading the Bible!

St. Thérèse of Lisieux
October 1

St. Thérèse of Lisieux

1873–1897 • France

Thérèse was born to Zélie and Louis Martin, who later were known as saints. She was lively and cheerful and grew up with four older sisters, but sadness overclouded her at the age of four when her mother died. Her older sister Pauline became like a second mother to her. But when Pauline left home to become a Carmelite nun, little Thérèse fell terribly ill. She turned to the statue of Mary in her room and pleaded for Mary's help. Suddenly, the statue gave her a smile full of such radiance and love that Thérèse was instantly cured.

Thérèse knew from a young age that Jesus was calling her to become a Carmelite nun. When she was fifteen years old, she and her father asked the Carmelites if she could enter, but they told her to return when she was twenty-one. Thérèse desperately wanted to become a nun as soon as possible. Doing up her hair to appear older, she visited the bishop to request permission to enter the convent. The bishop was impressed by the eager girl and told her he would consider her request.

But this was not enough for Thérèse.

She accompanied her father to Rome for an audience with the pope. There, she was sternly warned not to speak to the pope. But nothing could stop her from speaking what was in her heart. She knelt at the pope's feet and tearfully begged him to let her enter the convent. Everyone was shocked that Thérèse had been so daring. The pope kindly told Thérèse that she must do as the superiors of the convent told her. But Thérèse would not give up. She pressed his knees and told the pope that if he gave his permission, everyone would have to do as he said. The pope gazed into Thérèse's eyes and said, "Well, well, you will enter if the good God wills it." God did will for Thérèse to enter the Carmelite convent early. The bishop gave Thérèse his permission less than a month after she returned from Rome.

Thérèse's time in the convent was ordinary. None of the sisters knew that this little nun was an extraordinary saint! Thérèse knew that she was like a little child and could not do great, extraordinary things on her own. So she practiced her "little way," which meant that every little thing she did, she did for love of God. The prioress ordered Thérèse to write down her life in a book, which we can read today to learn all about her little way. She died a holy death from illness, offering her suffering to God with love.

St. Thérèse of Lisieux, help me to follow your little way out of love for God!

Feast of the Guardian Angels
October 2

Feast of the Guardian Angels

God loves you very much, and He has given you a very special gift—a Guardian Angel of your very own to watch over you and to guide you. Everyone has a Guardian Angel, including you and me.

Do you pray to your Guardian Angel?

Your Guardian Angel is always with you and loves you. Your angel has been watching over you ever since you were in your mother's womb and will stay with you until you draw your last breath. Your angel knows you better than even your best friend knows you.

Become friends with your Guardian Angel!

Ask your angel for help when you are in trouble. Ask your angel for guidance when you are not sure what is wrong and what is right. Pray to your Guardian Angel, and your angel will protect you and help you to do what is right.

Every morning when you awake, kneel down next to your bed and say this prayer to your Guardian Angel:

Angel of God,
My guardian dear,
To whom God's love
Commits me here,
Ever this day,
Be at my side,
To light and guard,
To rule and guide.

Today is a special day to remember your Guardian Angel and to say thank you for everything your angel does for you.

Dear Guardian Angel, thank you for always being at my side to watch over and protect me!

Bl. Edmund of Scotland

October 3

Bl. Edmund of Scotland

c. 1070–c. 1100 • Scotland

Edmund begged for God's forgiveness on his knees. He fixed his eyes on the crucifix and meditated on how Jesus had shed His blood on the Cross to wash sinners' souls clean. So wrapped was he in his prayers that he did not feel the cold of the stone slabs of the chapel floor. With a sorrowful groan, he bowed his head. For Edmund's sins, Jesus had died.

In the midst of his sorrows, love stirred in Edmund's heart: love for the Savior who in His great mercy had died to forgive Edmund's sins.

Edmund remembered the days when he had plotted for the Scottish throne. After his eldest brother and his father, Malcolm, had died in battle, Edmund and his uncle Donalbain had seized the throne from Edmund's older half-brother Duncan. Donalbain had promised Edmund all of Scotland after he died. He also promised to let him rule half of the kingdom while Donalbain lived. And so Edmund had agreed to his uncle's terrible plot, and Edmund's half-brother had been murdered. After less than three short years of ruling Scotland together, both Donalbain and Edmund were overthrown by Edmund's own younger brother Edgar and another uncle. Donalbain had been put to death, but Edmund was allowed to flee to a monastery in England to live his life as a monk.

Edmund had entered the monastery with his soul heavy with anguish. His dreams of ambition were crushed, and he had barely escaped with his life. Many a lonely night Edmund spent in his cell, reflecting on the past and how he had sinned.

But Jesus had spared his life and given him a second chance.

Edmund went to confession and confessed his terrible sins to a priest, who, through the power of Jesus, forgave him. As Edmund stepped out of the confessional, his eyes were bright and clear, and his back was straight as the weight of anguish was lifted from him.

For the rest of his life, Edmund spent his days in prayer and penitence. Everyone agreed that the wickedness of Edmund had disappeared and that he had become a very holy man. At his death, he requested that his body be buried in chains as a sign of his sorrow for his sins. His holy death gives hope to all who seek God's mercy and forgiveness for their sins.

Bl. Edmund of Scotland, help me to turn to Jesus for mercy and the forgiveness of my sins!

St. Francis of Assisi
October 4

St. Francis of Assisi

1181–1226 • Italy

Francis of Assisi was a fun-loving young man who wished to become a knight and win glory. On his way to battle, Francis had a dream in which Jesus told him to return to Assisi. So the next morning, Francis turned his horse about and returned to Assisi, where he waited to see what Jesus wanted of him.

As Francis was praying before a crucifix in an old little church called San Damiano, Jesus spoke to Francis from His Cross. He told Francis to rebuild His home, which was falling into ruin. Looking at the church's crumbling walls, Francis thought that Jesus was telling him to rebuild the chapel stone by stone. But Jesus wanted Francis to fix more than just the physical walls of the church. He had plans for Francis to build up His Church throughout the world.

Francis lived the way that Jesus had lived. He gave all of his money to the poor and called "Lady Poverty" his wife. He befriended all of God's creatures, including the animals. Because he loved Christmas, Francis started the tradition of creating a nativity scene, with Mary, Joseph, and baby Jesus. If you have a nativity scene in your home during Advent and Christmas, you have St. Francis to thank for it!

Many people began to follow Francis so that they, too, could live like Jesus. They gave all that they had to the poor, begged for food and whatever they needed, and preached about Jesus' love. With so many people joining him, Francis went to the pope to ask permission to start a new order.

At first, the pope did not listen to Francis; but then he had a dream: the great pillars of the church were falling. But then there was Francis, holding up the collapsing Church! The pope gave Francis his permission, and Francis founded the Franciscans to live as Jesus had and to spread His love to all the world. Francis even set out as far as Egypt to try to convert the sultan, who was fighting Christians during the Crusades. Impressed by Francis, the sultan promised to treat his Christian prisoners kindly, though he did not become a Christian, and let Francis return home unharmed.

Two years before Francis's death, a seraph angel with six wings appeared to Francis as he prayed. Blinding rays of light shot forth from the angel and pierced Francis's side, feet, and hands. From then on, Francis bore the stigmata, the Holy Wounds of Jesus' Crucifixion, until he died a holy death.

St. Francis of Assisi, help me to live like Christ!

St. Faustina Kowalska
October 5

St. Faustina Kowalska

1905–1938 • Poland

A simple Polish nun, Sr. Faustina Kowalska did not seem at all remarkable. She had grown up in a poor family and had finished only three years of school. Her duties at the convent were to cook, garden, and watch at the convent gate. But this simple nun had remarkable love for Jesus. Nothing made her happier than being with Jesus in the Eucharist.

On the evening of February 22, 1931, Sr. Faustina felt a sudden presence in her room. There stood a man dressed in white. Her heart leapt as she recognized Jesus. He held up His right hand in blessing. His left hand touched His breast, from which streamed rays of red and white light.

Silently and full of awe and joy, Sr. Faustina gazed on Jesus. Then, Jesus spoke to Sr. Faustina, saying, "Paint an image according to the pattern you see, with the signature: Jesus, I trust in You. I desire that this image be venerated, first in your chapel, and then throughout the world. I promise that the soul that will venerate this image will not perish." Sr. Faustina confided to the priest who heard her confessions what Jesus had told her. Together, they commissioned an image of Jesus as He had appeared to Sr. Faustina.

Jesus also instructed Sr. Faustina to write down in her diary all that He told her. He wanted Sr. Faustina to be the messenger of His Divine Mercy to the whole world! He taught her a special chaplet to pray at 3:00 p.m., the Hour of Mercy when He had died on the Cross. He also wanted His Divine Mercy to be celebrated the first Sunday after Easter.

Sr. Faustina experienced great union with God. Her heart was full of love for Him, and she spent her life spreading the devotion to Jesus' Divine Mercy to sinners throughout the world. In her last days, she suffered from tuberculosis and died a holy death at the age of thirty-three, the same age that Jesus had died on the Cross.

Almost thirty years after her death, the archbishop of Krakow sent Sr. Faustina's diary to the Vatican. This Polish archbishop would one day become Pope St. John Paul II. When he was pope, he instituted the Feast of the Divine Mercy on the first Sunday after Easter, just as Jesus had asked. Jesus wants us to be devoted to His image of Divine Mercy and to pray the Divine Mercy chaplet so that He can shower His mercy on the whole world.

St. Faustina Kowalska, help us to trust in Jesus' mercy!

Bl. Marie-Rose Durocher

October 6

Bl. Marie-Rose Durocher

1811–1849 • Canada

Eulalie Durocher was the tenth of eleven children in a Canadian family blessed by God—the children received a wonderful education, which helped three of Eulalie's brothers to become priests and her older sister Séraphine to become a nun. Eulalie entered the boarding school at the local convent because she wanted to be a nun too. But her health was too weak, so she had to return home and live with her family. God was teaching Eulalie patience.

Soon after Eulalie's return, her mother died. In her sadness, Eulalie discovered why God had sent her back home. She had to take care of her family now that her mother was gone. One of her three brothers who had become priests invited the family to live in his parish home, and Eulalie became the housekeeper. She was a housekeeper for over ten years, and in that time, she learned about the needs of the people of the parish and beyond. Eulalie discovered that many families were not blessed with the same wonderful education that she had received when she was young. There were many poor children in the countryside who had no one to teach them. Eulalie felt that God was calling her to form a religious community dedicated to educating children.

With the help of a priest, Eulalie became a nun and formed the Sisters of the Holy Names of Jesus and Mary. Eulalie took the new name Marie-Rose and became the congregation's superior. The sisters' special mission was to teach children, and they moved into a building that was to become their school.

Mother Marie-Rose faced many challenges in her school. An outspoken priest named Charles Chiniquy, who would later leave the Church to become a Protestant minister, wanted to control Marie-Rose's nuns and their school. Marie-Rose saw that what he wanted would do more harm than good. As the leader of her community, she put her foot down. She would not allow Fr. Chiniquy to interfere with what was best for her students. Fr. Chiniquy became angry and said mean things about Marie-Rose and her nuns in public. But Marie-Rose did not let his words bother her. She knew that she was doing what was best for her students. Even more importantly, she was doing what God wanted.

Mother Marie-Rose suffered from weak health and illness all of her life, but that did not stop her from doing her best to carry out the mission that God had given her. She spent the rest of her life educating children until she died a holy death.

Bl. Marie-Rose Durocher, help me to carry out God's mission for my life!

Our Lady of the Rosary
October 7

Our Lady of the Rosary

1571 • Marian Feast Day

Pope Pius V clutched his rosary beads in heartfelt prayer. He had ordered all the Roman churches to pray the Rosary both day and night.

They must pray for victory.

An important battle was taking place—the Battle of Lepanto.

The Ottoman Empire had brought together a great force of ships and was threatening to take over all of Europe. City after city had fallen to their troops; the Ottomans had reached as far as the walls of Vienna in Austria and had even landed in Italy, hoping to capture Rome itself. Their ships had not lost a battle in more than one hundred and fifty years and were therefore called "invincible." If the Ottomans prevailed, Europe would no longer be a Christian land. Only Don John of Austria's fleet of ships stood in the way. The Ottomans' ships greatly outnumbered Don John's. And so the pope knew that Don John needed all the prayers he could get!

On the day of the Battle of Lepanto, Pope Pius V was working hard with his cardinals. Suddenly, he ran to the window and gazed out into the sky.

"A truce to business," the pope cried. "Our great task at present is to thank God for the victory which He has just given the Christian army." Through the power of the Rosary, the outnumbered Christian ships had defeated the Ottomans! Hundreds of miles away in Rome, Pope Pius V miraculously knew of the victory on the same day. Mary had granted the Christian forces success in battle!

In gratitude to Mary, Pope Pius V instituted the Feast of Our Lady of the Rosary to celebrate Mary and the power of the Rosary.

You, too, can pray the Rosary. The Rosary is a very powerful help when we need to ask for God's protection. Mary's Rosary can help you win victory over sin!

Our Lady of the Rosary, grant me victory over sin!

St. Denis

October 8

St. Denis

d. c. 254 • Italy

Denis was a bishop who lived during the Roman persecution of Christians. Denis loved Jesus so much that he wanted other people to know and to love Jesus as much as he did. The people of Gaul (modern-day France) had not heard about Jesus. And so the pope sent Denis to the Gauls, so that he could preach the Good News and help the Gauls know and love Jesus.

Denis, along with a few companions, made the long journey from Rome to Gaul. Finally, Denis settled in what is now Paris, where he preached to the Gauls about Jesus. He explained to them that Jesus is God, and that Jesus loved them so much that He had died for them so that they could one day be with Him forever in heaven. Many Gauls believed in Jesus because of Denis's words, and so Denis spent many years baptizing the Gauls and giving them the sacraments.

Now, the Gauls were under the control of the Roman Empire, and Denis was so successful at converting the Gauls to Christianity that the Roman governor of the area began to notice. He ordered Denis's arrest, and Roman soldiers dragged Denis and his companions before the governor. The Roman governor ordered Denis to deny Jesus and worship the Roman gods.

But Denis refused.

Jesus had loved Denis so much as to die for him, and so Denis would love Jesus so much as to die for Him too.

The Roman soldiers marched Denis and his companions to the top of a tall hill called Montmartre, the "mount of the martyrs." There, Denis and his companions were beheaded.

An ancient legend tells us that after he was beheaded, Denis picked up his own head, carried it high, and walked for two thousand paces until he put it down again! A chapel was built at that very spot where it is said he finally rested.

St. Denis, help me to know and love Jesus!

St. John Henry Newman

October 9

St. John Henry Newman

1801–1890 • England

John Henry Newman was a highly respected Anglican priest at the University of Oxford in England. He and a group of other thinkers saw that the Church of England (also known as the Anglican church), which had broken away from the Catholic Church far back in the days of Henry VIII, was in need of reform and renewal. So he started a reform called the "Oxford Movement," which was meant to be a rebirth for the Church of England. He studied and studied to find ways to bring the Anglican church closer to the Church that Jesus had founded on earth. But the more he studied, the more he saw that the English church was not the true Church. His studies showed him that the Catholic Church was Jesus' true Church.

Now Newman had a hard choice to make.

If he became a Catholic, he would lose his important position in the University of Oxford. Not only that, he would lose all of his friends, because, in those days, the English did not like Catholics. But Newman knew that he had to do what was right and true.

Newman went on a retreat to a small village three miles away from Oxford called Littlemore. There, he spent three years praying and wrestling with the truth. Finally, he sank down on his knees before a visiting Catholic priest and asked to enter the Catholic Church.

All of Newman's Anglican friends became angry at Newman for becoming Catholic. But Newman knew that God was the most important friend he could ever have. And so Newman went to Rome, where he became a Roman Catholic priest and joined the Oratorians, the order of the cheerful saint Philip Neri. The pope asked Newman to return to England and start Oratories there.

Newman founded two Oratories in England and wrote many important books, including a work explaining why he converted to the Catholic Faith. His dearest wish was to help Anglicans and Catholics understand each other and to bring Anglicans to the Catholic Faith. He wrote that "heart speaks to heart," and that speaking from one's loving heart to another's heart is the best way to bring people to Jesus.

The pope made Newman a cardinal so that he could continue the important work of reviving the Catholic Faith in England. Newman taught and defended the Catholic Faith to the English until he died a holy death.

St. John Henry Newman, help my heart speak to other hearts about Jesus!

Sts. Eulampius and Eulampia
October 10

Sts. Eulampius and Eulampia

d. 310 • Modern-day Turkey

Eulampius and Eulampia were brother and sister. They lived during the time of the Roman persecution. The Christians were hiding in mountain caves to avoid capture, and the young Eulampius was caught trying to bring food to them. The pagan official tried to convince Eulampius to give up his faith in Jesus. But Eulampius refused, and the official ordered him to be cruelly flogged.

His young sister Eulampia had been desperately searching for her brother when she heard of his capture. The soldiers paraded Eulampius in the streets after his painful flogging. With a cry, Eulampia broke through the crowd and embraced him, shedding tears over his wounds. The soldiers saw that she, too, was a Christian, and so they arrested her and threw the siblings into prison.

No matter what the soldiers did or said, nothing could convince the two siblings to give up their faith in Jesus. They trusted in Jesus and knew He would take care of their souls. It was better for them to suffer here on earth and be forever with Jesus in heaven than to suffer forever the pains of hell because they had turned away from Him.

Seeing that Eulampius and Eulampia would never give up their faith in Jesus, the soldiers tossed them into a cauldron of boiling oil. To the soldiers' great astonishment, Eulampius and Eulampia remained unharmed. They sang praises to God with their youthful voices and stepped out of the cauldron without a burn mark on them.

Despite this great miracle, the pagan official's heart remained hardened. He ordered Eulampius and Eulampia to die by the sword, and the brother and sister became glorious martyrs for Jesus. Two hundred people who had witnessed the siblings' courage and faith became Christians. They, too, died for their faith in Jesus, and they sing their praises to God along with Eulampius and Eulampia in heaven.

Sts. Eulampius and Eulampia, help my faith in Jesus inspire others to love Him!

St. Philip the Deacon
October 11

St. Philip the Deacon

Biblical figure

Philip was one of the seven men ordained deacons by the Apostles. He was a great miracle-worker, and he preached the joyful news that Jesus is the Son of God, who died for our sins and rose from the dead.

An angel of the Lord spoke to Philip and told him to travel the desert road south from Jerusalem. Philip did what the angel asked. All alone, he traveled the desert road until he found a eunuch reading the prophet Isaiah and puzzling over the prophet's words. The eunuch was a faithful Jew who served in the court of the Queen of Ethiopia. He had gone to Jerusalem to offer sacrifice to God. Prompted by the Spirit, Philip ran up to the eunuch and asked him if he understood what he was reading.

"How can I, unless someone instructs me?" was the eunuch's reply.

So Philip hopped into the eunuch's chariot, and the eunuch showed Philip the Scripture passage he was reading. It was Isaiah's prophecy about Jesus, how "like a sheep he was led to the slaughter." Philip told the eunuch all about Jesus and how the prophet had foretold that He would die on the Cross to save us from our sins.

As they were traveling, the eunuch spied water in the desert. He ordered the chariot to a halt and asked to be baptized. Down into the water they went, and Philip baptized the eunuch, whose sins were all cleaned and his soul made newborn. At that instant, an angel snatched Philip away, and he vanished from the eunuch's sight. The eunuch continued on his journey to Ethiopia, rejoicing over the miracle and the goodness of God.

Philip continued to the town of Caesarea, proclaiming the Good News of Jesus all throughout his travels. Many years later, St. Paul, the Apostle to the Gentiles, visited Philip and his four daughters in their home in Caesarea. All four of Philip's daughters had consecrated themselves as brides of Christ and had the gift of prophecy. Philip proclaimed the Good News of Jesus until he died a holy death.

St. Philip the Deacon, help me be always ready to preach the Good News of Jesus!

St. Wilfrid
October 12

St. Wilfrid

634–709 • England

Fourteen-year-old Wilfrid left home for the king of Northumbria's court because his stepmother was unkind to him. At court, the queen especially favored Wilfrid. And so Wilfrid asked the queen for her help to enter the monastery. Not only did the queen help him become a monk, but she also helped him eventually travel to Rome. Wilfrid became a priest and later the bishop of York in Northumbria (now part of England).

As the bishop of York, Wilfrid governed and watched over his flock of Christians. But some of the English bishops, and even the king, tried to challenge his authority and divide his church and the faithful Christians under his care.

Bishop Wilfrid would not stand by and watch his flock being taken away!

He made the long journey to Rome and presented his case to the pope. The pope decided in Bishop Wilfrid's favor, and Bishop Wilfrid returned to England with the pope's ruling. The king of Northumbria said that he would do what the pope ordered, but that he would also throw Bishop Wilfrid in prison for having lied to the pope! The king did this because he considered Bishop Wilfrid his enemy.

The king eventually released him on the condition that Bishop Wilfrid leave Northumbria. And so Bishop Wilfrid became a missionary among the pagans in the south of Great Britain and brought many souls to Jesus.

Eventually, Bishop Wilfrid was invited to return to Northumbria. Now Bishop Wilfrid saw that even the pope's authority was being challenged by the bishops and the king. And so, for a second time, he made the long journey to Rome to speak to the new pope.

The pope again sided with Bishop Wilfrid. This time, when Bishop Wilfrid returned, the other bishops in England submitted to the pope's authority. Bishop Wilfrid rejoiced that the bishops in England now followed the pope as they ought. Bishop Wilfrid remained a defender of the pope until he died a holy death.

St. Wilfrid, please watch over the pope and bishops of the Church!

St. Edward the Confessor
October 13

St. Edward the Confessor

1003–1066 • England

Edward was the son of the Saxon king of England when the Danes invaded and seized the English throne. Ten-year-old Edward was sent to his uncle's faraway court in Normandy to protect him from the enemy Danes.

An exiled prince who had lost his country and his home, Edward learned not to put his trust in power, kings, and riches. Instead, he put his trust in God. Edward avoided the temptations of his uncle's court, loved going to Mass, and was faithful in his prayers. He grew into a man of honor and virtue.

When Edward was in his forties, the Danish king in England died, and the English people asked Edward to return and be their king. And so the exiled prince returned home to take the throne.

Because of all his suffering, Edward did not take being king for granted. He wanted to be a good and just king to bring peace to England. He knew that a good king served his people, so he took care of the poor in his kingdom. One of his servants was caught three times stealing from the king, and three times the king let him go, saying that the servant needed the gold more than he did.

Legends say that St. John appeared to King Edward disguised as a beggar. The king had no gold on him, so he gave the disguised beggar the ring from his finger. Later, St. John appeared to two pilgrims and gave them the ring to return to the king, with the promise that St. John would see him again in heaven!

King Edward made a promise to God to visit St. Peter's tomb in Rome, but he discovered that his people needed him too much for him to leave England. The pope released him of his promise but told the king that he should build a church to St. Peter in England instead. And so Edward built a new St. Peter's Abbey outside of London, where the great Westminster Abbey now stands.

The abbey was dedicated to God only a week before King Edward died, and he was buried at the abbey after his holy death.

St. Edward the Confessor, help me trust God instead of riches and power!

Pope St. Callistus I

October 14

Pope St. Callistus I

d. 223 • Italy

Callistus had an unusual beginning for a future pope. He was not a Christian from a pious family, nor did he receive the best education.

Callistus was a Christian slave.

His Roman master had entrusted Callistus with a large sum of money to start a bank. But when the bank lost all of the money, Callistus boarded a departing ship to run away because he knew he would be blamed for the bank's failure. The ship was stopped, and Callistus dove into the cold waves to escape. But he was captured and dragged back to his master, who had Callistus sentenced to a life of backbreaking labor in the mines.

But God was watching over Callistus.

Pope Victor and a virtuous Christian widow ransomed the Christians serving in the mines, Callistus among them. The next pope, Pope Zephyrinus, made Callistus his deacon. During the time he served Pope Zephyrinus, Callistus took charge of an underground burial site for Christian martyrs that to this day is called the Catacombs of St. Callistus.

When Pope Zephyrinus died, Callistus became the next pope. He preached especially the forgiveness of sins, saying Jesus forgave great sins if the sinner was sorry. Callistus I was pope for five years when a riot broke out between the Christians and the pagans in Rome. In the middle of the riot, Pope Callistus was thrown from the top of a high tower because he was a Christian, and he became a glorious martyr for Jesus!

Pope St. Callistus I, help me to trust that God watches over me!

**St. Teresa de Ávila
(St. Teresa of Jesus)**
October 15

St. Teresa de Ávila (St. Teresa of Jesus)

1515–1582 • Spain

A seven-year-old Teresa de Ávila and her older brother were running away. She had convinced her brother that they should be missionaries for Christ. Fortunately, their uncle found them on the road outside of town and brought them home before they fell into trouble. After that, Teresa showed few signs in her childhood that she would one day become a great saint!

As a young girl, she was more interested in parties and attention than in the love of God. When she was eleven, her mother died. A grief-stricken Teresa was sent to a convent for her education. Afterward, she decided to become a Carmelite nun. She thought that being a nun would protect her from distractions and help her lead a holy life. But being holy at the convent was not as easy as she thought. Many nuns did not care about leading a holy life, and so they would spend too much time on their appearance; they would gossip; they would entertain guests. In the convent, Teresa found it much easier to spend time impressing her friends with her lively conversation than talking to God through prayer. Sometimes she did not pray at all.

Then, Teresa became terribly ill and began to pray. In her prayers, she received visions and ecstasies. During this time, she felt that she was completely united with God. These visions and ecstasies frightened her because she did not believe she was worthy of such graces. But her confessor told her not to be frightened, because her visions came from God. In one of her visions, an angel holding a long spear of gold appeared to her. He pierced her heart with the spear, and Teresa felt consumed with the fire of love for God. Teresa wrote about her spiritual experiences and the life of prayer.

Teresa decided that she must do all that she could to make the Carmelite convent a place where nuns could strive for holiness without distraction. This meant returning to earlier rules of poverty and simplicity. Many of the nuns resisted. They did not want to give up their lives of comfort. Finally, Teresa was allowed to found her own convent, named after St. Joseph, in Ávila. There, the nuns lived in poverty, as originally intended. They even went without shoes. Teresa's reforms to the Carmelite order attracted other women desiring holiness to become nuns. Soon, Teresa was starting other convents. She even started monasteries for Carmelite monks with the help of another saint, St. John of the Cross. All throughout her work, Teresa was persecuted by those who did not want to see the convents reformed, but she triumphed through God's grace. She founded new convents until she died a holy death. St. Teresa de Ávila, please help me grow closer to Jesus through prayer!

St. Margaret Mary Alacoque
October 16

St. Margaret Mary Alacoque

1647–1690 • France

Ever since she was little, Margaret preferred praying to Jesus in front of the Blessed Sacrament to playing childhood games. At the age of nine, she became ill and bedridden for four years. She made a promise to Mary that, if healed, she would become a nun. After Our Lady miraculously healed her, Margaret took Mary as her Confirmation name in memory of her promise.

Her father died when she was still young, and the family property fell into the hands of her relatives. They treated Margaret Mary and her mother like servants in their own home. Margaret Mary would cry in the corner of the garden because they would not let her go to Mass when she wanted. Her heart was also sorrowful for her mother, who suffered much under this treatment. When Margaret Mary prayed in front of the Blessed Sacrament, Jesus would appear to her and console her. Margaret Mary thought that Jesus appeared to everyone. She did not know she was special!

When she turned seventeen, the family property was restored to her brother. Her brother wanted her to marry. Margaret Mary did not know if she should keep her promise to become a nun since she was so young when she had made it. One evening, she went to a masked ball. As she was leaving, Jesus appeared to her. He was suffering, His back scourged as in His Passion. He reproached her for not keeping her promise to Him.

Margaret Mary knew then that she really was meant to be a nun. She joined the Order of the Visitation, and soon, Jesus appeared to her and showed her His Sacred Heart. It burned with love for the world. But then, Jesus told her that most people ignored Him. He had given His heart to humanity, and yet most rejected Him! So He asked Margaret Mary to spread devotion to His Sacred Heart through the celebration of the Feast of the Sacred Heart, the reception of Holy Communion on the first Friday of every month, and adoration for an hour in front of the Blessed Sacrament on Thursday. The holy hour would console His Sacred Heart, which had been abandoned at the Garden of Gethsemane.

At first, the other nuns in the convent did not believe that Jesus had appeared to Margaret Mary. But then a newly elected mother superior believed in Margaret Mary's visions, and the convent celebrated the Feast of the Sacred Heart. Margaret Mary Alacoque died a holy death, and almost 150 years later, the Feast of the Sacred Heart was established for the whole Church. St. Margaret Mary Alacoque, help me to console Jesus' Sacred Heart with my prayers!

St. Ignatius of Antioch

October 17

St. Ignatius of Antioch

c. 50–c. 107 • Syria

Ignatius was a friend of the Apostles. He learned all about Jesus from St. John the Apostle. Every loving word St. John spoke about Jesus imprinted itself into Ignatius's heart. St. Peter himself ordained Ignatius as bishop of Antioch. Antioch was the first place that the followers of Jesus Christ called themselves "Christians."

At that time, the Roman emperors persecuted Christians all throughout the empire, which included Antioch. Ignatius spoke brave words to his fellow Christians and encouraged them to remain strong and true to Jesus. He told them how much Jesus loved them and wanted them to be with Him in heaven. More than anything, Ignatius wanted to die serving Jesus to show his love for his Savior and be with Jesus forever in Heaven.

When Ignatius was an old man, he finally received his wish.

The Roman emperor Trajan came to Antioch. Roman soldiers arrested Ignatius and dragged him before the emperor. The emperor ordered Ignatius to worship him as a god and to deny Jesus as the one true God. Ignatius stood tall and refused. He knew that there was only one God: Father, Son, and Holy Spirit. He would never deny his love for Jesus.

The emperor ordered Ignatius put in chains, sent to Rome, and cast into the Colosseum to become food for wild beasts. This did not frighten Ignatius. Instead, Ignatius rejoiced! His wish would come true! He would die a martyr for Jesus.

On Ignatius's long trip to Rome, Christians gathered to say goodbye to their beloved bishop. After long days of travel, the soldiers would rest at towns along the way, where Ignatius would write letters to his fellow Christians. He encouraged them to stay true to their love for Jesus and begged them not to try to save his life. Ignatius explained that he was happy to become food for the wild beasts, because that way, he would go straight to heaven and see Jesus.

Finally, Ignatius reached Rome, and the emperor's sentence was carried out. With a prayer of love for Jesus on his lips, Ignatius died in the Colosseum as a glorious martyr for Jesus!

St. Ignatius of Antioch, help me to stay true to my love for Jesus!

St. Luke the Evangelist
October 18

St. Luke the Evangelist

Biblical figure

Luke was a Greek physician. He probably learned his medical skills as a slave and worked to earn his freedom. One of the first Christian converts, he was a friend of the Apostles and, in particular, of St. Paul, who called Luke "the beloved physician" (Col. 4:14).

Sailing with Paul to Greece and Rome, Luke shared the joyful news that Jesus died for each and every one of us to free us from our sins.

When Paul was arrested for preaching the Word of Jesus, Luke visited him often to keep him company. During this time, Luke wrote the book of the Acts of the Apostles, which is a book about the beginnings of the Church. You can read this book in the Bible!

Luke was faithful to Paul and was the last to stay at his side when Paul was martyred. Afterward, he continued his travels, sharing his love for Jesus with everyone he met.

Tradition says that he paid visits to the Blessed Virgin Mary. He wrote the Gospel of Luke in the Bible, which includes special stories about Mary and the birth of Jesus that only she could have told him!

It is said that Luke was a wonderful painter and that he painted the earliest pictures of Mary. He also painted pictures with his words, as the Gospel of Luke is the longest and most beautiful of the Gospels.

Artists often show Luke with an ox at his side. That is because he begins his Gospel with the story of the angel Gabriel's appearance to Zechariah as he was burning incense to God in the Temple. Zechariah was a priest, and priests sacrificed oxen to God, making the ox a symbol of the priesthood.

St. Luke, help me to learn more about Jesus by reading your Gospel!

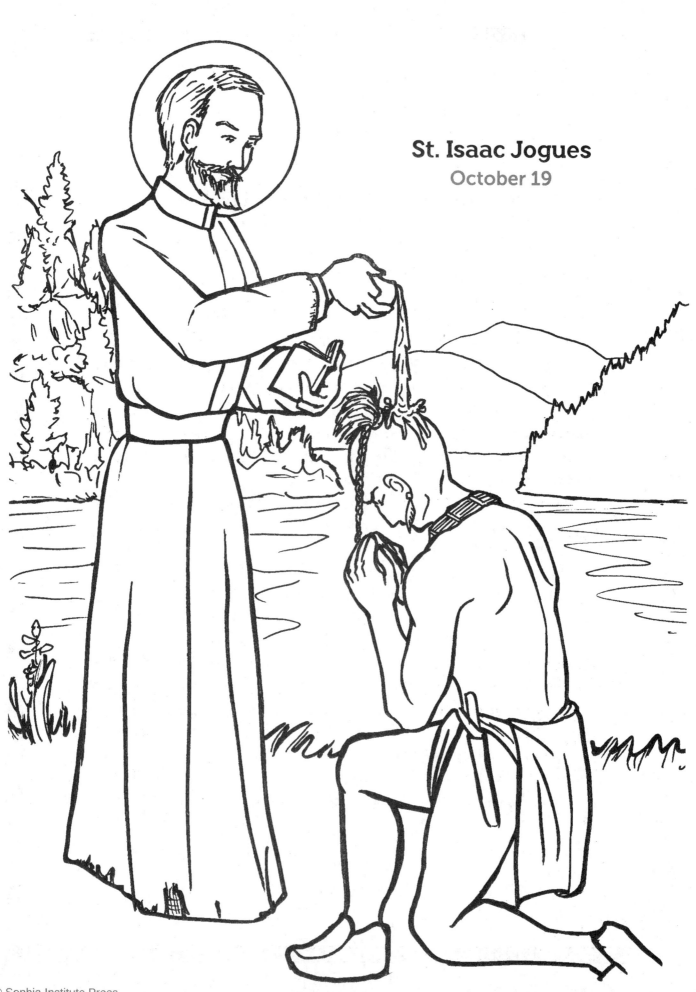

St. Isaac Jogues
October 19

© Sophia Institute Press

St. Isaac Jogues

1607–1646 • France

Isaac Jogues watched from the thickets as the Iroquois captured his companions. He had no thoughts of escape. He was a priest and could not leave behind his fellow French missionaries and the newly baptized Hurons. Isaac Jogues called out to the Iroquois warrior guarding the prisoners and was made a prisoner himself.

Isaac Jogues was a French Jesuit priest who came to Canada to preach to and baptize the Hurons. The greatest of joys had flooded his heart when he had first stepped onto the Canadian shore and said Mass. This was where he was supposed to be, bringing new souls to Christ.

The mission was always in danger. Any time that there was illness or crop failure, the Hurons blamed the "black robes," as the Jesuit priests were called. But Isaac Jogues and his fellow missionaries ate with the Hurons, tended to their sick, and lived among them. Slowly but surely, they brought many Hurons to Jesus, baptizing them in the name of the Father, the Son, and the Holy Spirit.

Isaac Jogues and his fellow missionaries were on their way to get medical supplies when they were captured by the fierce Iroquois. The Iroquois cruelly tortured the French missionaries, and Isaac Jogues lost his fingers. Bravely, he endured his suffering, comforting his fellow prisoners and hearing their confessions. Dutch settlers arranged for Isaac Jogues's escape, and he boarded a ship and returned home to France.

At first, no one recognized Isaac Jogues, so much had his suffering changed him. He received special permission from the pope to say Mass without his fingers (because he could not hold the Eucharist properly), and the pope called Isaac Jogues a martyr for Christ. But Isaac Jogues's heart was back at the Canadian settlement he had left behind. He could not abandon those many souls who had never heard about Jesus. He returned to the missionary settlement in Quebec and asked to be a missionary to the Iroquois.

Peace treaties were being made between the French and the Iroquois, and Isaac Jogues was made an ambassador to the Iroquois. This time, he was welcomed by the Iroquois, and he said Mass and continued his missionary work among them. But then, illness broke out among the Iroquois, and their crops suffered. They blamed Isaac Jogues and put him to death, and Isaac Jogues became a glorious martyr for the Faith! St. Isaac Jogues, help me to not be afraid to suffer for Jesus!

St. Paul of the Cross
October 20

St. Paul of the Cross

1694–1775 • Italy

The two boys spluttered and struggled in the river. Fear clutched Paul's heart—he and his brother John Baptist had fallen in, and now they were drowning! Out of nowhere, the most beautiful woman appeared. She extended her hand to them and pulled the two boys out of the river. Paul knew that the woman was the Blessed Virgin Mary and that she was watching over him. From his childhood, Paul dedicated himself to prayer and the service of Jesus and Mary.

One day, after receiving Holy Communion, Paul had a vision of himself wrapped in a black tunic. On his breast was a badge shaped like a white heart with a cross on top. Inside of the heart were three nails, in memory of the nails in Jesus' hands and feet, and the words, "The Passion of Jesus Christ." The Blessed Virgin appeared and handed him the tunic, and from then on, Paul was filled with the desire to found a religious order dedicated to Jesus' Passion, His suffering and death on the Cross. Paul became a priest and founded the Passionists, who wore the white heart from his vision on their tunics. His brother John Baptist also entered the order, and the two brothers lived the life of prayer and sacrifice of the Passionist brothers.

Paul of the Cross's life was marked by miracles. Once, when he was preaching to a large crowd in the square, sudden storm clouds gathered, and a torrent of rain burst upon the people. Paul raised his crucifix and said a blessing. The sky cleared, and the square completely dried! The people rejoiced in God's miracle!

Another time, Paul needed to send a very important letter by messenger on horseback. The rider said he could not take the letter because the waters of the river en route to his destination were too high to cross. But Paul told the rider not to fear and to carry his letter. The rider trusted Paul because he knew of his holiness. When the rider came to the river, he fearlessly spurred his horse onto the water. The horse's hooves dashed across the top of the water without sinking! The people on the riverbanks saw this and marveled at the miracle.

Paul of the Cross remained the leader of his order, the Passionists, until he died a holy death. St. Paul of the Cross, help me to think of Jesus' suffering and death on the Cross!

St. Ursula and Her Maidens

October 21

St. Ursula and Her Maidens

d. 451 • Britain

In a church of the German city of Cologne can be found a stone with an ancient inscription. The stone honors the spot where Ursula and her maidens died for their Faith long ago.

Legend says that the pagan king of England requested that the British king Maurus give his daughter Ursula to his son in marriage. The king of England's messengers made many promises of wealth and friendship if Ursula came to England to be the prince's bride, but threatened danger and ruin if she refused. King Maurus was anxious because the king of England and his son were pagans, and he was a Christian king whose daughter was especially dedicated to God. But Ursula agreed to become the prince's bride if he would be instructed in the Faith and baptized. And so the agreement was made, and while the prince learned about the Faith, Ursula would make a pilgrimage to Rome.

Ursula embarked on her ship with eleven maidens to accompany her and set sail across the North Sea. Great winds arose and brought Ursula's ship to the great Rhine River, and Ursula and her maidens passed through the city of Cologne on their way to Rome.

After they had seen Rome and its holy sites, Ursula and her maidens traveled back north to meet her promised prince. But when they returned to Cologne, the barbarian Huns were pillaging the country and attacking the city. Seeing Ursula and her maidens, the Huns rushed upon them to take them as their brides.

But Ursula stood tall among her maidens and declared in a ringing voice to the Huns that she and her ladies were Christian maidens and would not be forced into marriage. When the Huns saw that Ursula and her maidens would not become their brides, they put the maidens to death, and so they became glorious martyrs for the Faith.

A great church was built over that holy place where the maidens died, and a stone was inscribed in their memory so that pilgrims could come to pray and remember the maidens.

St. Ursula, help me to remain pure and chaste for Christ!

**St. John Paul
the Great**
October 22

St. John Paul the Great

1920–2005 • Poland

Karol Wojtyła was a young man when the Nazis took over his home country of Poland during World War II. The Nazis closed the Polish universities and seminaries to destroy Polish identity. The Polish people needed to cling to hope during these dark days. Karol helped to start a secret theater company, which put on plays to inspire the Polish people, give them hope, and remind them who they were. More importantly, he entered the seminary in secret to study for the priesthood.

At the end of World War II, the seminaries opened again. Now a priest, Karol served as a chaplain for Krakow University and would take students out hiking and kayaking, where they would bless God in the air and the sunlight. Later, Karol became a professor; then, the archbishop of Krakow in Poland; and soon after, a cardinal.

In 1978, a new pope had been elected: John Paul I. But only thirty-three days after his election, the pope died of a heart attack. The cardinals gathered once again to select a new pope. This time they chose Karol Wojtyła, and he became pope, taking the name John Paul II in honor of the pope who had just passed away.

Pope John Paul II traveled more than any other pope in history. From country to country, he drew in large crowds. He would tell the crowds, "Be not afraid!" and invited them to welcome Jesus into their hearts. Often, he had a special message for the young people, whom he especially loved. He started World Youth Day, which is a gathering of young people from all over the world to celebrate Jesus together. The pope also wrote many important works, most especially on the importance of love and marriage.

Near the end of his life, John Paul II became very sick with Parkinson's disease. The disease made him shake, and he was very weak. But he would still go out to preach to crowds of people and bless them with the Sign of the Cross with his trembling hand. He offered his suffering to Jesus until he died a holy death.

St. John Paul the Great, help me not to be afraid to welcome Jesus into my heart!

St. John of Capistrano
October 23

St. John of Capistrano

1386–1456 • Italy

John of Capistrano had been betrayed and was now a prisoner. The governor of Perugia, John had tried to make peace with enemies at war with his city, but they had broken the truce and made him a prisoner of war. During his imprisonment, John had a dream that forever changed his life. St. Francis of Assisi appeared to him and told him he must become a Franciscan.

When John was released from prison, he became a Franciscan monk. He followed St. Francis's example and became a great preacher, speaking to tens of thousands of people. Everywhere he went, he spread devotion to Jesus' Holy Name, and lived a life of great sacrifice and prayer.

The pope ordered John to preach for a crusade against the Muslim Ottomans, who had invaded Europe and were threatening the city of Belgrade. Three years before, the Ottomans had captured the great city of Constantinople, capital of the Eastern Roman Empire, which had withstood the attacks of eastern armies for nearly a thousand years. If the Christians did not fight off the Ottomans, then the Ottomans would take over Europe and persecute Christians.

Through his preaching, John raised an army of peasants and commoners to be led by John Hunyadi, a Hungarian general. John Hunyadi routed the enemy by sea. John of Capistrano, at the age of seventy, was in charge of the land forces. He prayed to the Holy Name of Jesus and led the army to a stunning victory by land over the professional Ottoman troops. Because of this victory, John of Capistrano is often called "the Soldier Saint."

Soon after his victory, John of Capistrano became ill and died a holy death.

St. John of Capistrano, help me turn to the Name of Jesus for protection!

St. Anthony
Mary Claret
October 24

St. Anthony Mary Claret

1807–1870 • Spain

Anthony was a weaver's son, and at the age of twelve began to practice his father's trade. But when he turned twenty-two years old, he knew that God was calling him to something else. He listened to God's call to enter the seminary and become a priest.

Because of his health at that time, Anthony could not become a hermit or a missionary abroad. Instead, he became a missionary to his own people. He walked all through northeastern Spain, carrying only a Bible and a change of clothes in his rucksack. His poor way of living and his sermons touched his listeners' hearts and inspired them to lead good lives. He founded the Congregation of the Missionary Sons of the Immaculate Heart of Mary, also known as the Claretians.

Because of his success as a preacher, Anthony Claret was named archbishop of Santiago in Cuba and had become strong enough to travel. There was much work for Anthony in Cuba. He preached against slavery and visited the poor and the sick, and once again, his words touched people's hearts. But not everybody liked that he was fighting sin and corruption, and he made many enemies. Someone even attacked him! But Anthony survived the attack, glad to have suffered for Jesus.

Isabella II, the queen of Spain, now called Anthony back to Spain to hear her confessions and raise her children in the Catholic Faith. Anthony came as she asked, although he did not live in the rich court. He lived a poor and simple life, and when he was not at court, he visited the prisons and tended to the poor and the sick.

But it was a time of political unrest in Spain. Isabella II was banished, and because the queen was banished, so was her confessor. Anthony Claret went to Rome until he retired in a monastery in France and died a holy death. It is thought that he preached ten thousand sermons during his life.

St. Anthony Mary Claret, help me become a missionary to my own people!

St. Tabitha
October 25

© Sophia Institute Press

St. Tabitha

Biblical figure

Tabitha was a widow in Joppa who did many good works for the love of Jesus. She cared for the sick, gave alms to the poor, and watched over the orphans. Many long hours she would spend sewing tunics and cloaks to give to other poor widows to wear when their clothes became worn and threadbare.

One day, Tabitha grew sick and then died. The other Christian disciples washed her body and laid it out in preparation for burial. The other widows Tabitha had cared for gathered around her, and their tears mingled with their prayers.

The Christian disciples had heard that St. Peter the Apostle was preaching in the nearby town of Lydda. They sent two messengers to St. Peter, asking him to come without delay.

As soon as St. Peter heard the news of Tabitha's death, he got up and traveled to Joppa. As he entered Tabitha's room, all the widows gathered around him, their faces streaming with tears. They lifted up the tunics and cloaks that Tabitha had made for them and showed him all the good she had done for them out of love.

With a comforting glance, St. Peter sent everyone out of Tabitha's room. He knelt down and prayed to Jesus, his Lord. Then, he turned to Tabitha's body and said, "Tabitha, rise up."

Tabitha's eyes opened. She sat up.

It was a miracle! St. Peter had raised Tabitha from the dead through Jesus' power. St. Peter reached his hand out to Tabitha, and she took it. He lifted her up and called all the disciples and the widows back into the room.

When everyone saw Tabitha alive and well, there was great rejoicing. News of how St. Peter had raised the widow Tabitha from the dead spread all throughout Joppa. Many who did not yet believe in Jesus were baptized because of St. Peter's great miracle.

St. Tabitha, help me to care for others out of love for Jesus!

St. Lucian
October 26

St. Lucian

d. c. 250 • Modern-day Turkey

Lucian was a pagan who worshiped false gods. He studied to be a magician and practiced magic to harm others. Practicing real magic is a sin against the First Commandment because magic comes from demons and powers that are opposed to God. To practice magic is to stand against the one true God.

One day, Lucian cast a spell against a Christian maiden who had dedicated herself to Jesus. The maiden made the Sign of the Cross, and Jesus shielded her so that the spell fell aside without doing her any harm.

Lucian was astonished.

He saw that the Sign of the Cross and the Christian God were more powerful than his magic.

Lucian burned his magic books in the middle of the city and publicly proclaimed that Jesus was the true God. Then, he studied the Christian Faith as hard as he had studied magic. He was baptized, and his past sins were washed away.

For a time, Lucian lived a quiet life of solitude and prayer. He knew that his soul was newborn and that he needed to practice a life of virtue to grow strong in his new Christian life. When he felt strengthened by God's grace, he went out proclaiming that Jesus was the true God, the merciful God who had forgiven his sins.

The Roman emperor passed a law that commanded Christians to worship the Roman gods or face death. Lucian was arrested and thrown into prison. But Lucian was strong in his faith and ready to die for Jesus so he could be with Him forever in heaven.

The judge told Lucian he would be released if he denied Jesus and worshiped false gods. But Lucian already knew that Jesus was the true God and more powerful than the false Roman gods. He refused to deny Jesus and lose his soul. Lucian endured torture and then was put to death, becoming a glorious martyr for Jesus.

St. Lucian, help me to worship God above all other things!

St. Elesbaan of Ethiopia
October 27

St. Elesbaan of Ethiopia

d. c. 555 • Ethiopia

Elesbaan was the noble Christian king of Axum in Ethiopia. His kingdom spanned the shore of the Red Sea deep into the continent, and he ruled his people with wisdom and justice.

The nearby Homerite Kingdom was ruled by a cruel king who persecuted the Christians in his kingdom. He banished the bishop, St. Gregentius, and destroyed the church in the city of Taphar. The Christians wept over the ruined stones of the church and begged the emperor Justin for help. The emperor turned to King Elesbaan for assistance, and the king agreed to save the Christians in the Homerite Kingdom.

King Elesbaan gathered his army and prayed to all the holy martyrs in heaven. He cast out the cruel king and placed a Christian king on the throne. Then, he called back St. Gregentius to watch over his Christian flock once more. Then, he went to the stones of the ruined church of Taphar and ordered it to be rebuilt, laying the first stone of the new church himself.

Back to his great capital city of Axum did Elesbaan return, and for many more years did he rule his kingdom with wisdom and justice. But his heart spent more and more time thinking about the things of God, and perhaps he remembered the love he felt when laying the first stone of the new church in Taphar. So he left his kingdom in the care of his son, the rightful heir, and sent his golden crown to the Church of the Holy Sepulchre in Jerusalem as a sign he was offering his kingship up to God.

One night, in secret, Elesbaan snuck out of the palace and went to a holy monastery on a lone mountain. He brought nothing with him but a mat and a single cup to drink from. When he entered the monastery, he acted like the humblest of the monks, and never once gave a single order as if he were still king. There, he spent the rest of his life in prayer and sacrifice until he died a holy death.

St. Elesbaan, help me to offer all of my worldly possessions to God!

Sts. Simon and Jude
October 28

Sts. Simon and Jude

Biblical figures

Sts. Simon and Jude were two of Jesus' Twelve Apostles. Simon was called "the Zealot," because he was a righteous follower of Jewish law. Jude, who is also called Thaddeus (and who should not be confused with Judas the traitor), was Jesus' cousin.

Simon and Jude followed Jesus through Galilee as He preached the Good News of His Father's Kingdom. They ran away in fear when Jesus was arrested and put to death on the Cross, but they rejoiced when Jesus appeared to the Twelve Apostles after His Resurrection. They watched Jesus ascend to heaven, His last command ringing in their ears: "Go, therefore, and make disciples of all nations, baptizing them in the name of the Father, and of the Son, and of the holy Spirit." They knew that they must go to the ends of the earth to share their love for Jesus and to baptize all people into God's family.

Both Simon and Jude went far and wide to preach and baptize as Jesus had commanded them. Jude also wrote the Letter of St. Jude, which you can read today in the Bible.

There is a legend that the king of Edessa had begged an artist to paint Jesus, but the artist could not capture Jesus' glorious and shining expression. And so Jesus imprinted a piece of cloth with an image of His face and sent Jude to Edessa to give His image to the king. Later, Jude went to Persia to continue preaching Jesus' love to the world.

It is said that Simon first preached about Jesus to the people of Egypt, but then went to Persia to join the Apostle Jude. Many Persians were baptized and became Christians, but the Apostles' success stirred up the jealousy of the pagan priests, who raised the crowds against Simon and Jude. No one knows for sure how the two Apostles were martyred, but many say that Simon was sawed in half and Jude was hit with a club. And so artists often paint Simon holding a saw and Jude holding a club to show the ways they gloriously died for Jesus.

Sts. Simon and Jude, help me to preach about Jesus' love far and wide!

Bl. Chiara Badano

October 29

Bl. Chiara Badano

1971–1990 • Italy

The young Chiara was pretty and fun and embraced life with laughter. For eleven years, her parents had prayed to have a child, and Chiara was their biggest blessing. When she was little, her dream was to be a flight attendant and see all the wonderful things in this world. Everything in life brought her joy, and she loved to play tennis, hike, swim, dance, and spend time with her friends.

At nine years old, Chiara joined a group called *Focolare*, which is a movement dedicated to bringing people together in Jesus' love. Her heart was filled with love for the suffering and forsaken Jesus, and she wanted to be His bride. Chiara's joy-filled face shined so bright with the love of Jesus that the founder of the Focolare movement gave Chiara the nickname of Luce, which means "light" in Italian.

When Chiara was sixteen, a terrible pain shot through her shoulder as she was playing tennis. At first, she thought nothing of it, but when the pain did not go away, she went to the doctor's office. Chiara had a rare form of bone cancer. When she found out, Chiara said, "It's for you, Jesus; if you want it, I want it, too."

From then on, Chiara met all her suffering with joy because she could offer it to Jesus. When other patients at the hospital were sad, Chiara would take them on walks to make them feel better, even though every step was painful to her. Her friends would visit her in the hospital to comfort her, only to find that it was she who brought them comfort. A local bishop heard about Chiara and went to visit her. He was amazed at her deep brown eyes, which were like deep pools of light. He asked her where her light came from. She answered simply, "I try to love Jesus as much as I can."

During her illness, Chiara comforted her mother. When she was eighteen and knew she would die soon, Chiara asked her mother to help her prepare for her funeral. Chiara called her funeral her wedding, because when she died, she would be united to Jesus forever. She would wear a white dress with a pink waist, and she said she did not want people crying, but singing at her funeral. "When you're getting me ready, Mum," Chiara said, "you have to keep saying to yourself, 'Chiara Luce is now seeing Jesus.'" After she received the sacraments, her final words were, "Ciao, Mum, be happy, because I am," and she went to heaven to be united with Jesus forever. Bl. Chiara Badano, help me shine the light of Christ for others!

Bl. Oleksa Zarytsky
October 30

Bl. Oleksa Zarytsky

1912–1963 • Ukraine

Fr. Oleksa was a Greek-Catholic priest in Ukraine under the Soviet regime. The leaders of the Soviet government persecuted anyone who did not agree with them. Because the Soviet government did not believe in God, it persecuted anyone who did.

The Soviet authorities arrested Fr. Oleksa because he was a parish priest. He suffered terrible conditions in prison for many years, and all the people of his parish missed his tender care for their souls. Fr. Oleksa wrote loving letters home to his elderly father, to his friends, and to his flock. He explained that Jesus was very near to his heart and that he could feel Jesus' love.

Then, Fr. Oleksa was let out of prison. He knew that the persecuted Catholics in the Soviet Union greatly needed priests to bring them the sacraments, most especially Jesus' Body and Blood in the Eucharist. He wanted to bring them Jesus, so that they, too, could feel Jesus' love.

Always keeping an eye out for the secret police, Fr. Oleksa traveled to Kazakhstan, the gulags of Siberia, and the Ural Mountains through Russia to bring the sacraments to those who needed them. He knew that nothing was more important than receiving the Eucharist, Jesus' Body and Blood. He knew that receiving the Eucharist would give people the strength to love Jesus and stay true to Him in the midst of the terrible persecution.

In secret, he heard his people's confessions for many hours so that their sins could be forgiven. Then, he would say Mass at night in people's homes, sometimes as late as 4:00 a.m. Throughout the suffering and the persecution, he always smiled a peaceful smile and brought comfort to others.

Finally, Fr. Oleksa was discovered and arrested by the secret police and thrown in a concentration camp. There, he endured great suffering. He was able to sneak out a letter that said, "Our Lady has visited me and said: My dear son, still a little suffering. I will come soon to take you with me." Soon after, he died in the comforting arms of Jesus and Mary, a glorious martyr for the Faith.

Bl. Oleksa Zarytsky, help me always desire Jesus' love in the Eucharist!

St. Foillan
October 31

St. Foillan

d. 655 • Ireland

Foillan was an Irish monk who fled the wars in Ireland and became a bishop of a monastery in England.

But his were not peaceful times.

War broke out between the chiefs and kings of the region, and Foillan's monastery was right in the middle of the rival armies. The monastery fell to the soldiers, who stole all its sacred treasure—the sacred vessels of the Mass, the relics of the saints, and the holy books of Scripture painstakingly copied down by hand—and took the monks captive. Foillan barely escaped with his life.

Foillan raised money to ransom his brother monks from the enemy and also recovered the relics and sacred books. These sacred treasures of the Church he carried onto a ship, and, along with his brother monks, he sailed to the land of the Franks, trusting that God would care for him and the monks and help them build a new monastery.

While Foillan and his monks were welcomed in the Kingdom of the Franks, they did not stay there long but made their way to the monastery of Nivelles in Belgium, which had been founded by St. Itta and St. Gertrude, a noble widow and her daughter who had given up the world to become nuns.

As a bishop, Foillan greatly helped the nuns by saying Mass at the monastery, and his sacred books and relics also were great treasures for the nuns, as they revered the Holy Word of God and the saints. Through St. Itta's help, Foillan was able to found a new monastery nearby: the monastery of Fosses.

One day, Foillan came to Nivelles from Fosses to sing Mass for the nuns. On his way back, he and his companions were waylaid in the forest by bandits and slain. St. Gertrude recovered Foillan's body. She took some relics of St. Foillan and then buried his body in the monastery of Fosses.

St. Foillan, help me to revere the things of God!

All Saints' Day
November 1

All Saints' Day

Feast Day of the Church

Today, we celebrate all of the saints in heaven.

Everyone who is in heaven is a saint.

There are many saints whom we know about, but there are many, many more whom we do not know about. All sorts of people are saints: priests and nuns, mothers and fathers, children and grown-ups.

But all the saints have one thing in common: they love God more than anything else. If we learn about the saints, then we also will learn how to love God more than anything else.

The saints are God's friends, and they are our friends too!

They are waiting for us to get to know them, and they are ready to help us when we are in trouble. So if you ask them, the saints will say special prayers to God just for you.

Today, say a prayer to your favorite saint. Maybe it is the saint you are named after. Or maybe it is the saint on whose feast day you were born. Or maybe it is one of the saints you have read about in this book!

Say hello to your favorite saint and ask him or her to show you how to love God more and more every day. That way, when you reach the end of your days and die with the love of God in your heart, you can be a saint in heaven too!

Blessed Virgin Mary, Queen of angels and of the saints, *pray for me.*

Sts. Peter and Paul, *pray for me.*

Sts. Josephine Bakhita and Marcus Chong Ui-Bae, *pray for me.*

Sts. Catherine of Siena and Patrick, *pray for me.*

Sts. Pancras and Gianna Molla, *pray for me.*

Sts. Joan of Arc and Agnes, *pray for me.*

(name your own saint), *pray for me.*

The Commemoration of
All the Faithful Departed
(All Souls' Day)
November 2

The Commemoration of All the Faithful Departed (All Souls' Day)

Feast Day of the Church

Today, we pray in a special way for all those who have died. The souls of the faithful departed have special need of prayers to help them get to heaven. We can ask God to be merciful on the departed souls and give them the life of His grace.

Did someone you know pass away this year? Say a special prayer for him or her.

Pray for all those in your family who have died.

Pray, also, for those who have no one else to pray for them and who are forgotten by those on earth. In purgatory, souls from every time and place are being purified so that they can be holy enough to enter heaven. These souls will especially be thankful for your prayers.

There is a special blessing given to departed souls in purgatory if you visit a Catholic cemetery today, or during the rest of the week, and pray for them. You can earn for these souls an indulgence, which means that they will spend less time suffering in purgatory!

You can pray this prayer for the dead:

Eternal rest grant unto them, O Lord,
and let perpetual light shine upon them.
May they rest in peace.
Amen.

Remember, if you pray for the souls in purgatory then they will pray for you too!

Dear Lord, grant the souls of the faithful departed eternal rest in peace!

St. Martin de Porres
November 3

St. Martin de Porres

1579–1639 • Peru

Martin was the son of Juan de Porres, a Spanish nobleman, and Ana Velasquez, a freed black slave from Panama. When Martin was two, after the birth of his little sister, Juana, their father abandoned them. The family grew up in poverty, with Martin and Juana's mother working as a laundress.

As Martin grew older, people mocked him for being of mixed race. But even at the young age of eight, Martin remembered the priest at Mass saying, "We were all made in God's image and likeness." He would tell Juana that God was concerned about the color of people's souls, not the color of their skin.

He became an apprentice to a barber-surgeon (someone who practiced medicine as well as cut hair) and learned to care for the sick. One day, when Martin was alone in the barber-surgeon's office, a man was carried in with a deep cut in his head. The people who carried him in wanted the barber-surgeon, not a twelve-year-old boy. But to everyone's amazement, Martin bandaged the wound, and the man was able to walk home.

Martin spent many hours at night praying before a crucifix that hung above his bed. He knew he wanted to give his whole life to God. So when Martin was fifteen, he went to live with the Dominicans in Lima at the convent of Santo Domingo. One night, he was praying in front of the Blessed Sacrament when the step he was kneeling on caught fire. Despite all of the chaos the fire caused, Martin did not even notice and continued kneeling in prayer.

The Dominicans gave Martin the duties of caring for the sick and the clothes room. When Martin was twenty-four, the Dominicans made him a religious brother, and he took charge of the infirmary. Later on, he founded a residence for orphans and abandoned children.

When an epidemic struck Lima, the young novices (those who had just entered the order) were locked in a separate part of the convent to prevent the spreading of disease. Martin miraculously passed through the locked doors to take care of the sick. Martin performed many other miracles: he could heal others instantly, and he could be in two places at once. Light would fill the room when he prayed, and his ecstasies would lift him into the air. When Martin turned sixty, he fell ill and endured terrible pain. He suffered for almost a year and then died a holy death. He was so famous for his miracles that crowds flocked to his body and took pieces of his habit for relics. St. Martin de Porres, help me to remember that everyone is made in God's image and likeness!

St. Charles
Borromeo
November 4

St. Charles Borromeo

1538–1584 • Italy

From a young age, Charles Borromeo knew that God was calling him to serve the Church. He entered the monastery at the age of twelve, and when he was only twenty-two, he moved to Rome to serve his uncle, Pope Pius IV, as an important Church official.

At this time, the Church was facing many struggles. Some priests and religious wanted to live easy, sinful lives instead of trying to be holy. Charles knew that if priests lived sinful lives then the people would find it easier to fall into sin. But if priests lived holy lives then the people would be inspired to be holy too. And so Charles Borromeo worked hard to reform the Church and to encourage priests and religious to live holy lives by living the way Jesus did—in service, love, and poverty.

Another struggle the Church was facing was the Protestant Reformation. Many people were leaving the Church to join the new Protestant religions. Charles Borrormeo worked hard within the Church to help keep people true to the Faith.

The pope made Charles Borromeo the archbishop of Milan, and Charles brought his reforms to his new flock.

But not all the priests in Milan liked Charles Borromeo's reforms.

One day, when Charles Borromeo was leading his household in evening prayer in his chapel, a priest snuck in with a gun and pointed it at the archbishop before the altar. The gun went off, and everyone thought Charles Borromeo had been shot. But Charles Borromeo refused to let his people interrupt their prayers to check on him. Only when their prayers were finished did the people rush to his side and see that the bullet had bounced off him, without breaking his skin. Many of the priests were inspired by their brave and holy archbishop.

A plague descended on Milan, and Charles Borromeo marched barefoot through the city streets praying that God would have mercy on their sins and lift the plague. At the hospitals, he cared for the sick and knelt at their bedsides. The other priests of the city had been too scared of catching the plague to serve the sick at the hospital. But after watching their holy bishop, they, too, tended to the sick. After a time of much prayer, the plague disappeared from Milan. Charles Borromeo served as God's faithful servant until he died a holy death.

St. Charles Borromeo, please give priests the courage to lead holy lives!

St. Guido Maria Conforti
November 5

St. Guido Maria Conforti

1865–1931 • Italy

In the dark and quiet church, the little boy stared up at Jesus on the crucifix above the altar. He looked at Jesus, and Jesus looked at him. To the little boy, it seemed that Jesus was telling him many things.

The little boy's name was Guido Maria Conforti. Every morning before school, Guido would stop by the church. He would sit down on the ground and gaze at the crucifix. The years went by, and the boy grew into a young man—and he never stopped visiting the church and listening to Jesus speak to his heart.

Guido's love for Jesus on the Cross grew deeper and stronger. It was before the crucifix that he first felt the stir of a special call in his heart. Jesus called and Guido listened. Jesus was calling Guido to be a priest!

When Guido told his family that he wanted to be a priest, his father was disappointed. He had been sending Guido to school so he could take over the family farm. But Guido's mother was happy, and she helped him with her many prayers.

When Guido became a priest, God spoke to his heart again—Guido was to found an order of missionaries, which he named the Xaverian Missionaries. The pope called Guido to Rome and told him he was to become the archbishop of Ravenna. At first, Guido did not want to be archbishop; he wanted to go to China with his missionaries. But the pope told Guido that he must be a missionary at home. And there was a lot of mission work for Guido to do in Ravenna. People were forgetting to live the Catholic Faith, and so Guido helped his people learn about the Faith and about Jesus' love for them.

After only two years, Guido had to resign as archbishop because of weak health. He was made bishop of Parma, where he would not be forced to work beyond his strength. Guido brought the crucifix from his boyhood church to his bishop's residence. There, he was often found kneeling enraptured before the crucifix—he could neither hear nor see anything but Jesus.

Near the end of his life, Guido was able to travel to China and visit his Xaverian Missionary brothers preaching the Gospel. He died a holy death after a life of being a missionary to those at home and listening to all that Jesus told him in his heart.

St. Guido Maria Conforti, help me to listen to all the things Jesus tells me in my heart!

Bl. Thomas Ochia Jihyoe
November 6

Bl. Thomas Ochia Jihyoe

c. 1602–1637 • Japan

Thomas Ochia Jihyoe bid farewell to his beloved Japan. He had been studying to be a priest, and like many priests in Japan, he had been expelled from the country because Christians were being persecuted terribly. Thomas's own parents had been martyrs for the Faith. He held their memory close to his heart and knew that he must be ready to die for his Faith, just as they had.

Thomas continued his studies for the priesthood first in Macau and then in the Philippines, where he entered the Augustinian order and became a priest. But his beloved country was never far from his mind. He knew that the faithful Japanese Christians were suffering, and that they needed a priest to give them the grace, comfort, and strength of the sacraments. And so Thomas returned to Japan at the risk of his own life.

Thomas disguised himself, adopting the name Kintsuba, and took a job in Nagasaki, the region with the most Christians in Japan and where many brave martyrs had died for love of Jesus. Working for the governor, Thomas was free to visit the Christians in prison. He gave them the sacraments and reminded them that Jesus had not forgotten them and that soon they would be with Jesus in heaven in reward for their faithfulness.

The governor of Nagasaki, however, grew to suspect that there was a Christian serving the prisoners. So Thomas had to flee from the city. Then, his identity was discovered. Thomas hid in a small cave where no one could find him. The governor of the city had all of his people out looking for Thomas. Wanted posters hung on every post and tree throughout Japan. Now everyone knew what Thomas looked like!

But that did not keep Thomas away from the Catholics suffering for Jesus. He would sneak out at night to visit the faithful Catholics. He wore many disguises to avoid capture, and he led the soldiers on many a wild chase. Finally, he was captured as a suspected Christian, and he revealed that he was Thomas Ochia Jihyoe, the priest they were looking for.

The Japanese officials cruelly tortured Thomas, trying to force him to give up the Faith. But nothing they could do would make him deny his love for Jesus. Thomas died a glorious martyr for the Faith and joined the other brave martyrs in heaven. Bl. Thomas Ochia Jihyoe, help all of those who are persecuted for Jesus!

St. Ernest of Mecca
November 7

St. Ernest of Mecca

d. 1148 • Germany

An abbot in Germany, Ernest was more suited to prayer and sacrifice than battle. But war loomed on the horizon. Soldiers gathered for the Second Crusade to fight in the Holy Land. But Ernest knew that it would not be swords and spears that would bring peace to the Holy Land, but prayer and the love of God.

He resigned as abbot of his monastery to join the Crusade. His parting words to his monks were, "The death I am destined to die matters little, so long as it allows me to suffer for the love of Christ."

He went on crusade not to fight a physical battle, with heavy armor and the sword.

The battle he would fight was to be a spiritual one.

His armor would be the Word of God, and his victory would come from prayer. He knew the soldiers would need a priest to tend to them. When they were dying on the battlefield, he would be there to hear their confessions and give them the Eucharist to help them get to heaven. When leaders made important decisions in battle, he would speak to them of the Word of God to remind them to do what was right.

The Second Crusade ended in defeat for the Christian army. Legend says that Ernest was captured on the battlefield and taken to Mecca, the holiest city for Muslims. There, Ernest preached of Jesus and His love and mercy to all who would listen.

There, too, he was put to death, a glorious martyr for the Faith. God had granted Ernest his wish: to suffer for the love of Christ. Now, he would be with Christ forever in heaven.

St. Ernest of Mecca, help us to do all things for love of Christ!

Bl. John Duns Scotus
November 8

Bl. John Duns Scotus

1266–1308 • Scotland

John Duns Scotus was a clever and subtle theologian. He studied at the Universities of Oxford and Paris and became a Franciscan friar. His last name is Scotus because he was born in Scotland.

Duns Scotus liked to puzzle through difficult problems about the Catholic Faith that no one else could figure out. He would write many lectures and treatises on these problems, and his writings helped explain important things about the Faith.

His most important writing is about Mary's Immaculate Conception. He explained that Mary must have been formed in her mother's womb without Original Sin, because one day, Jesus would be born of her flesh. Jesus is so holy, Duns Scotus explained, that it is only fitting that Jesus' Mother not be stained by sin. After all, she carried Jesus in her womb for nine whole months.

"But did not Mary need to be saved by Jesus, like everyone else?" many theologians asked. How could Jesus save Mary from sin if she had been conceived without Original Sin before Jesus was even born?

But Duns Scotus had worked out that puzzle too.

He explained that God is outside of time. God applied the grace earned from Jesus' Passion and death on the Cross to Mary before Jesus was born. All things are possible in God! The University of Paris, where Duns Scotus was a professor, accepted his answer to the puzzle and began to teach all of their students about Mary's Immaculate Conception.

Near the end of his life, Duns Scotus was sent to teach at a university in Germany, where he died a holy death. Over five hundred years later, Pope Pius IX used Duns Scotus's writings to declare officially the doctrine of Mary's Immaculate Conception.

Bl. John Duns Scotus, help me grow closer to Mother Mary!

Dedication of the Basilica of St. John Lateran

November 9

Dedication of the Basilica of St. John Lateran

324 • Rome

Today, when we think of where the Pope lives in Rome, we think of St. Peter's Basilica, in the Vatican.

But the popes in Rome did not always live inside the Vatican.

The first church in which the popes lived was the Basilica of St. John Lateran. In fact, the Lateran Basilica is still the pope's cathedral, which means that, even to this day, it is still the official church of the pope.

The history of the Basilica of St. John Lateran goes all the way back to the early 300s, when Constantine became emperor of Rome. Constantine ended the persecution of Christians and gave the pope the palace of the Lateran family. And so this palace became known as the Lateran Basilica and was dedicated to Jesus the Savior. Later on, it was also dedicated to both St. John the Baptist and St. John the Evangelist. This makes the Basilica of St. John Lateran the oldest basilica in Rome, the first home of the popes, and the most important church in Rome.

The Lateran Basilica was so splendid that it was known as "the golden basilica." Today, beautiful ancient mosaics color the basilica's walls. Great columns, flanked by twelve giant statues of the Apostles, lead to the basilica's greatest treasure: the high altar.

This altar is precious because, according to legend, the wooden altar used by St. Peter is encased inside. This means that the marble altar the pope uses today contains the altar used by the first pope!

When we celebrate the dedication of the Basilica of St. John Lateran, we celebrate the unity of all Catholics under the pope, who is the representative of Jesus on earth.

Dear Lord, please bless the pope, your representative on earth!

St. Leo the Great
November 10

St. Leo the Great

c. 400–461 • Italy

St. Leo the Great was a brave and strong leader of the Church. He not only guarded the Church on spiritual matters; he also guarded Rome against barbarian invaders!

Leo was a pope, a successor of St. Peter. Jesus had made St. Peter the leader of the Twelve Apostles and of the Church on earth. Therefore, the pope is the visible shepherd of his flock, the Church. Pope Leo guided the Church by guarding the truths of the Faith. Many false and dangerous lies about Jesus and what He taught were spreading throughout the Church. But Pope Leo was there to set his flock straight and to teach the truths Jesus passed down to His Apostles. Pope Leo wrote down many of his teachings. They were important in instructing the faithful about Jesus. They explained that Jesus was fully God and fully man and that He died to save us from our sins.

But soon, Pope Leo had to defend his flock from another dangerous foe. In 452, Attila the Hun invaded Italy with his barbarian army. Attila was a ferocious warrior and conqueror. Everyone in the Roman Empire was afraid of Attila the Hun. The emperor of Rome sent Pope Leo as one of his messengers to negotiate with Attila as his army rode south toward Rome. No one knows what Pope Leo and Attila the Hun said to each other. Some say that when the pope and Attila met, there appeared behind the pope a huge man dressed in priestly robes and holding aloft a fearsome sword to defend the city. Some said the man was St. Peter, the first pope, defending his successor; others said it was St. Paul, with his sword. Whatever happened, Attila was so impressed by the grey-haired pope that he decided to leave Rome in peace.

Only three years later, other barbarian invaders—the Vandals—attacked Rome. Pope Leo could not stop the Vandal army from plundering the city. But he begged the king to spare the lives of the Romans and not to burn the city down. The Vandal king agreed, and when he and his army left Rome, Pope Leo helped rebuild the city. Pope Leo died six years later in 461. He wished to be buried near the tomb of the first pope, St. Peter the Apostle, and was therefore buried in St. Peter's Basilica, where St. Peter is buried.

St. Leo the Great, guard us from anyone who tries to take us away from Jesus!

St. Martin of Tours
November 11

St. Martin of Tours

c. 316–397 • Modern-day Hungary

Martin's father was an officer in the Roman army and wanted his son to be a soldier too. But Martin did not want to be a soldier. As a young boy, he had learned about Jesus. Now he was studying to be a Christian and did not want to fight in battle. But when Martin turned fifteen, his father forced him to join the Roman army.

Stationed at the city of Amiens, Martin rode up to the city gate in his soldier's garb and cloak. The day was cold with the bitter wind, and the ground crunched with frost. At the gate, Martin saw a naked beggar shivering in the cold and the wind. None of the people paid any attention to the beggar as they passed him by. Martin was but a poor soldier and did not have much, but he took his sword and cut his soldier's cloak in half. He wrapped the torn cloak around the beggar's shivering shoulders. When Martin returned to the garrison, the other soldiers pointed and laughed at Martin and his torn cloak.

But God rewarded Martin for his generosity. That night, Jesus appeared to Martin in a dream. He was surrounded by angels and wore half of a torn cloak. Jesus explained that by giving his cloak to the beggar, Martin had clothed Christ Himself. After his vision of Jesus, Martin was baptized. A number of years later, he was free to leave the army and wished to visit his parents.

On his way home, he was attacked by robbers in the mountains. One of the robbers lifted his axe to strike Martin down, and Martin faced him calm and unafraid. Another robber asked Martin how he could be so brave in the face of death. Martin replied that he was a Christian and that Jesus would take care of him in this life and the next. The robbers were so impressed with Martin that they let him go. One of them even became Christian and entered a monastery.

At home, Martin converted his mother to the Christian Faith. Martin lived for ten years in a monastery and was then appointed bishop of Tours. There were many pagans in Tours who worshiped trees and had temples to false gods. Through many miracles, Martin converted the pagans, and they cut down their tree-idols and built churches over the temples. Martin served the Church as bishop of Tours until he died a holy death.

St. Martin of Tours, help me remember that what I do for others, I do for Jesus!

St. Josaphat

1580–1623 • Lithuania

Ever since he was a little boy, Ioann loved to say his prayers. He learned an old language called Old Church Slavonic and memorized the prayers and chants of the Church.

As he grew up, he worked hard for a merchant to earn a living. The merchant was so impressed by Ioann's work that he wanted him to marry his daughter. But Ioann never forgot his love of God, nor his call to a life of prayer, so he entered the Monastery of the Holy Trinity, became a priest, and took the name Josaphat. He became known far and wide for his holiness, and many came to visit him for his wise advice.

In eastern Europe, where Josaphat lived, many of the churches did not want to be a part of the Catholic Church in Rome under the leadership of the pope. They instead had their own Patriarchs whom they followed instead of the pope. But Josaphat knew that the Roman Catholic Church was the Church Jesus had founded on earth, and that the pope was Jesus' representative on earth. Jesus had promised that the gates of hell would never prevail against the Church under the pope's leadership. And so Josaphat and the members of his monastery remained Eastern Catholics in union with the Church in Rome.

Josaphat became archbishop and worked to unite the Eastern churches with the Church in Rome. He wrote a catechism to teach the people about the Faith, and he preached to bring together the East with Rome. But some people were angry at Josaphat for trying to unite East and West.

One day, an angry mob gathered outside of Josaphat's home. They carried torches and clubs and broke into Josaphat's home, attacking his attendants. Josaphat rushed out to beg them to stop their violence. The mob did not listen to Josaphat; instead, they attacked him. And so the holy archbishop Josaphat became a glorious martyr for the Faith.

St. Josaphat, help unite the Eastern and Western Churches!

**St. Frances
Xavier Cabrini**
November 13

St. Frances Xavier Cabrini

1850–1917 • Italy

The small, determined Italian nun disembarked from the ship in New York. She did not speak any English, but she was on fire with the love of God and ready to serve the Italian immigrant community in the United States.

Ever since she was a little girl, Frances Xavier Cabrini had wanted to be a missionary. At first, she wished to bring the message of Jesus' salvation to China and had brought her request to Pope Leo XIII. But the pope had told her, "Not to the East, but to the West." He knew that God had special plans for Frances Xavier Cabrini and that her pluck and common sense would help the Italian immigrant community, which was struggling to find its footing in the United States.

The first thing Mother Cabrini and her six Missionary Sisters of the Sacred Heart (the order of sisters she founded) did was establish an orphanage. They did not have enough money, so they had to beg door-to-door for donations before they could even open the orphanage. Mother Cabrini was untiring in God's service. She crossed the ocean thirty times in twenty-eight years to found hospitals, schools, and orphanages all over North and South America and Europe. Eventually, she became a U.S. citizen.

The sisters who worked with Mother Cabrini knew that she was especially blessed by God. One of the sisters had painful varicose veins in her legs. The doctor advised her to wear elastic stockings always to help relieve the pain. After several years of suffering, the sister snuck out a pair of Mother Cabrini's cotton stockings. When she put them on, her legs immediately improved!

The next day, Mother Cabrini noticed the sister walking about light on her feet. She asked the sister why her legs were feeling better, and the sister had to confess that she was wearing a pair of Mother Cabrini's stockings! Ever humble, Mother Cabrini told the sister not to be foolish enough to think that her stockings could have caused such a miracle. Instead, the sister's own faith must have healed her. Then, Mother Cabrini told the sister not to say anything about the miracle.

Mother Cabrini served the poor, the sick, and the orphaned until she died a holy death. She was the first U.S. citizen to be canonized a saint.

St. Frances Xavier Cabrini, help me to be untiring in God's service!

St. Nicholas Tavelic
November 14

St. Nicholas Tavelic

c. 1340–1391 • Croatia

Nicholas was a Franciscan friar in Croatia who more than anything wanted to be a missionary in the Holy Land, where Jesus had once lived and walked. At that time, the Holy Land was not a safe place for Christians because the Muslims who lived there did not let Christians publicly proclaim their faith in Jesus.

But Nicholas wanted to preach the Gospel of Christ to those of the Muslim faith. So he traveled the great distance from Croatia to the Holy Land and joined the Franciscans there, who were able to live in peace in their monastery on Mount Zion in Jerusalem as long as they did not preach in public.

The Franciscan friars took care of the holy Christian sites in the Holy Land for Christian pilgrims. They did not go out into the street to preach the Good News of Jesus, but instead, they proclaimed Jesus' love through their good acts and loving service to others.

But after a few years of caring for the Christian sites in Jerusalem, Nicholas realized that very few of the local Muslims were growing to know the Faith of Jesus. His heart yearned to be a witness to Christ and to proclaim the Good News of Jesus' love and mercy to all. Nicholas gathered a band of fellow friars, and together they decided to go out and proclaim the Gospel at the risk of their own lives.

Nicholas wrote out on a scroll the proclamation of the Christian Faith: he declared that Jesus is the Son of God, true God and true man. Then, Nicholas and his band of friars went boldly into the city of Jerusalem and began to proclaim the Gospel of Jesus. Before long, Muslim soldiers arrested the friars and dragged them to the judge.

Before the judge, Nicholas unrolled his scroll and declared the Christian Faith, each word ringing brave and strong. The judge grew angry that the friars were proclaiming the Christian Faith in his presence. He told the friars that they must give up their faith or be sentenced to death. Together, Nicholas and the friars cried out that they were ready to die for Jesus.

And so the judge handed Nicholas and the friars over to be tortured. But no matter how cruelly they were treated, or how many times they were asked to renounce their faith, Nicholas and his friars stood strong. They became glorious martyrs for the Faith, showing to the world their love for Jesus.

St. Nicholas Tavelic, help me show the world my love for Jesus!

St. Albert the Great
November 15

St. Albert the Great

c. 1200–1280 • Germany

God gave Albert a brilliant mind and a love for all types of knowledge. A Dominican priest, Albert pursued science and philosophy and showed how all knowledge reflects the grandeur of God because God is the source of all knowledge. Albert became a famous professor at the Universities of Cologne (in Germany) and Paris.

One of Albert's students was a large, silent man. The rest of the class thought this man was a bit slow and foolish.

But Albert knew better.

He recognized genius when he saw it, and he watched his student's progress with a sparkle in his eye.

This large, silent man was Thomas Aquinas, who became one of the Church's most brilliant theologians. Together, Albert and Aquinas worked through many thorny problems of philosophy and theology.

The pope made Albert the bishop of Regensburg in Germany. The university lamented to see Albert go. After only a few years as bishop, Albert received the pope's permission to retire, and he returned to teaching, much to the joy of his students.

News reached Albert that his treasured student, Thomas Aquinas, had died. This filled his heart with great sorrow, and he fell to weeping whenever Aquinas was mentioned. When some thinkers began to attack the reputation of Aquinas's theological work, Albert was the first to rise to his former student's defense.

At the onset of old age, Albert's sharp mind gradually weakened. He was forgetting one thing after the next. Albert's mind was one of his most prized possessions. God was asking Albert to make the great sacrifice of his mind and talents so that Albert would know that everything he had came from God and must return to God. Albert died a holy death among his fellow Dominican friars in Cologne.

St. Albert the Great, help me offer my studies to God!

St. Gertrude the Great
November 16

St. Gertrude the Great

1256–1302 • Germany

At the age of five, young Gertrude was put in the care of Benedictine nuns at the abbey of St. Mary of Helfta. The devout nuns raised Gertrude in their quiet atmosphere of prayer and contemplation, and the young girl, too, took the veil.

Gertrude had a curious and agile mind. She read and wrote in Latin at a time when few people knew how to read, and she gave herself to the study of science and philosophy.

But Jesus wanted more from Gertrude.

He was calling her to give herself to Him alone and be His special bride.

One day, when she was twenty-six years old, Gertrude was walking down the hall and bowed before an elderly nun as she passed her by. When she raised her head, Jesus stood before her! Jesus explained to Gertrude that He had come to comfort and save her, and the sweetness of His presence filled her heart.

When Jesus left, Gertrude understood how unworthy she was of His gifts, and she determined to do only those things that brought her closer to Jesus. From then on, she read the Scriptures and the Church Fathers, and the music she sang was always filled with the praises of God.

On the Feast of St. John the Evangelist, Jesus appeared to her with St. John, the beloved disciple. The disciple instructed Gertrude to lay her head on Jesus' breast, just as he had during the Last Supper. Resting her head against her Savior's chest, Gertrude exclaimed at hearing the tender beating of Jesus' Sacred Heart. St. John explained that the graces of Jesus' Sacred Heart would renew the world with the warmth of His divine love.

Gertrude continued to receive visions of Jesus and Mary throughout her life. She wrote down her revelations in a book called *Herald of Divine Love*. She had a deep love for Jesus' Sacred Heart and offered all of her sufferings for sinners and the holy souls in Purgatory. Jesus also performed many miracles through her. Many of the Benedictine sisters who were ill were cured through her prayers. Gertrude dedicated herself to the love of Jesus' Sacred Heart until she died a holy death.

St. Gertrude the Great, help my heart be renewed by Jesus' divine love!

St. Elizabeth of Hungary
November 17

St. Elizabeth of Hungary

1207–1231 • Hungary

Elizabeth was the daughter of the king of Hungary. When she was only four years old, she was engaged to marry the prince of Thuringia and went to live with her future husband's family. When the ruler of Thuringia died, she and the prince, whose name was Ludwig, were married at the ages of fourteen and twenty-one and became the next rulers of Thuringia.

Even though the marriage had been arranged by their parents, Elizabeth and Ludwig deeply loved each other. Their marriage was a happy one, and they had three children. The couple would hold hands when they prayed at night, and they took care of the poor together.

Elizabeth, in particular, saw it her mission to take care of the poor and the sick, because she knew that when she took care of them, she took care of Christ. Elizabeth founded a hospital at the foot of the mountain on which her castle stood. There, she would go daily to look after the sick herself. She passed out bread to the hungry and gave her fine clothes and jewels to the poor. The people at court made fun of Elizabeth because they did not think her behavior was befitting a noble lady, but Ludwig supported her in all the good she did.

One day, Elizabeth brought a dying leper into the castle. To comfort and give him peace, she laid the leper in her bed.

But then Ludwig found out what she had done. This time, he thought, Elizabeth had gone too far. He rushed to the bed and pulled down the bedsheet. But as his hands gripped the fine sheets, God gave him the grace to see that the leper was really Jesus Himself. Jesus had said in the Gospel of Matthew, "Amen, I say to you, whatever you did for one of these least brothers of mine, you did for me." And so Ludwig realized that to serve this poor leper was also to serve Jesus, and he marveled at the kindness and mercy of Elizabeth's heart.

Great sadness befell Elizabeth when Ludwig went off to war and died from the plague. She thought all joy had left her life. But she turned to God, and He gave her strength. She dedicated herself to Him as a Franciscan tertiary and refused to marry again, even though her family tried to convince her to find another husband.

Elizabeth spent the rest of her days in prayer and sacrifice. She offered all her sorrows to God and served the poor and the sick until she died a holy death. St. Elizabeth of Hungary, help me to see Jesus in the poor and the sick!

St. Rose-Philippine
Duchesne
November 18

St. Rose-Philippine Duchesne

1769–1852 • France

Philippine Duchesne's eyes grew wide as the priest told stories of his adventures in the New World, where he had brought the Gospel to the Native Americans, who had never heard of Jesus. As she left the church, she dreamed of someday becoming a missionary in America to share Jesus' love with others. Many years would go by and she would suffer many trials before this dream came to pass.

Philippine studied with Visitation nuns at their convent on a mountainside. Through her time with the kind, prayerful nuns, Philippine discovered that God, too, was calling her to join the order. Her family was large and wealthy, and her father did not want her to become a nun. He pulled her from the convent school, and she spent the last years of her education studying at home. But that did not keep her from listening to God's call, and she entered the Visitation order when she turned nineteen.

But Philippine was not a nun for long before the terrors of the French Revolution struck and the revolutionaries closed all the convents. Philippine and the other sisters had to flee. For ten years, Philippine cared for the poor and the sick, living her life as a nun out in the world. When the revolution was over, she joined the sisters of the Society of the Sacred Heart.

Now the dream God had placed in Philippine's heart since she was a child was about to come true. Philippine's mother superior sent her and four other sisters to Louisiana in America to be missionaries. The journey was long, and Philippine fell so sick she almost died! When the sisters finally landed, they discovered that the bishop had not prepared a place for them. So they traveled to Saint Charles, Missouri, where they built a log cabin and opened a school.

For many years, Philippine Duchesne shared the Gospel of Jesus in the harsh, pioneering conditions of the Midwest. She founded six other houses, along with schools and orphanages, and worked to serve the Native American communities. When she turned seventy-one, Philippine was asked to join a mission evangelizing the Potawatomi tribe in Kansas. Because she could not learn the language, she spent her time there in prayer, and her holiness was an inspiration to the people in the tribe. The little children called her "Woman-Who-Prays-Always." Her last years were spent in quiet retirement dedicated to prayer. St. Rose-Philippine Duchesne, help me to bring God's love to others through service and prayer!

St. Barlaam of Antioch

November 19

St. Barlaam of Antioch

d. 304 • Syria

Barlaam was a peasant laborer, a steady and simple man. He did not have much: he never went to school, and he had no riches. But Barlaam did have the most important thing of all—an unwavering faith in Jesus.

At that time, the Roman emperors persecuted Christians for not worshiping the false gods of Rome, and so Barlaam was arrested and dragged before the judge.

The judge looked Barlaam over. He saw Barlaam's poor clothes and rough hands. He did not think much of this Christian peasant. With a wave of his hand, the judge explained to Barlaam that all he had to do was offer incense in the fire before the idol, and he would go free.

But Barlaam shook his head. He explained in his plain and steady way that he would never worship false gods and give up his faith in Jesus.

The judge laughed at Barlaam's simple words. Then, he smiled a cruel smile. Barlaam was only a peasant; he would give in under torture. He ordered the guards to punish Barlaam with all sorts of cruel tortures. But Barlaam endured everything with his steady strength. He did not cry out or beg for mercy but remained loyal to his faith in Jesus.

The judge's cruel smile dropped into a frown. He could not let others know that this poor peasant had withstood the torture. That would make the judge appear weak! He must make the world believe that Barlaam had given up his faith in Jesus.

So the judge hatched a plan.

He ordered Barlaam's hand to be filled with incense. Then, he gripped Barlaam's wrist and held his hand over the fire before the idol. He thought that when Barlaam flinched in pain, he would drop the incense, and so everyone would think that he was offering sacrifice to a false god and had denied Jesus.

But Barlaam did not flinch. Although the flames licked, seared, and burned, he held his hand steadily over the fire and kept his fist closed. The judge watched with disbelief as the fire roasted Barlaam's hand right off!

Now everyone could see that Barlaam had unwavering faith in Jesus and that he loved Jesus more than anything—more than his right hand and more than his own life. Defeated, the judge saw that nothing would make Barlaam give up his faith in Jesus. Barlaam was executed and became a glorious martyr, showing the world the strength of simple, unwavering faith. St. Barlaam of Antioch, help my faith in Jesus never waver!

St. Edmund
November 20

St. Edmund

c. 841–870 • England

Edmund was the young king of East Anglia, a kingdom in England. He was crowned the monarch at the young age of fifteen by the holy bishop Humbert of Elmham. Even though Edmund was so young, he was a good king and wished the best for his people in all things.

Despite Edmund's many responsibilities and worries as king, he always found time to talk to God in prayer, knowing that God would give him the strength to be a good ruler. He dedicated a year of his life to memorizing the book of Psalms in the Bible so that songs of praise to God would always be on his lips.

For fifteen years, King Edmund reigned in peace and justice, but this peace was shattered when the Vikings invaded East Anglia, led by Ivar the Boneless and his brother Ubbe. The Vikings slaughtered Edmund's people and ransacked the monasteries. During all the fighting, the holy bishop Humbert was killed and became a glorious martyr for the Faith.

Ivar the Boneless sent a messenger to Edmund's court demanding that Edmund surrender his hoard of gold and treasure and become his underling or die. King Edmund wished to fight and die rather than surrender, but when he saw that the Viking forces were too great and would slaughter all of his men, he sent his army home so that they would not shed their blood in vain.

The Vikings captured Edmund, bound him in chains, and brought him before their leaders. They promised to spare his life if he swore to be loyal to Ivan the Boneless instead of to his people and his Christian Faith. King Edmund declared that he would rather die than be unfaithful to God and to his people.

The Vikings then cruelly tortured Edmund, but throughout all his suffering, Edmund unceasingly called out to Jesus. Edmund became a glorious martyr for the Faith, with Jesus' name the last word on his lips.

St. Edmund, help Jesus' name be always on my lips!

Presentation of the Blessed Virgin Mary

November 21

Presentation of the Blessed Virgin Mary

Marian Feast Day

Joachim and Anne brought their young daughter, Mary, to the temple steps. They had prayed to God to give them a child, and they had promised to dedicate their child to Him if He answered their prayer. After their beautiful baby, Mary, was born, they kept her home with them for three precious years. Now they were bringing the three-year-old Mary to the Temple to dedicate her to God's service.

The little girl climbed up the Temple steps with the light of love in her eyes. She did not cry at leaving her parents because she knew she was going to serve God, whom she loved above all else.

The high priest led little Mary to the steps of the high altar, and she prostrated herself entirely before the altar, offering herself to God alone.

The high priest was amazed.

Never had such a young child been so ready to give herself so completely to God.

From that day on, Mary served in the Temple. Her days and nights she spent singing psalms in praise of God, reading the Scriptures, and keeping vigil before God's altar. She decorated the Temple and wove the veils and priests' robes with her hands.

All at the Temple recognized Mary's holiness and grace. And at the Temple she stayed until she was betrothed to Joseph. Then, the angel Gabriel appeared before her to announce that she was full of grace and had been chosen to be the Mother of God.

If it is hard to understand how so young a girl would be so ready to give herself to God, we must not forget that God had saved Mary and preserved her from Original Sin. She lived full of grace, her heart ever turned to God.

Hail Mary, full of grace, help my heart be ever turned to God!

St. Cecilia
November 22

St. Cecilia

3rd century • Rome

The music was playing for her wedding, but Cecilia was singing a hymn to God in her heart. A Roman maiden from the noble patrician class, Cecilia had promised Jesus that she would never marry and so be His alone. But her parents were forcing her into marriage with the noble Roman Valerian. With her heart's song, she sang to Jesus that she desired Him alone and that she knew that He would protect her as His bride.

The moment they were alone together, Cecilia told Valerian of her promise to God and that she had a guardian angel to defend her. Valerian was astonished and asked if he could see the angel. Cecilia said that he would if he was baptized a Christian. Valerian did as she asked. When he returned, he found Cecilia on her knees praying, and beside her stood her brilliant guardian angel. Valerian also knelt beside her, and the angel placed two crowns of lilies and roses on their heads, for soon the two would become martyrs for the Faith.

Valerian's brother Tiberius also became a Christian, and together they buried the Christians who were martyred under Roman persecution. The two brothers were caught and became martyrs for Jesus. Cecilia knew that her turn would soon come. She gave all her wealth to the poor and recovered the brothers' bodies and buried them in her villa. The Roman soldiers caught Cecilia and dragged her to the pagan temple, but she refused to offer sacrifice to false gods.

And so the Roman authorities ordered her death. They locked her in the Roman baths of her villa and lit the flames under her baths so hot that Cecilia would suffocate. Abandoned in her baths a day and a night, Cecilia remained unharmed by the heat and the flames. Seeing this, the Romans lowered the heat, and a soldier entered with a sword and struck her the three times allowed to him by Roman law. Yet Cecilia still was not dead. She lay on the floor of her baths for three days. Many Christians came to visit her to give her comfort, but instead, she gave them comfort with her joyful words. She was ready to go to heaven to be with Jesus. On the third day, she went to heaven, a glorious martyr for the Faith!

St. Cecilia, help me always sing a hymn to God in my heart!

Bl. Miguel Agustin Pro
November 23

Bl. Miguel Agustin Pro

1891–1927 • Mexico

Miguel was a fun-loving Mexican boy, always cheerful and delighting in boyish pranks. One day, he suffered a fall, which knocked him unconscious. His worried parents rushed to his side, and when he came to, he immediately asked for his favorite Mexican sweetbread, *cocol*. From then on his friends and family nicknamed him "Cocol."

Simultaneously playful and prayerful, Miguel heard God's call in his heart to become a priest, and so he entered a Jesuit seminary. One year later, the Mexican Revolution broke out. This revolution sought not only to transform the Mexican government, but to change the hearts of the people by stamping out their deep Catholic faith. The Jesuits fled the country, and Miguel finished his studies abroad and was ordained a priest in Belgium.

After his ordination, Fr. Miguel suffered terrible and painful stomach problems, and so his superior sent him back to Mexico, hoping that Fr. Miguel would recover by returning home. Soon after Fr. Miguel returned to Mexico, the Mexican government passed a new law forbidding any worship in public. Fr. Miguel saw that God had sent him to serve the faithful Catholics who were suffering under a government seeking to destroy their faith. He hoped one day to die for Jesus and offer his life to bring his beloved Mexico back to Christ.

To serve the faithful in secret, Fr. Miguel put on disguises and rode about on his bicycle or walked on foot to give the faithful Holy Communion. At one time, he dressed up as an office worker, another time as a mechanic, and yet another even as a beggar! He would sign his letters with the name "Cocol," his old nickname, to hide his identity.

Eventually, he was discovered, and when a failed attempt was made to assassinate a government official, Fr. Miguel was arrested and falsely accused of the crime. He was sentenced to death without a trial. A government officer leading Fr. Miguel to his death begged for forgiveness. Fr. Miguel gave the officer not only his forgiveness, but his thanks. Fr. Miguel knew that his sacrifice would bring his beloved Mexico back to Jesus.

Bravely, Fr. Miguel refused the offered blindfold and stood before the firing squad. Holding his arms spread wide like a cross, he cried out, "Long live Christ the King." Then, forgiving those who were putting him to death, he became a glorious martyr for the Faith. Even though it was forbidden, thousands of brave Catholics lined the street to say farewell to their brave priest as his body was taken to its burial. Bl. Miguel Agustin Pro, help me to bring others to Jesus!

St. Andrew Dung-Lac
and His Companions
November 24

St. Andrew Dung-Lac and His Companions

c. 1795–1839 • Vietnam

The Vietnamese people did not come to know the Catholic Faith until missionary priests made the long and hard journey to Vietnam to share their love for Jesus. The Vietnamese emperors did not like seeing so many of their people convert to the new Faith brought to their country from overseas. For three centuries, the emperors persecuted Catholics in Vietnam, putting to death their own people as well as those missionaries who brought the Faith to their shores.

One of these brave martyrs was Andrew Dung-Lac. When he was twelve years old, he learned the Faith from a catechist who had been asked to care for him. Andrew became a priest and faithfully served his flock until the emperor ordered the arrest of all Catholic priests. Andrew's parishioners dearly loved their priest, and they scraped together the little money that they had to buy his freedom. But this freedom lasted only a short while, and Fr. Andrew Dung-Lac was arrested again, along with a fellow priest, and put to death, becoming a glorious martyr for the Faith.

Another brave martyr was Fr. Joseph Marchand, a missionary priest from the Paris Society of Foreign Missions. He risked his life to come to Vietnam and teach its people about Jesus' love for them. The Seminary of Foreign Missions in Paris invited Fr. Joseph Marchand to return to Paris as their rector. This would have been a great honor and would have meant a life of safety for Fr. Joseph. But he turned down the position. He knew that God wanted him to spread the Gospel to the people of Vietnam. After Fr. Marchand had spent ten years as a missionary, a royal decree was passed ordering the arrest of missionary priests, and Fr. Joseph Marchand was arrested and cruelly tortured, becoming a glorious martyr for the Faith.

A Vietnamese official named Michael Ho Dinh Hy was one of the few Catholic officials in Vietnam. Born Catholic, he raised his family in the Catholic Faith and helped his son become a priest by sending him to a seminary in Indonesia. When the emperor outlawed all missionary activities, Michael Ho Dinh Hy helped missionary priests travel through Vietnam to serve the faithful. Finally, he, too, was arrested and became a glorious martyr for the Faith. St. Andrew Dung-Lac and companions, help me to love Jesus more than my own life!

St. Catherine of Alexandria
November 25

St. Catherine of Alexandria

d. 305 • Egypt

Catherine was the daughter of the governor of Alexandria. Alexandria was a city of ancient learning in Egypt, and Catherine was a brilliantly educated young woman, knowing not only the ins and outs of the arts and sciences but also the important truths of the Faith.

The emperor Maxentius came to Alexandria and ordered all the Christians to sacrifice to the pagan gods in the temple. Those who would not sacrifice, he put to death. Catherine knew that she must do all that she could to save her fellow Christians. She entered the emperor's court, and in a voice that never wavered, Catherine denounced the emperor's persecutions and with clear argument explained the truth of the Christian Faith. The emperor was angered by her words, but he could not answer her arguments. So, with the intention of proving Christianity false, he summoned the great philosophers and thinkers of the court to hold a debate with Catherine.

All the great scholars filed into the court. All stood against Catherine, who was alone and unafraid. Despite all their wise words and all their clever sayings, Catherine was far wiser and cleverer than they. She soundly trounced their false arguments. In fact, so convincing was she that many of the scholars became Christian themselves. Emperor Maxentius was incensed. His plan had backfired. Because he could not win his fight the fair way, he threw Catherine into prison. But even in prison, Catherine did not stop trying to win others to the Faith. She spoke to the soldiers and her fellow prisoners, and won many hearts for Christ.

Legend says that the story of Catherine's wisdom even reached the empress's ears. She was curious to meet this brave and wise young woman, and so she visited Catherine in prison. Catherine told the empress all about her love for Jesus, and proved to her that Jesus was God and He had come down from heaven to die so that all could enter heaven. The empress's heart responded to Catherine's words, and she became a Christian. Later, she, too, would become a martyr for the Faith.

In his fury at Catherine's converting so many people to Christianity, the emperor ordered Catherine to be tortured on a large wheel with long, terrible spikes. But when the guards brought the wheel down to Catherine's prison, she prayed to God, and the wheel burst into pieces. The emperor ordered her beheading, and Catherine became a glorious martyr for the Faith, her death winning countless souls for Christ. St. Catherine of Alexandria, help me to do all I can to know and defend my Faith to others!

St. Sylvester Gozzolini
November 26

St. Sylvester Gozzolini

1177–1267 • Italy

Sylvester was born to a wealthy noble family, and his father had sent him to the university to gain fame and glory. But Sylvester's heart did not care for the glory of this world—he yearned to serve God as a priest. When he went home and told his father about his vocation to the priesthood, his father was so upset with Sylvester that he disinherited him and never spoke to him again. This must have pained Sylvester deeply, but Sylvester knew that he must obey God's call.

Sylvester became a priest, but his life was still full of worries and worldly cares. One day, as he prayed at a funeral, Sylvester realized that it was the fate of all earthly things to return to the dust of the earth. Better it would be to live for the spiritual life alone, a life completely dedicated to the things of God and heaven. And so he left the city, went to the mountain, and lived in a cave far away from the worries and cares of the world. In the solitude of his cave, Sylvester dedicated his life to the things of God and of heaven.

Other men, inspired by Sylvester's holy example, wished to join him in his life of prayer and solitude. Sylvester understood that God was calling him to found a monastery, but he did not know which monastic rule to follow. Different monasteries follow rules of prayer and work, which are passed down to them from their founding saints. Sylvester did not know which saint's rule God was calling him to follow.

Tradition says that while Sylvester was deep in prayer, many holy founders appeared to him in a vision. Each saint showed the different rule he had established and the habits or robes of his order. But none of these rules touched Sylvester's heart, and so he merely bowed his head and was silent. Finally, surrounded by his monks, St. Benedict—the founder of the Benedictine order—appeared to Sylvester and presented to him the Benedictine rule and habit. Sylvester's heart leapt for joy. He knew that God was calling him to be a Benedictine monk. He thanked the holy founder, St. Benedict, and gratefully accepted his rule and his habit.

After the vision, Sylvester founded a monastery on Monte Fano and followed the Benedictine rule. The pope approved of Sylvester's new order, which became known as the Sylvestrines, or, informally, the "blue Benedictines." Sylvester led his order until he died a holy death.

St. Sylvester, help me yearn for the things of God and of heaven!

St. Bilhildis

November 27

St. Bilhildis

c. 630–c. 710 • Germany

When little Bilhildis was three years old, she was sent to her aunt to be taught the Catholic Faith and receive baptism. But right before the priest was ready to baptize little Bilhildis, the barbarian Huns attacked the country. In the fright and devastation, everyone forgot about baptizing little Bilhildis. She returned home to her parents and grew up believing that she had been baptized!

When Bilhildis turned sixteen years old, her parents arranged her marriage with the pagan Duke of Franconia. Bilhildis was a faithful, virtuous wife, and she daily prayed that her husband would grow to know and love Jesus. But despite her prayers, her husband would not become Christian, and when he died, Bilhildis founded a convent and became its abbess. Many nuns joined her convent, and the abbess Bilhildis taught them how to live lives of virtue and holiness.

A few years later, three of Bilhildis's nuns were at their prayers when an angel appeared to them and revealed to them their abbess had never been baptized or confirmed. The angel then instructed the nuns to tell Bilhildis so that she could receive the Sacrament of Baptism. When they told Bilhildis what had happened, she was astonished and did not know if she should believe them. After all, her parents had been good Christians and had told her she had been baptized as a child.

She went to the bishop for advice, and he offered a Mass asking Jesus to reveal to him if what the three nuns said was true. The same angel then appeared to the bishop and told him that Bilhildis had never been baptized and confirmed. And so the bishop gave Bilhildis the sacraments she had never received: the Sacraments of Baptism and Confirmation.

Bilhildis received the sacraments with a grateful heart. She knew that God had sent His message to her through His angel because Baptism and Confirmation were so important. Baptism makes us sons and daughters of God and opens the gates of heaven to us by giving us God's grace. Confirmation gives us the special strength of the Holy Spirit and completes the graces we received in Baptism.

Bilhildis grew in virtue and holiness with the grace of the sacraments. She served her nuns as their abbess until she died a holy death.

St. Bilhildis, help me live out the graces of my baptism!

St. Catherine Labouré
November 28

O MARY CONCEIVED WITHOUT SIN PRAY FOR US WHO HAVE RECOURSE TO THEE

St. Catherine Labouré

1806–1876 • France

Nine-year-old Catherine Labouré was crying alone in her room before a statue of Mary. Her mother had just passed away. The young girl wiped her tears away, stood on her chair, and tenderly lifted the statue of Mary from the wall. She kissed it and whispered, "Now, dear lady, you are to be my mother." Little did she know the special care her Mother in heaven would give her.

When she grew up, Catherine joined the Daughters of Charity in Paris. One night, she awakened to a child's voice calling, "Sister Labouré, come to the chapel; the Blessed Virgin awaits you." The child was an angel, and he led her to the chapel, ablaze with candlelight. The Blessed Virgin Mary appeared with a rustle of silk and sat nearby. Under the angel's direction, Catherine knelt and rested her hands on Mary's lap. The Virgin Mary told Catherine that God wished to give her a mission, and they spoke for three hours before the Virgin Mary disappeared.

The next time Mary appeared to Catherine, she was inside a large oval frame, around which were these words: "O Mary, conceived without sin, pray for us who have recourse to thee." Within the frame, the Blessed Virgin stood on a large globe that represented the entire world, and with her feet, she crushed a serpent. On her fingers were many rings set with precious stones. Dazzling rays of light streamed forth from her rings.

Catherine noticed that some of the precious stones on the Virgin Mary's rings did not shine, so she asked why. The Blessed Virgin responded that the rays shining forth from her rings were precious graces. Those rings that did not shine represented graces for which people forgot to ask. As Catherine watched, the oval frame rotated. On the other side was a circle with twelve stars, within which was a large "M" crowned by a cross. Underneath were two hearts: the Sacred Heart of Jesus, crowned with thorns, and the Immaculate Heart of Mary, pierced by a sword.

Mary commanded Catherine to have a medal made bearing the images she had just shown her on the front and back. She promised many graces to those who wore her medal. According to the Virgin Mary's instruction, Catherine told the priest who heard her confessions, and through his help, the local archbishop ordered the medals made. Mary showered so many blessings on those who wore her medal that people soon began calling it the "Miraculous Medal." Catherine remained under the care of the Blessed Virgin until she died a holy death.

St. Catherine Labouré, help me never to forget to ask Mary for God's graces!

Our Lady of Beauraing

November 29

Our Lady of Beauraing

1932–1933 • Marian Apparition

On the evening of November 29, in the humble town of Beauraing in Belgium, Fernande and Albert Voisin were walking to pick up their sister Gilberte from school. They were joined by their friends, sisters André and Gilberte Degeimbre.

When they reached the school, Albert spied a bright light near the grey, stone railroad bridge. It was a white-robed lady with eyes of deepest blue. Bright rays shone around her head like a crown, and over her arm was draped a rosary. She floated in the sky as though walking on a cloud. Albert pointed out the lady to the girls, crying, "Look! The Blessed Virgin, dressed in white, is walking above the bridge!"

The girls thought he was joking, but the amazement in his face caused them to look. They gasped. They could see the white-robed lady too! Then, Gilberte Voisin stepped through the convent school door and wondered what everyone was staring at so intently. Then, she, too, saw the floating lady.

The children went home and told their families what they had seen. Reports of the children's vision spread throughout the town of Beauraing. Almost every day, the five children went to the convent school garden and saw the white-robed lady in the sky. For the first three days, the lady did not speak. Then, Albert asked the lady if she was the Immaculate Virgin. The lady nodded her head and opened her arms. Albert asked the Blessed Virgin Mary what she wanted from them. Then, Our Lady spoke her first words to the children: "Always be good."

The Blessed Virgin Mary appeared to the children thirty-three times between November 29 and January 3. Though crowds followed the children, they could not see Mary. But they could see how the enraptured children were almost thrown to their knees at her coming. As a test, a doctor held a lit match under little Gilberte Voisin's hand during a vision. Not only did Gilberte not feel a thing, but her hand was completely unharmed!

On the last day of her apparitions, Mary opened wide her arms and revealed to the children her golden heart surrounded by glittering rays. This golden heart was the Immaculate Heart of the Mother of God. Our Lady told the children to "pray, pray very much," and asked for a chapel to be built for pilgrims. Then, she wished the children goodbye and told each one of them a message meant only for him or her. Every year, thousands of pilgrims go to Beauraing, and many are miraculously healed or converted to the Faith. Our Lady of Beauraing, help me always be good!

St. Andrew the Apostle

Biblical figure

Two men were with John the Baptist when he pointed to a man walking by and said, "Behold the Lamb of God." One of these men was Andrew, who looked with wonder and curiosity at the man John the Baptist had pointed out. What sort of man was a lamb, let alone God's lamb? This man must be pure and innocent, Andrew thought, and able to take away the sins of many. Andrew and his companion decided that they must follow this man and find out who he was.

The man, who was Jesus, turned around and saw that the two men were following Him. He asked, "What are you looking for?"

At first, Andrew and the other disciple did not know what to say, but then they replied, "Teacher, where are you staying?"

"Come, and you will see," was Jesus' reply. And so Andrew and the other man spent the rest of the day talking to Jesus.

Andrew's heart was on fire after his time with Jesus. He rushed to find his brother Simon and exclaimed to him, "We have found the Messiah." He brought Simon to Jesus. Jesus gave Simon a new name: Peter. One day, Peter would become the first pope.

Later, Andrew and Peter were fishing in the Sea of Galilee. Jesus called to them, "Come after me, and I will make you fishers of men." Immediately, both brothers dropped their fishing nets and followed Jesus as His disciples. Andrew felt in his heart that he was willing to leave everything to follow Jesus, His new Master, the Lamb of God.

Andrew became one of the Twelve Apostles. After Jesus' Ascension, Andrew traveled far and wide to share the love of Jesus and to baptize in the name of the Father, Son, and Holy Spirit.

Tradition says that Andrew preached the Gospel of Jesus in Greece and Asia Minor. For his preaching, he was bound by ropes and crucified on an X-shaped cross, becoming a glorious martyr for the Faith. Andrew is honored as the first Apostle Jesus called to follow Him.

St. Andrew, help me to answer Jesus' call!

St. Edmund Campion

December 1

St. Edmund Campion

1540–1581 • England

Edmund Campion was the most admired and sought-after student at Oxford University. Even Queen Elizabeth I was impressed by the young and talented Edmund. A life of fame awaited him. Young and thoughtless, he gave up his Catholic Faith and joined the Church of England to ensure the queen's favor.

But then Edmund's conscience started bothering him. Was the admiration of others worth the price of his soul?

He realized it was not.

Edmund left England for Ireland and returned to his Catholic Faith. Then, he went to Rome and became a Jesuit priest.

The faithful Catholics in England were suffering persecution for not joining the Church of England, and many English Catholics were wavering in their faith, not sure if they should follow the queen or the pope. But Edmund knew that Jesus had left His Church under the authority of the pope, not under the authority of kings and queens. Risking his life, Edmund, along with other Jesuit priests, traveled to England to comfort the suffering English Catholics and give them the sacraments to strengthen their souls.

In England, Edmund traveled from Catholic home to Catholic home to say Mass for the faithful in secret. Bravely, he preached to the English Catholics and was called "the Pope's Champion." The English authorities chased Edmund, and he had many near escapes. He would hide in secret rooms called "priest holes" in manor houses and ride on horseback through the countryside, evading the spies hunting him down for the reward upon his head.

Finally, Edmund was discovered by a spy and arrested after spending only little over a year in England. At first, he was imprisoned in the Tower of London, but then he was taken to a private estate. There, Queen Elizabeth visited the priest who had once been her favorite. She told him that if he gave up his allegiance to the pope, she would reward him greatly. Edmund explained that he was ever her loyal subject and she his queen, but that his first loyalty was to God and then to the souls he served as a priest.

Once again, Edmund was imprisoned in the Tower and there tortured on the rack. Undergoing a fake trial for show, he was sentenced to death by hanging, along with two other Catholic priests. Because he was faithful to God, the pope, and the Catholic Faith, Edmund became a glorious martyr for Christ.

St. Edmund Campion, help me to prize God above all other things!

Bl. Maria
Angela Astorch
December 2

Bl. Maria Angela Astorch

1592–1665 • Spain

Young Jeronima Astorch's parents died when she was very young, so she was raised by her nurse, who dearly loved the joyful and playful little orphan. As a young girl, Jeronima enjoyed reading, most especially her breviary, a book containing the psalms and prayers of the Church.

Jeronima entered the Capuchin convent and took the name Maria Angela. Her heart sang with joy as she joined the nuns in chanting the psalms. When she sang, she felt close to the angels, joining them in their song of joy and praise of God.

Maria became the mistress of the novices, which meant that she was to teach the new young women who entered the convent how to grow in love for God and to live in holiness.

During this time, Maria received a vision of a great and beautiful heart hovering in the air. The Blessed Virgin, holding the sweet baby Jesus, stood on one side of the heart, and St. Francis of Assisi (the founder of the order) stood on the other, all gazing with shining eyes at the floating heart. Maria's own heart blazed with love at the sight of this beautiful heart. She knew it was the heart of Jesus, and her own heart flamed with a great burning to be united to His. From then on, Maria's soul overflowed with the deepest love for Jesus as her mystical Groom.

At the age of thirty-three, Maria was elected as the abbess of her convent and became like a mother to all of her nuns. Even though she was their leader, she was always the first to sweep, wash the dishes and the laundry, and bring in the firewood. Maria founded a new convent and was its abbess for sixteen years. She and her nuns endured many difficulties, including a plague and a flood, but all throughout, she cared for the souls of her nuns, striving to bring them ever closer to Jesus.

Near the end of her life, she resigned as abbess, and her life became a simple one dedicated to prayer. She died after singing, with her nuns, the hymn "Sing, my tongue, the Savior's glory"—a song to Jesus in the Blessed Sacrament.

Bl. Maria Angela Astorch, help my heart burn with love for Jesus!

St. Francis Xavier
December 3

St. Francis Xavier

1506–1552 • Spain

Francis Xavier was young, athletic, and talented. Ambitious, he wanted to make a success of himself as a scholar at the University of Paris. There, he befriended a fellow student named Ignatius, who would one day be known as St. Ignatius of Loyola. Ignatius spoke to Francis about God, telling him that nothing was more important than heaven and its spiritual treasure. At first, Francis did not listen; he wanted success on earth, not in heaven. But eventually, Ignatius's holiness and his words touched Francis's heart, and he realized that he was meant to be a priest. Together, Ignatius and Francis founded the order of the Society of Jesus, also known as the Jesuits.

Francis traveled to India as a missionary to preach the Faith of Jesus to the Indian people, who did not know Christ. Francis went to the poorest of the poor and told them that Jesus had been poor like them and was with them in their suffering. Always cheerful, Francis lived with the poor, shared their food, and took care of the lepers there. He even miraculously healed some who were sick. Francis's words and acts touched the Indians' hearts because he lived just like them. Many were baptized and believed in Christ.

While Francis was preaching in India, a man named Anjiro sought him out. Anjiro was from Japan, and he told Francis all about his country. Anjiro's stories set Francis's heart on fire. He wanted to travel to Japan and tell the Japanese people about God's love for them.

Francis faced many struggles when he arrived in Japan. The language was unlike anything he had ever heard, and it took him a year to learn. The Japanese people also did not respect his life of poverty. To them, poverty was not a sign of holiness. Francis realized that the Japanese people needed to respect him in order to listen to him. So he dressed in rich priestly vestments and gave the finest gifts to their leaders. By adopting these local customs, Francis found that he reached more souls for Christ. While the Japanese leaders were friendly to Francis, they did not want him to make their people Christian; therefore, they made it illegal for the Japanese to practice Christianity. Nevertheless, about two thousand Japanese people converted to the Christian Faith. Because of Francis Xavier, the Japanese came to know Jesus.

The Japanese told Francis Xavier about China, and he realized that there were even more people who had never heard about Christ. Francis Xavier decided to travel to China and share God's love with the Chinese. He sailed to China, but the Chinese did not allow him to land on the mainland, so he waited on a nearby island. There, Francis Xavier caught a fever and died a holy death before he could preach to the Chinese people. St. Francis Xavier, help us to spread God's love to all people!

St. John Damascene

December 4

St. John Damascene

679–749 • Syria

John was an Eastern Christian who lived in the Muslim-ruled city of Damascus. Not only did he get along with his Muslim countrymen, but they held him in high honor, and he was an important counselor to the Muslim ruler, the caliph. A devout Christian and very learned, John wrote many important books about the Christian Faith.

At that time, the Christian emperor of the East passed a decree forbidding the public display and veneration of icons, which are images of Jesus, Mary, and the saints painted in great prayer and reverence. Some people believed to pray before an icon was to worship the image, just as the pagans worshiped false images ages before.

But John Damascene knew that Christians venerate, not worship, images. To venerate is to do honor and to pray to those the image represents. When we pray before an icon of Jesus, we are not praying to the icon, but to Jesus, whom the icon makes us think about. When we pray to the saints, we are not worshiping them, but asking them to pray for us, just as we ask the living to pray for us. We must all pray for each other to God, and we are very lucky to have the saints in heaven pray for us when we ask.

And so, when the emperor forbade the use of icons, John Damascene knew this was a mistake. The emperor had no right to forbid this ancient Christian practice of hanging icons in churches. John Damascene wrote books defending the veneration of icons, which angered the emperor.

So the emperor hatched a plot.

He forged a letter, using John Damascene's signature, stating that John Damascene wished to betray his ruler, the caliph. The emperor then sent this false letter to the caliph, who believed that his trusted counselor had betrayed him. Despite John's claims of innocence, the caliph ordered John's hand cut off. But when John Damascene prayed to the Blessed Virgin Mary, she miraculously restored John's hand to him. Seeing this, the caliph believed in John's innocence and asked John to remain his counselor.

But now John Damascene realized that God was calling him to a holier life than one of politics. He became a monk and entered the monastery of St. Sabbas, some eighteen miles away from the holy city of Jerusalem. There, he spent his days in prayer and writing in defense of the Faith until he died a holy death.

St. John Damascene, pray for me to God in heaven!

St. Sabbas
December 5

St. Sabbas

439–532 • Modern-day Turkey

When Sabbas was a young boy, his parents left him and his inheritance in the care of two uncles because his father was an officer who traveled with the army. But his uncles were greedy for Sabbas's inheritance and fought over his money. Sabbas saw that greed created ugliness and sin, so he gave up his inheritance to enter the monastery.

Sabbas's uncles felt ashamed and promised to return Sabbas's inheritance if he came home. But by that time, Sabbas had grown to love the life of prayer, and he realized that God wished for him to be a hermit.

There was a famous abbot, St. Euthymius, who led his hermits in the desert outside of Jerusalem. Sabbas became a student of Euthymius, and he lived alone in a cave for five years, praying and weaving willow baskets in exchange for food. After the abbot St. Euthymius died, Sabbas left for the Kidron Valley and lived in a cave at the bottom of a mountain. Other men joined Sabbas, and they built a hermitage. The patriarch of Jerusalem saw that all the hermits needed a priest to give the sacraments, and so he made Sabbas a priest. Sabbas tended with great love to the needs of his hermits.

Some of the hermits, however, were not happy with Sabbas as their leader because the Devil had sown rebelliousness in their hearts. And so those hermits fought and squabbled and feuded and argued. To keep the peace, Sabbas left his monastery for the desert to pray.

Sabbas found a large cave and lay down to spend the night. At midnight, he rose to sing the psalms and discovered two glowing eyes staring at him.

The eyes belonged to a great lion!

Without any fear, Sabbas prayed his midnight psalms, and the lion departed from the cave. The next morning, the lion returned while Sabbas was at his prayers. Sabbas invited the lion to stay, saying there was room enough for both, but the lion shook his mane, and, leaving the cave for good, went to find a new home.

Finally, the patriarch of Jerusalem ordered Sabbas to return to his hermitage. The rebellious monks grew so angry that they left the hermitage and tried to start their own. Sabbas felt so sorry for the rebellious hermits that he raised money and sent it to them. His forgiveness and kindness touched their hearts, and so they reconciled. Sabbas led his hermits until he died a holy death.

St. Sabbas, help me find peace in prayer!

St. Nicholas

December 6

St. Nicholas

d. 345 • Modern-day Turkey

From his youth, Nicholas desired to live a holy life. He fasted, prayed, and offered sacrifices to grow closer to God. When he was of age, he became a priest and served the people of the town of Myra. Nicholas inherited great wealth when his parents died, and he used his newfound riches to give to the poor.

One day, Nicholas heard of a poor man with three daughters. The man was so poor he could not afford to give his daughters dowries. Without dowries, the three daughters would never marry and so would fall into ruin because their father could not afford to feed and care for them.

Nicholas felt sorry for the three daughters. One night, he filled a pouch with coins and snuck out in the dark to the poor man's house. He tossed his coin-filled pouch through the open window, and it landed with a thump on the dirt floor.

The next day, the poor man discovered the pouch and rejoiced to see that inside was enough money for his eldest daughter's dowry. The family celebrated, and she happily married. After a time, Nicholas secretly tossed another pouch full of enough coins for the second daughter's dowry, and, finally, a third pouch for the youngest. Now all three daughters could marry and so were saved from ruin.

Later, Nicholas became the bishop of Myra. During this time, the Roman emperor Diocletian persecuted Christians. Because Nicholas defended the Faith and watched over the Christians in his care, rough soldiers arrested him and threw him into prison. Many years he spent in his dark and cramped prison cell. His only comfort was the love he felt for Jesus in his heart.

Finally, Constantine became the new emperor. Constantine was a friend to the Christians and declared Christians free to worship Jesus throughout his empire! A soldier yanked open Nicholas's prison door and announced he was at liberty to go. Nicholas rose from his knees, where he had been silently praying, and gave thanks to God for rewarding his faith and trust.

Bishop Nicholas returned to Myra and served his Christian flock until he died a holy death. There is a special tradition to celebrate his feast day. On the eve of St. Nicholas's Day, children put one shoe outside their door or in front of the fireplace. The next morning, they find their shoes filled with coins or small gifts in memory of the coins St. Nicholas gave to the poor man and his three daughters. Because of St. Nicholas's care for the poor, myths and legends grew about him, and he became known as Santa Claus and Good St. Nick. St. Nicholas, help me to give what I can to the poor!

St. Ambrose
December 7

St. Ambrose

c. 340–397 • Modern-day Germany

Born to a Christian Roman family in Gaul, Ambrose was raised with a deep love of his Faith by his widowed mother and his sister, who had consecrated themselves to God. A brilliant student and speaker, Ambrose studied law and became the governor of Milan, in Italy. At that time, some people waited until they were older to be baptized, and so Ambrose was still praying and preparing for his baptism.

The bishop of Milan had died, and a great crowd of priests and people had gathered in front of the church to elect a new bishop. But no one could agree on who the next bishop should be! A great argument arose, and violence threatened to break out. Ambrose was present and spoke peaceful words to calm the crowd.

Suddenly, a child in the crowd cried out, "Ambrose, bishop!"

The crowd fell silent. No one could think of a better man to be bishop than the wise Ambrose. Another person took up the cry, and then another. Soon, the entire crowd was calling for Ambrose to become bishop.

Ambrose was stunned. He had no desire to be bishop. Why, he was not even baptized yet! But he realized that it was God's will for him to be bishop, and he accepted God's greater plan for him. First, he was baptized, and then eight days later, Ambrose was consecrated bishop of Milan.

The first thing he did as bishop was to give away all his land and wealth to the poor. From then on, he dedicated himself to serving his church. People would flock to hear his homilies at Mass, and he especially preached the beauty and holiness of remaining unmarried for God. He was so eloquent that he was later known as "the Honey-Tongued Doctor," and artists often portray him surrounded by bees and honey. Another saint, named Augustine, listened to Ambrose's homilies and, through him, came to the Church.

As bishop of Milan, Ambrose defended the Church against both heresy and paganism. His writings and speeches all proclaimed that Jesus was both fully God and fully man, and that Christianity was the true Faith. He tirelessly served his church in Milan until he died a holy death.

St. Ambrose, help me to live the life God has planned for me!

The Immaculate Conception of the Blessed Virgin Mary
December 8

The Immaculate Conception of the Blessed Virgin Mary

Marian Feast Day

When the angel Gabriel appeared to Mary to announce that she was to be the Mother of Jesus, he greeted her with the words, "Hail, full of grace."

Mary was full of grace.

Not only had she never sinned, but she had been conceived without Original Sin, the sin we all inherit from Adam and Eve's Fall.

Why was she given this special gift? God saved Mary from the stain of sin because He knew that she would say yes to the angel's words. He knew that she would say yes to His will and become the Mother of Jesus.

For nine months, Mary carried Jesus in her womb. For nine months, her body gave Jesus life, and from her body, His body was made.

Jesus is holy. Jesus is God. It is only fitting that the Mother who bore Him should be pure and spotless. Like the Ark in the Old Testament that carried God's written Word, the Ten Commandments, inside it, Mary carried Jesus, God's Word made flesh, inside her.

Mary is the New Ark of the Covenant.

Because Jesus is sacred, Mary was made sacred to honor Him.

Today, we remember that Mary was conceived without sin. We celebrate Mary's Immaculate Conception because it helps us remember that Jesus' body is holy, so holy that God required Mary to be holy too.

Mary said, "My soul magnifies the Lord." Everything that Mary does is to make us look at Jesus. When we celebrate and honor Mary, we celebrate and honor her Son, because everything that she does brings us closer to Him.

Immaculate Mary, conceived without sin, pray for me now and at the hour of my death!

St. Juan Diego
December 9

St. Juan Diego

1474–1548 • Mexico

In Mexico, an Aztec boy was born named Cuauhtlatoatzin, which means "the Eagle-who-Speaks." Raised by his uncle, he married a young Aztec woman and lived humbly as a farmer. Like all Aztecs, the couple worshiped many gods. But the false Aztec gods were very different from the one, true God. They were violent and demanded human sacrifice.

Then, the Spaniard Hernán Cortés came and, along with him, the Franciscan friars. The friars spoke of Jesus, who loved us so much that He died for us. The love of Jesus spoke to Cuauhtlatoatzin's heart, and he and his wife were some of the first Aztecs to be baptized. They took the names Juan Diego and Maria Luisa. When Maria Luisa died, Juan Diego returned to live with his uncle. He lived a simple life of prayer, and early every Saturday morning, he made the hour-long walk to the Franciscan church near Mexico City to hear Mass in honor of Our Lady.

One Saturday morning, as he passed by Tepeyac Hill, he heard a gentle voice calling his name. Quickly, he climbed the hill, where he found the most beautiful woman he had ever seen. The woman told him that she was Mary, the Mother of God, and that she wished him to go to the bishop and ask him to build a church in her honor.

Juan Diego did as Our Lady asked. But he was just a humble man, so the bishop did not believe him and asked for a sign. On his return, Our Lady promised Juan Diego she would give him a sign the next day. The next morning, however, Juan Diego's uncle fell terribly ill, and Juan Diego stayed home. Finally, he went to fetch a priest to give his uncle last rites.

Our Lady appeared to Juan Diego on the road and promised that his uncle would be all right. Then, she pointed to the top of Tepeyac Hill and told him to gather the roses he would find there. These he gathered and showed to the bishop. But when he opened his tilma (a cloak), the roses tumbled to the ground, and imprinted on his tilma was a miraculous image of Our Lady. The bishop fell on his knees and gave thanks to Our Lady for her sign. Juan Diego returned home and found his uncle cured, just as Our Lady had promised.

The bishop built Mary's church on Tepeyac Hill, which housed Mary's miraculous image. Beside the church was a little hermitage for Juan Diego, who spent the rest of his life welcoming pilgrims to the church. Many miraculous healings occurred to those who prayed before Mary's image, and millions of Mexican Indians converted to the Catholic Faith. St. Juan Diego, help me humbly serve Jesus and Mary!

Our Lady of Loreto

Marian Feast Day

If you go inside the magnificent Basilica of the Holy House in Loreto, Italy, you will find a little house made out of stone. In a niche of the house is a black statue of Mary made of cedar wood and encrusted with jewels.

Tradition says that this little house has gone on a miraculous journey. It is the Holy House of Nazareth, where the Holy Family once lived.

The Blessed Virgin Mary was born in the little stone house. Its walls had witnessed the angel Gabriel announce to Mary that she was to be the Mother of God. Its walls had resounded with her humble yes.

When the Holy Family came to Nazareth after living in Egypt, they lived in the little house. Its walls witnessed Jesus growing up, from a small child into a man. It witnessed Mary's gentle smiles and Joseph's strong laughter. The light from the setting sun would shine through its western window on the Holy Family praying together.

For many centuries, the house of Nazareth stood, becoming a site for pilgrims. But then, after the Crusades, a host of angels picked up the Holy House and transported it far away so the house would not be destroyed.

First, the house was brought near a little town in Dalmatia. Then, the angels carried it to a wooded area near the town of Recanati, Italy. There, miracles occurred for those pilgrims that visited the Holy House. Finally, the house appeared in the Italian city of Loreto, and there it remained.

A great basilica was built around the Holy House. Thousands upon thousands of pilgrims go to visit the house and pray to the Holy Family that lived within its walls. They pray before Mary's statue over the altar, and Mary hears their prayers, which she brings to her Son. Through her intercession, many miracles happen for those who visit the house.

The popes hold the Holy House in great honor, and it is under their protection. Many saints have gone to visit the Holy House and Mary's statue, including St. Charles Borromeo, St. Francis de Sales, St. Ignatius of Loyola, and St. Alphonsus Liguori. A famous prayer of praise to Mary is called the Litany of Loreto and is promoted by the pope.

Our Lady of Loreto, please watch over my family!

Pope St. Damasus I
December 11

Pope St. Damasus I

c. 306–384 • Rome

Pope Damasus had just been elected the thirty-seventh pope.

But not everyone wanted Damasus to be the next pope. His election was opposed by a small, but powerful group who wanted someone else! But Damasus was the true pope, and the Roman emperor banished the false pope from the city.

The struggle at the beginning of Pope Damasus's papacy was just one of the many struggles he would face throughout his shepherding of the Church. Many false teachings about the Catholic Faith were spreading throughout the East and the West, and Pope Damasus staunchly defended the true Faith of Jesus.

Pope Damasus called the First Council of Constantinople to defend the truth that Jesus was fully God and fully man. St. Jerome attended that council, and Pope Damasus asked Jerome to come back to Rome with him and be his secretary. Pope Damasus and Jerome became close friends, and Damasus asked Jerome to translate the New Testament into Latin. At that time, the New Testament was mostly available in Greek, but the language that most people spoke was Latin. Pope Damasus wanted the Bible to be available in the language that most people could understand. And so under Pope Damasus, the Gospels were translated into Latin, and Latin became the official language of the Catholic Church, which it remains to this day.

Pope Damasus also wished to honor all of the glorious martyrs who had died for their love of Jesus. There were many, many martyrs who had died in Rome so that the world could come to know Christ!

Pope Damasus discovered these martyrs' tombs, built churches for them, and wrote epitaphs, or beautiful poems, over their graves. The wish of his heart was to be buried with the martyrs when he died, but he wrote that he would not wish to dishonor them, because he did not consider himself worthy to be buried beside them. Pope Damasus served as pope until he died a holy death at nearly eighty years old.

Pope St. Damasus, help me to get to know Jesus better by reading the Bible!

Our Lady of Guadalupe
December 12

Our Lady of Guadalupe

Marian Feast Day

Early Saturday morning, Juan Diego was walking by Tepeyac Hill on his way to Mass. A chorus of birds burst into song, and from a radiant cloud at the top of the hill a gentle voice called, "Juanito, Juan Diego!"

Curious, he climbed the hill, and there he found a beautiful woman dressed like an Aztec princess. Her blue-green mantle was spangled with the constellations, and tied around her waist was the sash that symbolized pregnancy among the Aztec people. The beautiful lady spoke to him in his own Indian language. "Juanito, my son, where are you going?" she asked. He explained that he was going to Mass. The beautiful lady then told Juan Diego that she was the Blessed Virgin Mary, the Mother of God, and that she wanted him to go to the bishop and ask that a church, dedicated to her, be built on Tepeyac Hill.

But when Juan Diego did as Our Lady asked, the bishop did not believe him. On his return home, Our Lady again met Juan Diego and instructed him to try again the next day. This time, the bishop asked for a sign that Juan Diego was telling the truth. Juan Diego met with Our Lady, and she promised to give him a sign on the next day.

But the next morning Juan Diego's uncle fell terribly ill, and Juan Diego stayed to watch over him. Finally, he went to fetch a priest to give his uncle last rites. Ashamed that he had missed his appointment with Our Lady, Juan Diego avoided Tepeyac Hill. But because he had not gone to meet her, Our Lady went to meet him. She came to him on the road and promised him that his uncle would be all right. Then, she pointed to the top of Tepeyac Hill and told Juan Diego to gather the flowers he would find there. On top of the hill, Juan Diego discovered beautiful Spanish roses miraculously blooming in the middle of winter. He gathered the flowers into his tilma to present to the bishop.

When Juan Diego met the bishop, he opened his tilma, and the roses tumbled out. The bishop fell on his knees. Imprinted on the tilma was the image of Our Lady! She looked exactly as she had when she appeared on Tepeyac Hill. And if you look closely into her eyes, you can see the images of Juan Diego and the bishop reflected in them. Because of the miraculous image, the bishop built a church on Tepeyac Hill dedicated to Our Lady of Guadalupe. To this day, you can visit the Basilica of Our Lady of Guadalupe and see her miraculous image on Juan Diego's tilma. Our Lady of Guadalupe, take care of me, your little child!

St. Lucy
December 13

St. Lucy

c. 283–304 • Italy

St. Lucy is one of the early Christian virgin martyrs put to death in the fourth century. She died for the Faith in Sicily, Italy, probably under the persecutions of Emperor Diocletian. She was a deeply beloved saint for the early Christians, and she is included in the prayers at Mass. If you listen carefully, you can hear her name mentioned shortly after the Consecration of Jesus' Body and Blood.

Many stories and legends have been handed down about Lucy's life. The most famous one is that Lucy would visit the catacombs, where the Christians hid from Roman persecution. The underground catacombs were dark, so she would bring candles to light her way as she brought food to those in hiding.

When Lucy's mother fell seriously ill, she engaged Lucy to a wealthy pagan man because she wanted to make sure that her daughter would be taken care of when she was gone. But Lucy did not want to marry a pagan. She wanted to be a bride of Christ! So she told her mother to visit St. Agatha's shrine to pray for a cure. St. Agatha was another virgin martyr, famous for her miracles.

Mother and daughter prayed at St. Agatha's shrine, and Lucy's mother was healed! To thank God for her cure, Lucy convinced her mother to let her give her money to the poor. When Lucy's suitor found out she had given away her money, he angrily reported her as a Christian. The Roman officials ordered Lucy to renounce her faith and worship the emperor. But she would not. She suffered many persecutions, even having her eyes put out, until she was put to death and became a glorious martyr for the Faith.

St. Lucy's feast day is a famous day of celebration. There is a long procession where the girls dress in white robes to symbolize the white robes of baptism, and they wear a red sash around their waist to symbolize St. Lucy's martyrdom. Finally, they crown themselves with wreaths and candles to remember that St. Lucy brought light to the people in the catacombs.

St. Lucy, help me bring the light of Christ to others!

St. John of the Cross
December 14

St. John of the Cross

1542–1591 • Spain

Alone in the dark prison cell, John reached out to God. In his soul, a song of love was stirring that he would put into words. In the darkness of his prison cell, John of the Cross discovered that the only guiding light he had was the love in his heart for God.

John of the Cross was born to poor silk weavers in Toledo, Spain. As he grew up, he tried out various trades, but he was not particularly good at anything, and so he was invited to serve the sick at the hospital in Toledo. He discovered through his work that God was calling him in a special way, and he entered the Carmelite order and became a priest.

At John's first Mass, he met Teresa de Ávila, the great reforming saint and nun who desired the Carmelite nuns to pursue lives of holiness. When John spoke to Teresa, her words inflamed his heart to seek holiness in the way that she described, and he worked to reform the Carmelite friars the way that Teresa worked to reform the Carmelite nuns.

But not all of the Carmelites liked John of the Cross's reforms. That is why some of these brothers ordered soldiers to seize him, beat him, and throw him into his dark prison cell! A jailer took pity on John and gave him a candle as well as paper, pen, and ink to write with. For over nine months, a candle his only source of light, John of the Cross wrote his mystical poems about the dark night of the heart's search for God.

St. Teresa de Ávila helped obtain his release, and John of the Cross dedicated his life to founding Carmelite monasteries under the rule of his reforms so that Carmelite friars could pursue greater lives of holiness. John himself experienced the deepest consolation and the mystical union of his soul with God in prayer.

But John of the Cross's life was always to be one of suffering, as he followed the way of the Cross, his namesake. His direct superior banished him to a faraway monastery. There, John of the Cross became terribly ill, and he was so neglected that his sufferings grew worse and worse. But his sufferings and his holiness were so great that even his enemies grew to acknowledge his sanctity, and he died a holy death.

St. John of the Cross, help my love for God be a guiding light!

St. Maria
Crocifissa di Rosa
December 15

St. Maria Crocifissa di Rosa

1813–1855 • Italy

Little Paola di Rosa's mother was a devout woman of faith who raised her daughter to love Jesus. Sadly, she died when Paola was eleven years old, and so Paola went to school with the Visitandine sisters. At seventeen, she returned to help her father, a wealthy factory owner, with his work. But her time with the sisters had shown her that God had called her to a life of service. She once said that her conscience would not let her sleep at night unless she had done something good that day.

Her father wished for Paola to marry, and he arranged many gentlemen suitors to ask for her hand. But Paola knew that she wanted to belong to God alone, and so she turned her suitors down one by one. She told the priest who was her spiritual adviser about God's will for her, and so the priest went to her father and told him that Paola was not called to marriage.

Paola cared for the spiritual needs of her father's workers. She organized retreats and catechism lessons for them to attend. But that was not enough for Paola. Paola saw that the Italian city of Brescia was full of many people who needed her care. She opened a shelter for poor women with her father's help. She began tending to the sick at the hospital, and soon, other women began to join her. They became the new order of the Handmaids of Charity, and Paola took the name Maria Crocifissa di Rosa.

War broke out between Italy and Austria, and the hospitals needed assistance more than ever. There were more and more patients, wounded and sick.

Enemy soldiers invaded the hospital, and Maria heard them outside the door. She clutched her crucifix to her heart. Then, she pulled open the door and held the crucifix up high. The soldiers, seeing the nun and the crucifix, felt ashamed. They backed out of the door and out of the hospital, leaving the sick unharmed.

Maria and her order of nuns served the poor and the sick until she died a holy death.

St. Maria Crocifissa di Rosa, help me not let a day go by without doing some good!

St. Adelaide of Burgundy
December 16

St. Adelaide of Burgundy

c. 931–999 • Modern-day Switzerland

Adelaide was the princess of the Kingdom of Burgundy. At fourteen years of age, she married Lothair, the heir to the Kingdom of Italy, as arranged by her parents. But her marriage did not last long. A rival to the throne, Berengar, had Lothair poisoned and then took over the kingdom. Berengar tried to force Adelaide to marry his son. She was beautiful and intelligent, and Berengar knew that if his son married Adelaide, the people of Italy would accept him as their new ruler.

Adelaide refused. She would never marry the son of the evil man who had killed her husband. And so Berengar had Adelaide locked up in a nearby castle on a lake.

But Adelaide was not without friends.

A priest named Fr. Martin dug an underground passage leading out of the castle. In secret, he led Adelaide to her escape into the wood. There she hid, while Fr. Martin fed her the fish he caught from the lake. Soon, a local duke took Adelaide into his castle for her protection. Adelaide, however, knew that she was still not safe. Berengar would find her. So she sent a message to King Otto of Germany for help.

Otto arrived with his army and forced Berengar from his ill-gotten kingdom, and Adelaide gave Otto her hand in marriage on Christmas Day. The people of Italy loved Adelaide, and so they happily welcomed Otto as their new ruler on account of his bride. The pope crowned Otto and Adelaide as Holy Roman emperor and empress, and together they ruled their joint kingdoms for twenty years.

When Emperor Otto passed away, Adelaide's stepson, Otto II, took the throne. The new emperor's wife did not like Adelaide, insulted her, and banished her from the court. Adelaide endured all without complaint.

When Otto II and his wife died, leaving their young son as emperor, Adelaide returned to the court and ruled as the child emperor's guardian. She provided for the poor in the kingdom, built monasteries, and sent missionaries out to those who had not heard of Jesus. At court, she lived a life of prayer and instructed her household in virtue. When the young emperor was old enough to rule, Adelaide retired to a convent and spent her life in prayer until she died a holy death.

St. Adelaide of Burgundy, help me to watch over those God puts into my care!

St. John of Matha

December 17

St. John of Matha

1160–1213 • France

Today was a holy and special day for John of Matha. Today was the day he would say his first Mass as a priest. His soul trembled as he said the words of Consecration and held the Body and Blood of Jesus in his anointed hands.

During this first Mass, God sent John the grace of an inspired vision: there stood an angel wearing a red and blue cross on his breast. The angel's hands rested on the heads of two captives bound in chains. Through his vision, John understood that God was giving him a mission. His mission was to found an order dedicated to ransom, or to purchase the freedom of those Christians enslaved by the Moors. (This was the time of the Crusades, and many Christians were held captive in the lands of the Moors.)

Before John of Matha started his new order, he wished to spend time in prayer and sacrifice. There was a holy hermit who lived deep in the wood of France whose name was Felix of Valois (who would also one day be known as a saint). John joined this holy hermit, and together the two spent their days in quiet prayer and sacrifice.

One day, when John and Felix were praying on the riverbank, a great white stag appeared to the two men in a vision. Between the stag's antlers was the red and blue cross that John had seen the day he said his first Mass. John then confided his mission to Felix and told him how he was to found a new order to ransom the enslaved Christians. So both John and Felix set off for Rome to ask the pope's permission to start the new order.

The pope received the two men with honor, having heard of their holiness. He granted John permission to start his new order, which was called the Trinitarian order. The Trinitarians were to wear white habits with a red and blue cross—the cross John had seen in his visions—on the breast.

For the rest of his life, John worked to free the enslaved Christians. He founded many Trinitarian monasteries throughout France, and he traveled back and forth from France to Spain and Tunis, purchasing the freedom of hundreds of slaves. He prayed and worked to free those in captivity until he died a holy death.

St. John of Matha, please help all find freedom through Jesus!

St. Flannán of Killaloe

December 18

St. Flannán of Killaloe

7th Century • Ireland

Flannán was the son of an Irish chieftain named Turlough. Instead of living the life of a chieftain's son, Flannán wished to dedicate himself to God. So he became a monk and joined the monastery of Killaloe, which the holy St. Molua had founded.

Irish legend says that one day, Flannán was tasked to work at a mill to make bread. Flannán worked late into the night, long after the sun had set. The steward of the monastery realized that he had forgotten to give Flannán a candle, and so he sent a young boy to see if Flannán needed one.

The boy saw light glowing through a crack in the mill's door, so he peeked through the keyhole, curious about where the light was coming from. There was Flannán, hard at work. But the light the boy saw was not coming from a candle, but from Flannán's own left hand, whose fingers shot forth streams of light!

The boy ran back to the monastery to tell the steward what he had seen, and when the abbot St. Molua heard the story of Flannán's shining left hand, he resigned his post as abbot and appointed Flannán to take his place.

Flannán was a holy abbot. He took good care of his monks, teaching them to lead lives of prayer and virtue. He also preached to the people about the Good News of Jesus so that they could know and love God. The people of Killaloe loved Flannán so much that they wanted him to be their bishop. And so Flannán made the long journey to Rome, where the pope consecrated him as the first bishop of Killaloe.

When Flannán returned to Ireland, he was such a good shepherd to his people and lived such a holy life that his father, the chieftain Turlough, wishing to follow his son's example, gave up his wealth and power and became a hermit. Flannán served the people of Killaloe as bishop until he died a holy death.

St. Flannán of Killaloe, help me bring others to Jesus by living a holy life!

Sts. Fausta and Anastasia of Sirmium

December 19

Sts. Fausta and Anastasia of Sirmium

c. 300 • Modern-day Serbia

Fausta and Anastasia were mother and daughter. They lived in Sirmium during the time of the Roman persecution of Christians throughout the empire.

Fausta was a holy and virtuous Christian widow whose heart held a deep love for Jesus. She passed on this deep love for Jesus to her daughter Anastasia, who also grew in holiness and virtue.

Nothing else is known about St. Fausta, but through her, we learn how important it is for parents to teach their children to love Jesus and to raise them to be saints!

Tradition says that Anastasia could perform healing miracles, and that she would visit the Christians thrown into prison because of the emperor Diocletian's persecution. There, she would heal them from their sickness and from their wounds in the name of Jesus.

Eventually, Anastasia, too, was arrested. But no matter how cruel or painful the torture, nothing could make her deny Jesus. Her deep love for Jesus, the gift of love that her mother had passed on to her, strengthened her to endure all trials. Anastasia died a glorious martyr for the Faith on Christmas Day.

The Church keeps Sts. Fausta and Anastasia ever present in her memory. In St. Peter's Square, where the pope lives in the Vatican, St. Fausta's statue can be seen adorning the colonnade.

If you listen carefully at Mass, you can hear the name of her daughter Anastasia mentioned in the prayers.

Sts. Fausta and Anastasia of Sirmium, help me to hold a deep love for Jesus in my heart!

Bl. Imelda Lambertini
December 20

Bl. Imelda Lambertini

1322–1333 • Italy

More than anything, nine-year-old Imelda longed to receive Jesus in the Blessed Sacrament. She loved Him with all of her heart, and she knew that by receiving Jesus in Communion, she would be completely united with Him. At that time, it was the Church's rule that a person had to be fourteen years old in order to receive Communion because the Church wanted to make sure that the person receiving Communion completely understood that the bread and wine of the Eucharist are truly Jesus' Body and Blood. But Imelda understood that Jesus is truly present in the Eucharist, and she found waiting for Jesus very hard.

Imelda asked her parents to let her live with the Dominican sisters so she could grow closer to Jesus. Even though Imelda was so young, her parents granted her wish because they could see that she belonged to God in a special way. The sisters happily received Imelda in the convent and let her wear their habit and sing their prayers.

Imelda asked if she could receive her First Communion. The sisters were touched that Imelda wanted to receive Jesus, but they told her that she was too young and needed to be better prepared. But Imelda insisted again and again, so the sisters went to ask the priest. But he also told Imelda that she was too young.

The nuns had just heard Mass on the vigil of the Feast of the Ascension. Imelda, now eleven years old, was kneeling alone in prayer. One of the nuns was clearing things from the altar when a consecrated Host floated from the tabernacle and drifted over to Imelda. Shining, it hung suspended over her head. Immediately, the nun rushed to find the priest, who also saw the shining Host floating over the kneeling Imelda. The priest understood that Jesus was telling him that Imelda was to receive the Eucharist.

And so the priest gave Imelda her First Holy Communion. Imelda's eyes had never left the Host, and now they shone with joy. The nuns left their little Imelda alone to pray. One of the nuns returned and called for Imelda to come for supper. But Imelda did not move. There was a gentle smile on her face. The nuns discovered that Imelda had experienced so much joy at receiving the Eucharist that she had gone straight to heaven! Jesus had called Imelda to be united with Him forever.

Nearly five hundred years after her death, Pope Pius X decreed that children at the age of reason (about seven years old) could receive Holy Communion, and, on December 20, 1826, he recognized Imelda as a blessed in heaven and made her the patron of First Communicants. Bl. Imelda Lambertini, help me long to receive Jesus in Holy Communion!

St. Peter Canisius
December 21

St. Peter Canisius

1521–1597 • Netherlands

During the life of Peter Canisius, Germany was facing a great crisis of faith. The new Protestant religion was sweeping through the land, and many people were leaving the Catholic Church.

Peter Canisius had left behind the promise of a brilliant career to join the Jesuit order, where he was taught by the holy founder St. Ignatius of Loyola himself. Peter knew that he must do all he could to preach to the German people that the Catholic Church was the true Church that Jesus had founded when He was on earth. And so Peter preached to the rich and the poor, the old and the young—especially to children. He even wrote three catechisms so that all could read and learn about the Catholic Faith.

Not only did Peter Canisius preach with words, he also preached with actions. He took special care of the sick, and when a terrible plague struck Vienna, where he was teaching, he tended to the sick and won the people's hearts. When he preached with words, he preached with great love. Since many Protestants had been born into their new religion, he understood that they did not know any other faith. Because of this, he was kind and gentle when he spoke to those of the Protestant faith, though he was never afraid to speak the truth.

Peter Canisius was not even afraid to preach to the Holy Roman emperor!

The emperor's son had appointed a Protestant minister to a high position at court. Peter went to the emperor and his son, and he told them that having the Protestant minister at court would confuse the faithful about the truth of the Catholic Faith. The emperor greatly respected Peter Canisius, and so he dismissed the minister. But from that day on, his son, who would become the future emperor, held a grudge against Peter Canisius. But Peter did not mind. He knew that whatever a future emperor thought of him was not as important as what God thought of him.

Peter Canisius understood that education in the true Faith was so important if Catholics were going to share the true Faith with their Protestant brothers and sisters. So he founded many colleges throughout Germany and Austria to teach the Faith. He also founded many seminaries to train priests. Throughout his life, he wrote and preached in defense of the Catholic Faith, until he died a holy death. Because of all of Peter Canisius's hard work, the Catholic Faith returned to Germany, and he is called one of the Apostles of Germany. St. Peter Canisius, please help me never be afraid to speak the truth with gentleness and love!

Bl. Jutta of
Disibodenberg
December 22

Bl. Jutta of Disibodenberg

c. 1084–1136 • Germany

Jutta knelt in her little room, holding her book of Psalms. She was an anchoress, which meant that she never left her little room in the monastery of Disibodenberg, where she gave her life to God in prayer.

When Jutta had been twelve years old, she had fallen terribly ill. When she returned to health by God's grace, she promised to God that she would be His alone and live a holy life. As she grew in beauty and years, her widowed mother tried to convince her to marry. Jutta belonged to a noble family, and she had learned music, needlework, and the fine arts of a medieval lady in preparation for marriage.

But Jutta remembered her promise to God and refused her suitors and a life of ease. And so she had been enclosed in the monastery as an anchoress at twenty years of age.

Every day, Jutta prayed the entire psalter, which is a book of psalms, and offered many sacrifices to God. She became known for her holiness and wisdom. Many people came to visit her outside her window, and God would heal them through Jutta's prayers.

Families sent their daughters to Jutta to be educated in holiness. One of her young pupils was a girl named Hildegard of Bingen. Jutta taught Hildegard to chant and pray the psalms, and together their souls would sing sacred music to God. Hildegard would grow up to become a famous composer of sacred music and would one day be recognized as a great saint.

A group of women gathered around Jutta, and she became their abbess. She guided them on their path to holiness until she died a holy death. Hildegard became the next abbess after her teacher's death, and she guided the women in her care, following Jutta's holy example.

Bl. Jutta of Disibodenberg, help my soul sing sacred music to God!

St. John of Kanty
December 23

St. John of Kanty

1390–1473 • Poland

Born a country boy in Poland, John of Kanty went to the University of Krakow and was such a good student that he eventually became a professor at the university, as well as a priest. He was simple and humble and possessed a deep love for the poor.

John of Kanty spent many hours in prayer, and sometimes he stayed up all night praying before God. Because he had such a deep devotion to Jesus' suffering and death, he wished to go on pilgrimage to the Holy Land, where he could visit the places where Jesus lived, died, and rose from the dead. In the Holy Land, he even hoped to receive the honor of becoming a martyr for Jesus and was saddened when he returned home from his pilgrimage safely. John of Kanty also made four pilgrimages to Rome on foot.

During one of his pilgrimages, a robber set upon him on the road and snatched John of Kanty's purse. Then, the robber demanded to know if John had any more money. Shaken, John replied that the robber had taken it all. And so the robber went on his way down the road.

But then, John gave a start.

He remembered that he had sewn some gold pieces into the hem of his robe in case of an emergency. Quickly, he fished out the gold pieces and raced after the robber. Calling out to the robber to wait, he held forth the gold pieces and breathlessly explained that he had yet more money to give. Astonished by the priest's generosity, the robber returned everything he had taken from John of Kanty to begin with.

In the later years of his life, John of Kanty offered great sacrifices to God so that he could live a holier life. He slept on the ground, did not eat meat, and dressed the poor with his own clothes, often giving them his shoes. At the end of his life, he gave away everything that he owned to the poor, and he died a holy death.

St. John of Kanty, help me to have a deep love for the poor!

The Holy Ancestors of Christ
December 24

© Sophia Institute Press

The Holy Ancestors of Christ

Feast of Jesus

God created Adam and Eve, the first man and woman, and placed them in the Garden of Eden. He gave Adam and Eve the gift of life, the gift of each other, and the gift of all of creation to watch over. Even more wonderful, God was their friend. The life of His grace belonged to them, and His home in heaven would be their home too. Only one thing did God command in return: Adam and Eve must not eat of the Tree of the Knowledge of Good and Evil.

Then, the serpent slithered into the garden. Its tongue hissed lies and temptations to Eve to eat the fruit of the forbidden tree. Eve said no to God's command. She ate the fruit and shared it with Adam. Adam and Eve rejected God; they rejected His friendship; they rejected His blessed home in heaven. They ate the fruit of death and became prisoners of the Devil and sin. Now we all are born with the Original Sin of our first parents, Adam and Eve.

But God loved us so much that He wanted to free us from the Devil and sin. At the moment of our first parents' disobedience, God promised to send us a Savior. He said to the serpent, "I will put enmity between you and the woman, and between your offspring and hers; they will strike at your head, while you strike at their heel" (Gen. 3:15). The promised Savior would be the offspring of the woman and would free enslaved humanity.

And so God worked through the history of mankind to bring about the birth of the promised Savior. He called Abraham—a descendant of Shem, the son of Noah—to enter the Promised Land. God told him that his descendants would be as numerous as the stars in the sky. Abraham, his son Isaac, and Isaac's son Jacob are the great patriarchs. From the tribe of Judah—Jacob's son—would King David be born. A man after God's own heart, David was the grandson of the faithful Ruth and the son of Jesse. God promised David that the Messiah would inherit his royal throne. From David's line was Joseph born, who was betrothed to the Blessed Virgin Mary.

When the angel Gabriel asked Mary to be the Mother of God's promised Savior, Mary said yes. Her yes undid the disobedience of Eve's no. Mary was the woman whose offspring God promised would strike the serpent. Jesus, through His death and Resurrection, freed mankind from the Devil and sin. Holy Ancestors of Christ, help me be ready to receive the Savior of the world into my heart!

The Nativity of the Lord
December 25

The Nativity of the Lord

Feast of Jesus

The stable was small, dirty, and smelled of animals. Joseph was worried. Mary was about to give birth, and, try as he might, he could not find a room in any of the inns. Then, he had remembered the stable in Bethlehem, and so here Mary would have her baby.

Mary's gentle eyes fell on Joseph, and they calmed the worries of his heart. Her gaze was filled with peace and trust because she saw the Father's hand in all things. She glanced at the wooden manger and their loyal donkey munching on the straw. In this humble place, the Son of God would be born.

Her heart was filled with the mystery of God's ways. His Son had not chosen to be born among the princes of the world, in luxury or riches; nor among the scholars of the world, with their scrolls and parchment. The Son of God had chosen to be born among the poorest of the poor. He would be born of Mary, God's lowly handmaid, and raised by Joseph, a humble carpenter.

Mary gave birth to Jesus, and the tiny infant nestled in her arms, close to her heart. Joseph bowed protectively over mother and child, and the warm light of God's love filled Mary's and Joseph's hearts with the gifts of joy and peace. They laid Jesus in the manger, and over the stable, a radiant star shone in the nighttime sky.

Soon, shepherds burst upon the Holy Family, full of excitement to see the newborn Jesus. They told Mary that they had been watching their sheep out in the fields when there suddenly appeared a majestic host of angels singing, "Glory to God in the highest." An angel had told them where they would find the Savior, the Messiah whom God had promised them. So with great haste, they had come to Bethlehem, and here they had found Jesus by the sign the angel had given them: an infant wrapped in swaddling clothes, lying in the manger.

Mary and Joseph were amazed by the shepherds' story, and Mary reflected on their words, keeping them close in her heart. Her baby was the greatest gift of love a mother ever could receive, but she also knew that Jesus was God's gift of love for the whole world. "For God so loved the world that he gave his only Son, so that everyone who believes in him might not perish but might have eternal life" (John 3:16). Dear baby Jesus, let the light of your love fill my heart with the gift of joy and peace!

St. Stephen
December 26

St. Stephen

Biblical Figure

The man stood before the Jewish priests and judges of the Sanhedrin, his face like that of an angel, fearless and bright. His ringing voice proclaimed that Jesus was the Messiah, whose coming all the prophets had foretold. The men of the Sanhedrin muttered darkly to each other. This man was declaring that Jesus, whom they crucified, was the promised Savior of the world.

After Pentecost, the Apostles, filled with the Holy Spirit, fearlessly went forth and preached the Good News. More and more men and women believed in Jesus and were baptized. The Apostles needed help serving the many new Christians and caring for their poor. And so they laid hands on seven men, filling them with the Holy Spirit and making them deacons. These deacons would help the Apostles by serving the poor. The foremost new deacon, filled with wisdom and the Holy Spirit, was Stephen.

Stephen preached to the crowds about Jesus. He performed many great wonders and miracles in Jesus' name. His words touched people's hearts so that they believed in Jesus and were baptized. Some Jews who did not believe in Jesus came from the synagogues to debate Stephen. But no matter what they said, Stephen's wisdom overcame all of their arguments. And so they dragged Stephen to the Sanhedrin and told lies and made false accusations against him.

Fearlessly, Stephen stood before the Sanhedrin and proclaimed Jesus as the Messiah, whom the judges and priests had betrayed out of the hardness of their hearts. All those in the Sanhedrin were furious at his words.

Suddenly, the heavens opened, and Stephen looked up. There shone the glory of God the Father, at whose right hand stood Jesus! Stephen proclaimed, "Behold, I see the heavens opened and the Son of Man standing at the right hand of God."

At this, the Jews covered their ears, rushed at Stephen, and cast him out of the city walls to stone him. Those present took off their coats and laid them at the feet of a man named Saul. Later, Saul would become Paul, the great Apostle who spread the Good News of Jesus throughout the world. But his heart had not yet seen the truth about Jesus, and he persecuted Christians.

As Stephen was being stoned, he cried out, "Lord Jesus, receive my spirit." And then he fell on his knees and forgave those who were stoning him, crying out, "Lord, do not hold this sin against them." Then, Stephen became the first glorious martyr to die for Christ. St. Stephen, help me fearlessly proclaim that Jesus is the Savior of the world!

St. John the Evangelist

December 27

St. John the Evangelist

Biblical Figure

John was the beloved disciple, the youngest of the Twelve. Jesus always called John to accompany Him in special moments: he was one of three disciples, along with Peter and James, to witness Jesus' Transfiguration, and he was called to watch with Jesus in the Garden of Gethsemane.

During the Last Supper, when Jesus changed bread and wine into His Body and Blood for the first time, John rested his head against Jesus' chest and heard Jesus' heart beating with love for the whole world.

John was the faithful disciple who never abandoned Jesus when He was in trouble. When Jesus was arrested in the Garden of Gethsemane, John did not run away. Instead, he followed the guards to where they held Jesus. He was there at Jesus' feet during the Crucifixion, and comforted Mary, Jesus' Blessed Mother. From the Cross, Jesus said to Mary, "Behold, your son," and to John, "Behold, your mother." Jesus was giving Mary to John to be his Mother, and so John cared for Mary as would a son.

The third day after Jesus died, Mary Magdalene proclaimed joyfully to all the gathered disciples that Jesus was risen and that she had seen Him! John raced to Jesus' tomb (Peter running close behind him) to see if it was true. When John reached the open tomb, he looked inside, but he let Peter enter the tomb first, since Peter was the leader of the Apostles. Then, John went inside and saw that the tomb was empty and the burial cloths put aside. He believed Mary Magdalene's words. Jesus had risen from the dead. When Jesus passed through the locked doors to visit the disciples, John's heart was radiant with joy.

Soon after, John, Peter, and the other disciples went fishing, but no matter how long and hard they tried, they could not catch any fish. Then, a stranger on the shore called out to them and instructed them to cast their nets one more time into the deep. This time, the fish rushed into the nets, which became so heavy that they were close to breaking. John looked at the stranger on the shore, and his heart recognized that it was Jesus. "It is the Lord!" John cried out.

John lived into old age on the island of Patmos. He wrote the fourth Gospel, which describes Jesus as the Son of God and flies to such heights of wisdom that John is symbolized with the eagle. He also wrote three letters and the final book of the Bible, Revelation. You can read all that John the beloved disciple wrote in the Bible. St. John the Evangelist, help me remain always faithful to Jesus!

The Holy Innocents
December 28

The Holy Innocents

Biblical Figures

An angel appeared to Joseph in a dream. "Rise," the angel commanded. "Take the child and his mother, flee to Egypt, and stay there until I tell you. Herod is going to search for the child to destroy him."

Joseph started awake, the angel's urgent command still clear in his mind. He went to where Mary was sleeping with the baby Jesus, gently shook her awake, and explained all the angel had told him. With haste, they prepared for their departure and loaded their faithful donkey with their few possessions. Anxious questions troubled Joseph. Would Jesus be safe? Where would they live in Egypt? Then, Mary's gentle hand rested on his arm, and her trusting gaze filled him with peace. The Father in heaven would look after them, and He would protect His Son, Jesus. And so the Holy Family fled into the night for Egypt.

In Jerusalem, King Herod was awaiting news from the three Wise Men. Earlier, they had come to Jerusalem seeking the newborn king of the Jews. Herod had pretended to be their friend and had sent them to Bethlehem, where the Messiah was prophesied to be born. The Wise Men were supposed to report back to Herod when they found the baby.

Herod feared that if another king was born, he might try to take Herod's throne! And so Herod was plotting to kill the baby Jesus when he discovered His identity. But after the three Wise Men had found Jesus in Bethlehem, an angel warned them, too, about Herod's plan, and so they went home by a hidden way.

When the Wise Men never returned to Jerusalem, Herod was furious. And so in his dark heart, he decided that he did not need to know the identity of the newborn Messiah to kill him. He would instead kill all the baby boys under two years old in Bethlehem. He ordered his soldiers to carry out his vile command. In Bethlehem, his soldiers committed the unspeakable evil that Herod had ordered.

All the innocent babies that died are called the Holy Innocents because they had done no wrong and had died for Jesus. Because of the angel's warning, the Holy Family escaped and lived in Egypt until Herod died and the angel told Joseph they could return home.

The Holy Innocents' pure souls rested in the bosom of Abraham, the father of the Jewish people, until Jesus opened the gates of heaven after His death and Resurrection. Now they are honored as saints in heaven because they shed their innocent blood for the Savior of the world. Holy Innocents, help my heart be as pure and innocent as yours!

St. Thomas Becket
December 29

St. Thomas Becket

1118–1170 • England

Thomas Becket was the best friend of King Henry II of England. They hunted together and joked and laughed. Thomas was the king's chancellor, which means that Thomas was the most powerful man in England under the king. He loved to dress in rich robes and ride in full wealth and splendor. Together, the king and Thomas worked hard to run the kingdom, and people marveled over how the king and Thomas seemed to agree about everything.

But Thomas was not only the king's chancellor; he was also a deacon of the Catholic Church. When the archbishop of Canterbury died, Henry II wished to appoint Thomas as the next archbishop. Thomas warned the king that, if appointed archbishop, he must serve God before the Crown. He knew the king well, and he knew that the king would wish to take away power that rightfully belonged to the Church. Thomas would have to protect the Church.

But Henry did not believe Thomas's warning. He believed that Thomas would do as he said because Thomas was his friend. The king appointed Thomas as archbishop of Canterbury, and at the urging of a cardinal of the Church, Thomas accepted his new position and was ordained a priest and then a bishop.

After being anointed archbishop of Canterbury, a change came over Thomas. He took off his rich, luxurious robes and prayed late into the night. When the pope sent Thomas his pallium, the cloak that was the symbol of the bishop's authority, Thomas went to receive it barefoot, as a sign of his humble service before God.

Not long after, everything that Thomas had warned the king about came to pass. First, the king wanted to take one thing from the Church, and then another. Each time, Thomas opposed the king and defended the Church. Henry II was livid. He could not believe that his old friend would not do as he said! He cried out in fury, "Will no one get rid of this troublesome bishop?" Four knights who overheard this outburst took his words as a command instead of a fit of anger, and they arranged to kill Thomas Becket.

Assassins entered the cathedral as Thomas was praying Vespers. Thomas commanded no one to defend him, and he refused the assassins' command to obey the king instead of God. And so Thomas became a glorious martyr for the Faith in Canterbury Cathedral. When Henry II heard of his old friend's death, he wept terrible tears, sorrowing that his words of anger had brought about Thomas's death. He stopped taking what belonged to the Church, and when he was an old man, the king walked three miles barefoot to make a pilgrimage to St. Thomas Becket's tomb. St. Thomas Becket, help me humbly obey God above all others!

The Holy Family of Jesus, Mary, and Joseph
December 30

The Holy Family of Jesus, Mary, and Joseph

Feast of Jesus, Mary, and Joseph

Jesus' laughter filled the Holy Family's humble home in Nazareth. Whenever Jesus laughed, Mary's and Joseph's hearts bubbled with joy; it did not matter how tired or sad they had been just a moment before. The young Jesus would laugh over the wonder of a tree or a flower, or the song of a house sparrow, and His laughter was always mingled with love. Mary and Joseph treasured Jesus' laughter, from His infant coos to the free laughter of His boyhood.

They also treasured Jesus' silence.

At times, Jesus would fall into a silence rich with unspoken words. Sometimes, He would go off alone into the quiet. In this silence, Mary and Joseph knew, Jesus was speaking to His heavenly Father.

We can imagine the Holy Family greeting the morning with prayer to God. Joseph would chant aloud the psalms, Mary would say to the Father, "Let it be done according to your word," and Jesus would say to His heavenly Father, "Thy will be done on earth as it is in heaven."

When Jesus was twelve, the Holy Family traveled in a caravan to Jerusalem to celebrate the feast of Passover. When Mary and Joseph left Jerusalem with the caravan, they thought Jesus was with relatives or friends. It was only after a day's journey that they discovered that Jesus was nowhere to be found. They had lost Jesus in Jerusalem! He could be anywhere in that busy and dangerous city!

Mary and Joseph rushed back to Jerusalem and desperately searched for Jesus for three days. On the third day, they went to the Temple, ready to pour out their sorrow to God and beg for His help. To their astonishment, there Jesus was, speaking to the teachers at the Temple. The amazed teachers were asking themselves who this young boy named Jesus was, who spoke with wisdom beyond His years.

Mary went to Jesus and asked Him in a quiet voice why He had caused them so much worry. Jesus answered, "Why were you looking for me? Did you not know that I must be in my Father's house?" Joyful that they had found Jesus, Mary and Joseph returned to their humble home in Nazareth. There, Jesus was obedient to His Mother and foster father, and He learned Joseph's trade as a carpenter. Together, the Holy Family prayed and worked and lived ordinary lives, offering everything they did with love to the heavenly Father. Holy Family, help me to offer my ordinary days with love to my heavenly Father!

Pope St. Sylvester I
December 31

Pope St. Sylvester I

d. 335 • Rome

St. Sylvester was pope in Rome when the Roman emperor Constantine declared Christians were free to practice their religion in the Roman Empire. This was a time for great rejoicing among Christians. All the blood the early martyrs shed had sown the seeds for the conversion of Rome. Now all Christians could share the love of Jesus with the whole world and practice their Faith in peace.

A wondrous legend is told of Pope St. Sylvester's works in this joyous time.

Two pagan priests sought an audience with Constantine. They tore their hair and wept over the fact that ever since Constantine had made the empire Christian, a terrible dragon in a cave had spewed a poisonous breath, and every day, three hundred people died from the dragon's noxious fumes. Emperor Constantine called Pope Sylvester and told him about the evil dragon, and Pope Sylvester promised that he would put an end to the dragon's terror. Trembling, the pagan priests declared that they would become Christian if Sylvester succeeded.

That night, St. Peter appeared to Sylvester in a dream and told him what he must do. The following morning, Sylvester entered the dark mouth of the dragon's cave. The pagan priests waited by the entrance of the cave, overwhelmed by the dragon's breath escaping from underground. But the pope descended unharmed until he reached the dragon, an evil glint in its snakelike eyes. Poisoned breath spouted from its lizard's snout and charred the stones and dried the underground pools.

Pope Sylvester cried out in a loud voice the words St. Peter had told him: "Satan, remain here until the Second Coming of Christ!" At the pope's words, the dragon was immobilized by the power of God, and Pope Sylvester bound and sealed the dragon's snout so that its breath could no longer poison those in the world above. Pope Sylvester returned to the daylight of the cavern entrance, where he found the pagan priests recovering from their faints. They were converted to Christianity on the spot, and countless pagans in Rome were baptized because Pope Sylvester had sealed away the dragon.

Magnificent churches were built in Rome during Pope Sylvester's papacy, and the Roman martyrs were honored. He defended the Church against the attacks of the Evil One and welcomed many souls to the Church until he died a holy death.

Pope St. Sylvester I, please watch over the Church and defend her against the Evil One!

Sophia Institute

Sophia Institute is a nonprofit institution that seeks to nurture the spiritual, moral, and cultural life of souls and to spread the Gospel of Christ in conformity with the authentic teachings of the Roman Catholic Church.

Sophia Institute Press fulfills this mission by offering translations, reprints, and new publications that afford readers a rich source of the enduring wisdom of mankind.

Sophia Institute also operates two popular online Catholic resources: CrisisMagazine.com and CatholicExchange.com.

Crisis Magazine provides insightful cultural analysis that arms readers with the arguments necessary for navigating the ideological and theological minefields of the day. *Catholic Exchange* provides world news from a Catholic perspective as well as daily devotionals and articles that will help you to grow in holiness and live a life consistent with the teachings of the Church.

In 2013, Sophia Institute launched Sophia Institute for Teachers to renew and rebuild Catholic culture through service to Catholic education. With the goal of nurturing the spiritual, moral, and cultural life of souls, and an abiding respect for the role and work of teachers, we strive to provide materials and programs that are at once enlightening to the mind and ennobling to the heart; faithful and complete, as well as useful and practical.

Sophia Institute gratefully recognizes the Solidarity Association for preserving and encouraging the growth of our apostolate over the course of many years. Without their generous and timely support, this book would not be in your hands.

www.SophiaInstitute.com
www.CatholicExchange.com
www.CrisisMagazine.com
www.SophiaInstituteforTeachers.org

Sophia Institute Press® is a registered trademark of Sophia Institute.
Sophia Institute is a tax-exempt institution as defined by the Internal Revenue Code, Section 501(c)(3). Tax I.D. 22-2548708.